AF600365

JUDICIAL EXPERTS: A SOURCE OF EVIDENCE IN ECCLESIASTICAL TRIALS

THE CATHOLIC UNIVERSITY OF AMERICA
CANON LAW STUDIES
No. 389

Judicial Experts: A Source of Evidence in Ecclesiastical Trials

A HISTORICAL SYNOPSIS AND A COMMENTARY

A DISSERTATION
SUBMITTED TO THE FACULTY OF THE SCHOOL OF CANON LAW
OF THE CATHOLIC UNIVERSITY OF AMERICA IN PARTIAL
FULFILLMENT OF THE REQUIREMENTS FOR THE
DEGREE OF DOCTOR OF CANON LAW

BY THE
REV. WILLIAM M. PICKARD, J.C.L.
PRIEST OF THE DIOCESE OF GALVESTON

THE CATHOLIC UNIVERSITY OF AMERICA PRESS
WASHINGTON, D.C.
1958

NIHIL OBSTAT:
John Rogg Schmidt, J.C.D.
Censor Deputatus

Washingtonii, D.C., die 26 aprilis, 1957

IMPRIMATUR:
✠ Wendelinus J. Nold, S.T.D.
Episcopus Galvestoniensis

Galvestonii, die 29 aprilis, 1957

Printed by the Abbey Press, St. Meinrad, Indiana, U.S.A.

JESU SOLI JUSTITIAE
ET IN HONOREM
MARIAE EIUSDEM SPECULI
HOC OPUSCULUM
DICATUM EST

FOREWORD

The primary purpose of any judicial process is the ascertainment of truth. For arriving at this truth several means are available, the most usual of which are the confession of the parties, the testimony of the witnesses, and documentary evidence. At times, however, it may be necessary or very useful to employ still another means, namely, the proof afforded through the examination and report of a judicial expert.

The use of experts is common in modern procedural practice, both civil and ecclesiastical. In civil law today, perhaps the most frequently employed experts are psychiatrists, called upon in criminal cases to examine the accused and to testify concerning his mental capacity. In canon law probably the most frequently used experts are urologists and gynecologists, who serve in matrimonial causes wherein impotence and non-consummation is claimed. Psychiatrists, too, are increasingly employed by the Church as experts in cases of alleged nullity of marriage due to insanity or to functional impotence.

It is the purpose of this dissertation to treat of the expert as a source of evidence in the judicial process of ecclesiastical tribunals (exclusive of the process of beatification or canonization). In the first part of this study the rôle of the judicial expert is traced historically from its beginning in Roman law until the promulgation of the present Code of Canon Law in 1918. In the second part is contained a commentary of the present law concerning judicial experts, with special attention given to the use of experts in matrimonial trials.

The writer takes this occasion to thank His Excellency, the Most Reverend Wendelin J. Nold, S.T.D., Bishop of Galveston, for the opportunity of graduate study in Canon

Law at the Catholic University of America. He also wishes to thank the members of the Faculty of the School of Canon Law, his classmates at the University, his parents, and all others whose scholarly guidance, helpful suggestions, kind encouragement and prayers have made this dissertation a reality.

TABLE OF CONTENTS

PART II

CANONICAL COMMENTARY

PART I

HISTORICAL SYNOPSIS

CHAPTER I

THE EXPERT IN ROMAN LAW

As he is known today, the judicial expert is a person possessed of a particular skill or knowledge, who is called into a judicial process in order that he may help the judge to establish some fact or to determine the true nature of a thing by conducting an examination and giving a report in accord with the principles of his art or profession. Did such an expert exist in Roman Law? Because such a great bulk of the Church's legislation was borrowed from Roman Law, it is important that one search in the earliest statutes of Rome for any instances in which experts were employed as an aid in the settlement of litigation. It matters not what such experts were called, or whether they functioned entirely as does the judicial expert of today. What is important is to find cases in which skilled persons were engaged to perform an examination and to make a report of that examination, thereby aiding in the discovery of truth, and contributing toward an equitable decision in the dispute.[1]

Article I. Expert Surveyors

The first known Roman legislation concerning experts is contained in the *Twelve Tables* (ca. 450 B.C.). There one finds that surveyors played the rôle of experts when they were appointed by the praetor to settle a boundaries dispute. When by their expert skill as *periti* they had established the boundaries, the surveyors were to report their findings to the praetor. The praetor was then to assign to

[1] As to whether the expert of Roman Law was simply a special witness, or only an advisor to the judge, or perhaps himself a *iudex*, cf. E. Robert Arthur, *Expert Witnesses, an Historical Study*, unpublished, typewritten dissertation, School of Canon Law, (unique copy in the archives division of the Catholic University of America Library, is #3283), (Washington, D.C.: The Catholic University of America, 1940) (hereafter cited as *Expert Witnesses*).

each party the land to which he was entitled, according to the testimony of the experts.[2]

Pomponius (ca. 150 A.D.) wrote that an action was granted against a court-appointed surveyor who was maliciously fraudulent in his report.[3]

Domitius Ulpianus († 228 A.D.), the famed jurist from whom nearly one-third of the *Digest* of Justinian was later compiled, wrote substantially the same thing that was contained in the *Twelve Tables*: "It is part of the duty of the magistrate in a case involving the boundaries of land to send surveyors, and by means of them, dispose of the question in accordance with justice. . . ."[4]

A letter from the Emperor Constantine (306-337) in 330 to Tertullian, a provincial governor, stated that, in a controversy over boundaries, "surveyors are to be commanded to go to the disputed place, in order that by the discovery of truth in this matter the dispute will be ended." This letter became embodied in the Theodosian Code,[5] and later also in the Justinian Code.[6]

Article II. Handwriting Experts

Another use of experts is indicated in a letter from the Emperor Justinian I (527-565) to the praetor Julian. This letter, written about 530, was incorporated in Justinian's collection of laws which was known as the Code.[7] Stating that in any comparison of handwriting as found in private letters and other non-public instruments on the one hand, and in public and official documents and instruments, on the other hand, there was abundant occasion for falsification, Justinian enacted certain rules to avert this falsification. He demanded that the experts employed for the *com-*

[2] *The Civil Law*, 11 vols., a translation by S. P. Scott; Vol. I, *The Twelve Tables* (Cincinnati, 1932), Table VIII, Law IV, p. 72.

[3] D. (11.6) (3.4).

[4] D. (10.1) 8.

[5] *Codex Theodosianus* (2.26) 1.

[6] C. (3.39) 3.

[7] C. (4.20) 3,4 and (4.21) 3,4.

parationes letterarum swear that the comparison they were about to make would be done, not for the sake of gain, nor in enmity to the party, nor for a bribe. These regulations were binding in every court of the Empire.

Article III. Expert Midwives

Because it was the pattern from which the Church's legislation was probably modelled, the most important Roman Law concerning experts was that which dealt with the place of midwives in determining pregnancy. This one finds in the *Digest* of Justinian[8] The *Digest* adopted the teaching of Ulpian, who had in turn used as his source an earlier imperial rescript sent to the *Praetor Urbanus*, Valerius Priscianus. The Emperor had been consulted in a case wherein the husband claimed that his wife, now separated from him, had become pregnant during this separation. The wife denied the charge. To solve the question the rescript suggested what is termed a "new counsel and remedy," namely, the praetor was to choose the home of a most reputable woman and send there the disputedly-pregnant wife to be inspected by *"tres obstetrices probatae artis et fidei."* Upon completion of their inspection, these skilled and honest midwives were to report their conclusions to the praetor, whose further action was to be determined by the majority opinion of the midwives.

This new procedure was later adopted by the *senatusconsultum*, which made it mandatory for the praetor in similar cases to summon midwives to conduct the physical examination of women. It was also of obligation for the praetor himself to appoint the midwives, not giving the parties the right to choose their own.

Conclusion

There can be no doubt that the Roman judicial system employed experts. From the dawn of systematic legal pro-

[8] D. (25.4) (1.4,5).

cedure, judges were humble enough to admit that in many fields they were less than expert. They were then, on occasion, compelled to seek help from persons more qualified than themselves, if the truth was to be ascertained. Thus it was that in settling controversies the courts of the Roman Empire engaged experts surveyors, handwriting specialists, and midwives.

CHAPTER II

THE EXPERT IN ECCLESIASTICAL LAW UNTIL THE TIME OF THE COUNCIL OF TRENT

The preceding survey of the Roman legislation governing the use of experts in judicial processes reveals the foundation upon which was built the ecclesiastical law of experts. In this matter, as in practically all others, the Church through its close association with the Empire assimilated for its own discipline what was already existent and evidently effective in the civil law of the Empire in which the Church had become established.

Being concerned chiefly with the health and growth of the infant Church in a pagan world, the Fathers and Councils of the Church bothered little with the less important issues such as specific legislation for the use of experts in trials! They were, and rightly so, more concerned with the defense of the faith from heresy than with the enactment of procedural rules.

Despite, however, the lack of legislation in the matter, experts must have been used whenever a case demanded it. The ecclesiastical judge, just as his counterpart in the civil law, undoubtedly sometimes found it necessary to seek the advice and testimony of men particularly skilled in some art or science. Prudence dictated such a course of action, and Roman Law offered its gift of experience in the matter. As an objective observer of the practice of the times, the ecclesiastical judge knew in which points the civil law was practical and effective, and in which points impractical and ineffective, and accordingly he benefited from that knowledge.

Slight indeed are today's traces of any church legislation regarding the use of experts in that bygone era. The sparse legislation that is retained offers grounds sufficient for asserting that from its very beginning the Church employed experts in certain controveries.

Article 1. The Expert in the *Decretum* of Gratian

The collection of Gratian (ca. 1140) contains the earliest trace of Church regulation concerning experts. Cyprian, in a letter written in 249 to Pomponius, dealt with the unhappy problem of concubinage among women who had dedicated themselves to the service of God by a vow of virginity.[1]

These women asserted that they remained virgins despite their cohabitation with men. As proof they offered the testimony of midwives witnessing to their virginity. Cyprian replied that the mere fact of physical integrity was no excuse for their action, for one could be defiled in soul even if the defilement were not evidenced exteriorly, and he reminded the bishop that midwives were, after all, capable of error in their inspection. *"Nec aliqua putet se posse hoc excusatione defendi, quod inspici et probari possit, an virgo sit: cum et manus obstetricum et oculi saepe fallantur. . . ."*

When these evil-doers had repented by giving up their illicit concubinage, they were, so continued Cyprian, to be diligently re-examined by midwives, and if found still to be virgins they were again to be admitted to the Church.

The value of this early letter cannot be overestimated. It was important enough to be included in Gratian's collection nine hundred years after its composition; it was commented upon by almost every writer on the *Decretum;* it was referred to by the glossators and commentators of the Decretals of Pope Gregory IX. The very wording of the letter shows the rather common usage of midwives in a controversy over virginity. Had not the guilty women themselves engaged midwives to establish their defense, even before Cyprian had been consulted?

The most noteworthy principle established by Cyprian

[1] Epistula IV, nn. 3, 4, *Corpus Scriptorum Ecclesasticorum Latinorum,* editum consilio et impensis Academiae Litterarum Caesareae Vindobonensis (72 vols., Vindobonae, 1866), Vol. III, Pars II, pp. 474-477.

was the fact that the hands and eyes of midwives could often be deceived. The *Glossa Ordinaria* of Gratian's Decree was concerned with this principle of Cyprian. The gloss investigated the various possibilities—when the testimony of a husband was to be believed, when that of his wife, when that of the *peritae matronae*, and concluded, "if two or three noble and upright women say that she is a virgin, not known by any man, their testimony is to be believed."[2]

The same glossator noted that, although Cyprian's argument against the reliability of testimony by sight was valid, inasmuch as the eye could readily be deceived, nevertheless the non-deception of the eye was of more frequent occurrence.[3]

Besides this important bit of legislation, the *Decretum* reveals other instances of the use of experts. In two canons, reputedly from the Frankish Bishop Rabanus Maurus to Heribaldus in 853,[4] the use of expert midwives is seen.[5] Despite the fact that these two canons were taken from a forgery of the Pseudo-Isidorian group, the *False Capitularies,* attributed to Benedict the Levite,[6] they attest to what was very likely the practice of the times. If the appointment of experts in such matters had not been a common occurrence at the time the forgeries were produced, the false decretals would probably not have been accepted as genuine. Rather, they would have been rejected as recog-

[2] *Decretum Gratiani* (Romae, 1582), gloss on c. 4, C. XXVII, q. 1, s.v. *obstetricum.*

[3] C. 4, C. XXVII, q. 1, s.v. *fallantur.*

[4] *Libri VII collecti ab Angesiso Abbati et Benedicto Levita ante annos octingentos,* Liber Sextus, c. 55, 91. Mansi, *Sacrorum Conciliorum; Nova et Amplissima Collectio* (53 vols. in 60, Paris-Leipzig-Arnhem, 1901-1927), XVII, Supplement, Columns 931, 937, *Capitularium Karoli Magni et Ludovici Pii.*

[5] C. 29, C. XXVII, q. 2; c. 1, C. XXXIII, q. 1.

[6] A. Van Hove, *Commentarium Lovaniense in Codicem Iuris Canonici,* 1 vol. in 5 toms., Tom. I, *Prolegomena* (2. ed., Mechliniae-Romae: H. Dessain, 1945), p. 237.

nizably spurious, and contrary to the ordinary teaching and practice.

Thus one may profitably study the canons involved along with their glosses. Briefly, these canons ruled that if *per iustum iudicium* it was proved that the husband was frigid, and hence not capable of rendering the marital debt, he and his wife could be separated, and the wife permitted to remarry. A gloss on the second of these canons stated that the proof of the non-consummation was to be obtained "*per aspectum corporis, si virgo est.*"[7] The conclusion of the gloss was that this corporal inspection was to be conducted by midwives. If they found that the woman was still a virgin, their testimony was to be preferred to all other proofs, even to the proof that might derive from the sworn testimony of the husband.[8]

Paucapalea in his *Summa* (written between 1140-1148) made no reference to experts, but thought that the *iustum iudicium* of this same decree meant merely what was mentioned in the following canon, namely, "*ut uterque eorum septima manu propinquorum, tactis sacrosanctis reliquiis, iureiurando dicat, ut numquam per commixtionem carnis una caro effecti fuissent.*"[9] He seemed to consider proof sufficiently given by means of the testimony of seven friends and neighbors of each spouse, independently of the testimony of skilled midwives as demanded by other commentators.

Rufinus († 1190) likewise disagreed with the gloss, calling not for experts, but for the *septimae manus* witnesses. Commenting on this same canon, he wrote that the necessary proof was to be obtained "*non utique candentis ferri vel ferventis aquae aut huiusmodi—quod prohibetur—sed septima manu propinquorum.*"[10]

[7] C. 1, C. XXXIII, s.v. *iudicium.*

[8] C. 1, C. XXXIII, q. 1, s.v. *probare.*

[9] Paucapalea, *Die* SUMMA *des Paucapalea über das* DECRETUM GRATIANI, herangegen von Dr. J. Friedrich von Schulte, (Giessen, 1890), C. 1, C. XXXIII, q. 1, s.v. *per iustum iudicium.*

[10] Rufinus, *Die* SUMMA DECRETORUM, herausgegeben von H. Singer

The Archdeacon Guido de Baiiso († 1313) thought that in this particular case (the frigidity, or impotence, of the husband) proof should be established not only by expert testimony, but also by the testimony of the *septimae manus* witnesses, because "the eye of the midwife is often deceived." This was not law, but merely his personal opinion, and was not held by all canonists. He referred to Goffredus de Trono († 1245) and Joannes Andreae (1272-1348), who both taught that the *purgatio septima manu* was unnecessary in the present case, since the inspection of the woman by midwives would suffice for proof.[11]

It should be observed that the difference of opinion regarding the use of experts or of the *septimae manus* witnesses concerned only this particular case where the wife had alleged that her marriage remained unconsummated in consequence of the impotence of her husband.[12] As will be seen later, the use of the *septimae manus* witnesses was demanded only when the woman claiming non-consummation was herself not a virgin.

If it was not a requirement of law, it was at least the practice of the times, to demand examination of the husband, as witness Hostiensis:

> Quid si mulier dicit quod vir non potest eam cognoscere, allegans super hoc defectum membri viri? In hoc casu dic virum inspiciendum per homines expertos et honestos, sicut dixi de muliere arcta ... feci inspici nedum per laicos sed etiam per clericos.[13]

For a complete picture of the use of experts in this period of Gratian, there are two canons of the *Decretum* that

(Paderborn: Schöningh, 1902), ad c. 1 ("*Quod autem*"), C. XXXIII, q. 1, s.v. *per iustum iudicium.*

[11] Guido a Baiiso, *Rosarium, seu in Decretorum Volumen Commentaria,* (Venetiis, 1577), ad c. 1, C. XXXIII, q. 1, s.v. *per obstetrices.*

[12] C. 1, C. XXXIII, q. 1.

[13] Hostiensis (Henricus de Segusio †1271), *Summa Aurea* (Lugduni, 1568), Lib. IV, tit. XIV, *de frigidos et maleficiis et de impotentia coeundi,* under "*Qualiter et quando divortium*" (hereafter cited *Summa Aurea*).

should be studied. As interpreted by the glossators, those canons insisted upon the skill necessary for midwives engaged in the *aspectio corporis.*[14]

The first of these canons (*Requisisti*) called for proof through the *septimae manus* witnesses in a case wherein both parties alleged non-consummation. The gloss, however, made it clear that such witnesses were used only if the woman was not a virgin. If she remained a virgin, then the judgment of the midwives as to her virginity was sufficient proof of non-consummation.[15]

The next canon (*Si quis accepit*) treated of the case wherein the wife alone, quite some time after her marriage, claimed that her husband had never consummated the union. Since the husband denied his wife's charge, so the canon stated, he was to be believed in preference to his wife. The reason for the preference, according to the canon was *"quia vir est caput mulieris."* Though this is to be honored as a Scriptural quotation,[16] it seems quite unsound as a basis for the preference afforded the man's testimony. It also appeared unsound to one of the glossators, who opined that the real reason for the preference lay in the commonly accepted principle, *"favendum est matrimonio."* The man testified for consummation, the woman against consummation. Thus the presumption favored the husband.

It was, however, merely a presumption, and as such had to give way to fact. So the husband's testimony could be undermined by contrary proof. This being so, the glossator distinguished two cases. In the first case, wherein the woman had lost her virginity before marriage, her later claim of non-consummation of marriage was to be disregarded in view of the husband's contention to the contrary. The *septimae manus* witnesses were of no avail in such a case, for the claim of non-consummation was not mutual.

[14] C. 2 (*"Requisisti"*), C. XXXIII, q. 1; c. 3 (*"Si quis accepit"*), C. XXXIII, q. 1.

[15] C. 2, C. XXXIII, q. 1, s.v. *septima manu.*

[16] Ephesians, 5:23.

In the second case, wherein the woman entered marriage a virgin, her later testimony of non-consummation was of equal worth with her husband's contrary claim of consummation. In this latter case, so concluded the glossator, belief was to be given to the one who established proof *per aspectum corporis.* Nevertheless, unless the women performing the inspection *"essent peritissimae, potius esset credendum viro."*[17]

Hence, although great weight attached to the husband's testimony, that fact in itself did not militate against the testimony of experts. On the contrary, the testimony of the experts was sometimes of prime importance; it could be the determining factor itself.

Article II. The Expert in the Decretals of Pope Gregory IX

The Decretals of Gregory IX (1227-1241) indicate a rather frequent use of experts in ecclesiastical trials, and show a development of rules governing experts. While the expert was consulted in many fields, he was most often employed in the matrimonial causes of alleged impotence and non-consummation.

Section 1. The Expert Surveyor

The expert surveyor of the Decretals, as in Roman Law, was to be selected not by the contending parties, but rather by the judge or his superior.

In July of 597,[18] Pope Gregory I (500-604) instructed a Bishop John to settle a boundaries dispute with the aid of a surveyor whom the Pope was sending. The two contending abbots were to accept the decision of the bishop, which decision was to be rendered according to the report of the skilled surveryor.[19] The *mensor* was liable if by his

[17] C. 3, C. XXXIII, q. 1, s.v. *tempore.*

[18] Jaffé, *Regesta Pontificum Romanorum* (2. ed. by F. Kaltenbrunner, to 590; by P. Ewald, 590-882; and by S. Lowenfeld, 882-1198; Lipsiae, 1885-1888, referred to as JK, JE, JL), JE, n. 1482.

[19] C. 9, X, *de probationibus,* II, 26.

false report he maliciously wronged one of the parties.[20] He was not, however liable "*de culpa . . . vel de neglegentia.*"[21] Gregory urged, but did not command, that the bishop be present for the surveyor's examination of the property. The bishop's presence was not absolutely necessary, wrote a commentator, because experts are "*quasi quidam testes, unde satis est ut videant et iudicio referant.*"[22]

The careful wording of this comment by Panormitanus (Nicholaus de Tudeschis, 1386-1453) leads to an important distinction made at the time by all the commentators on the Decretals of Gregory. They distinguished between the oath *de credulitate* required of experts, and the oath *de veritate* required of ordinary witnesses. The distinction is valuable, because it leads to a precise notion of the expert.

The oath *de veritate* was the type of oath required of first hand witnesses. They testified regarding what they had learned directly through their senses, and so had to swear to the *truth* of what they said. The oath *de credulitate* was demanded of what may be called "second hand" witnesses. Such witnesses testified chiefly not regarding what they had learned directly through their senses, but regarding what they had learned indirectly, through a judgment they arrived at by observing an effect and then reasoning to its cause. They were to swear, not to the *truth,* but to the *credibility* and probability of their judgment.

The eyewitness to the signing of a private letter would have sworn *de veritate,* while the handwriting expert, comparing an already signed letter with what he knew to be

[20] Dorna, *Die* SUMMA LIBELLORUM *des Bernardus Darna,* Vol. I, fascicle 1, CXXXI, p. 62—*Quellen zur Geschichte des Römisch-Kanonischen Processes im Mittelalter,* edited by L. Wahrmund (Innsbruck, 1905).

[21] Hostiensis, *Commentaria in Quinque Decretalium Libros* (6 vols. in 4, Venetiis, 1581), ad c. 9, X, *de praescriptionibus,* II, 26 (hereafter cited *Commentaria*).

[22] Panormitanus, *Commentaria in Quinque Libros Decretalium* (5 vols. in 7, Venetiis, 1588), ad c. 9, X, *de praescriptionibus,* II, 26, n. 7 (hereafter cited *Commentaria*).

the proper signature, would have reasoned from effect to cause, and so would have sworn *de credulitate.*

Upon this distinction the commentators rested their arguments for or against requiring an oath from experts. As was seen, Panormitanus referred to experts as "*quasi quidam testes.*" The Italian Cardinal Peter Paul Parisius (1473-1545) wrote of surveyors: "They are not properly called witnesses, because they make their depositions *de credulitate.*"[23]

Since they were not witnesses in the strict sense of the term, experts were not required to take an oath *de veritate.* This was the teaching of Hostiensis and of most of the canonists. Writing of ordinary witnesses, the Cardinal required that they touch the Sacred Gospels and swear to the truth of what they were about to say.[24] This oath he did not require of the *matronae peritae* when they testified as to their findings obtained from the physical inspection of women.[25]

SECTION 2. EXPERT PHYSICIANS

The expert physician was also employed at this time. The Abbot of Holy Trinity of Maleleone appealed to Innocent III for a decision on whether a certain priest was to be declared irregular for involuntary homicide. The priest in question surprised a thief looting his church. Chasing the thief, he managed to overtake him and hit him with a hoe just as a group of aroused parishioners arrived on the scene and themselves began to beat the luckless looter, who in a short time was dead.

The priest wondered if it was his blow that had caused

[23] *Repetitiones in Iure Canonico* (6 vols., Venetiis, 1587), Vol. IV, ad c. 9, X, *de praescriptionibus,* II, 26, at n. 10 (hereafter cited *Repetitiones*). Cf. also Baldus de Ubaldis, *Super Decretales* (Lugduni, 1547), ad c. 4 (*Proposuisti*), X, *de praescriptionibus,* II, 19, folio CLXVI, § 3.

[24] Hostiensis, *Summa Aurea,* Lib. II, *De testibus,* n. 5, "*Quid debent iurare.*"

[25] *Commentaria,* c. 6 (*Fraternitas*), X, *de frigidis et maleficiatis et de impotentia coeundi,* IV, 15, s.v. *districte.*

the man's death, and if he might not therefore have incurred an irregularity. He asked the abbot, who in turn presented the problem to the pope. In his reply, dated July 1, 1209,[26] the pope stated that the priest had not incurred the irregularity "if it should appear that the particular blow inflicted by him was both so slight in itself, and so minor in relation to that part of the body, a part in which, if one were lightly struck, one would not ordinarily die, that in the judgment of expert physicians it might be averred that such a blow was not lethal."[27]

Felinus Sandeus (1444-1503), at one time an auditor of the Rota, commenting on this rescript of Innocent, left some precise information concerning the use of expert physicians. What he said of this particular type of expert will, for the most part, apply to the expert of any other art or science.

Of first importance, Sandeus noted that in this particular case the judge was not free, but was bound to consult expert physicians. In general, though, when doctors were to be used by the court, Sandeus admitted that if the parties agreed upon one and the same expert he could be used. If they disagreed, the judge himself was obliged to appoint the *peritus medicus*.[28]

The appointed doctor was not merely to give his opinion, but was obliged to make a complete report, based upon his personal examination, and to state the reasons for his conclusions in the report.

Ordinarily at least two doctors were to be employed, but one would suffice: 1) if he was maintained at public expense for the people; 2) if the parties to the dispute agreed on

[26] Potthast, *Regesta Pontificum Romanorum, inde ab anno post Christum natum MCXCVIII ad annum MCCCIV* (2 vols. Berolini, 1874-1875), n. 3757 (hereafter cited Potthast).

[27] C. 18, X, *de homicidio voluntario vel casuali,* V, 12.

[28] F. Sandeus, *Commentaria in V Libros Decretalium* (3 vols., Venetiis, 1570), Vol. III, Column 1041, nn. 3 ff., ad c. 18, X, *de homicidio voluntario vel casuali,* V, 12 (hereafter cited Sandeus).

one and the same expert, and 3) if in the locality only one expert could be found.

This same commentator advised that the expert was to be believed provided he had at least one confirmatory witness (*contestem*). Therefore when testifying concerning the *peritia* of his particular art the expert was to swear "*de credulitate* ... unless he testified concerning a thing that was perceptible not only by a judgment of the intellect, but also by some one of the corporeal senses. . . ."

Finally, Sandeus reminded the judge that if the report of the experts was faulty, either because of their lack of skill or for any other reason, he was obliged to change his sentence to accord with the report of the more skilled experts.

SECTION 3. EXPERTS IN CAUSES OF IMPOTENCE AND NON-CONSUMMATION

The expert used in causes involving impotence and non-consummation occupied the most prominent place in the Decretals. In point of time, the first case is found in a letter of Pope Gregory VIII, written in 1187.[29] The pope was appealed to in a case wherein the wife swore that her marriage had not yet been consummated, and could not be consummated because of her husband's impotence. To confirm her contention, she offered the testimony of seven women who had examined her and pronounced her physically inviolate. The husband swore that his wife's charge was untrue.

Gregory replied that the "*iuramenta puellae et testimonia illarum septem mulierum, quae ipsam per experientiam virginem asseverant,*" were more deserving of belief than the husband's uncorroborated sworn testimony.[30]

This decision was in keeping with the teaching of the commentators on Gratian, namely, that in cases wherein the claim of non-consummation was contested by one of

[29] JL, n. 16081.

[30] C. 4, X, *de probationibus*, II, 19.

the parties, the best proof was that afforded by experts in confirmation of one of the parties.[31] As was previously seen, the man's sworn testimony alone would have been preferred to that of the woman had she lacked corroborating proof, for the presumption of the consummation of the marriage favored the husband.

In 1206 Pope Innocent III dealt with a similar problem.[32] The case was one of claimed non-consummation. The actual decision of the pope is not pertinent to this study, but his tacit approval of the consulting bishop's earlier mode of procedure is noteworthy. This bishop, before petitioning the aid of the pope, had sought to solve the matter by employing *"matronae . . . providae et honestae"* to inspect the woman. The case grew complex, so the pope's intervention was asked. In his reply, the pope casually reiterated the use of experts in the procedure of the lower court, as if such action of the inferior court were the expected thing.[33]

Sixteen years later Pope Honorius III[34] (1216-1227) dealt with a case wherein a dissolution of the bond was sought on grounds of non-consummation caused by the relative impotence of the husband. The wife stated that although she and her husband had cohabited for eight years, she still retained her integrity. She claimed that her husband was impotent. While he acknowledged that he had never been capable of consummating his marriage, he denied that he was absolutely impotent, claiming that he was capable of sexual relations with other women. To avoid any fraud in the matter, the bishop to whom the case was directed ordered that the wife be inspected *"a matronis bonae opinionis, fide dignis, ac expertis in opere nuptiali."* This done, the experts testified that the woman remained a virgin. Then the priest of the parish wherein the husband resided made inquiry concerning the husband, whether

[31] C. 1, C. XXXIII, q. 1, s.v. *probare.*

[32] Potthast, n. 2836.

[33] C. 6, X, *de frigidis et maleficiatis et de impotentia coeundi,* IV, 15.

[34] Potthast, n. 7832 (Persutti).

he had carnally known another woman. This inquiry was fruitless.

The wife insistently professed her desire to obtain a dissolution of the bond in order that she might remarry and become a mother. The bishop finally referred the case to the pope.

Honorius, having considered the matter, ordered that the couple was to continue to live together for three more years in an effort to consummate the marriage. At the end of this time a sentence of dissolution was to be pronounced if *"septima propinquorum manu firmatibus iuramento se comisceri carnaliter nequisse."* The gloss informs us that the oath of the *septimae manus* witnesses was a precaution added to the proof already given by the experts.[35]

The same Pope Honorius in 1225[36] was asked to settle a question concerning the repudiation of expert midwives. The case involved a young girl who had left her youthful husband to enter a convent, claiming non-consummation of her marriage. She fortified her claim by the testimony of certain women who, after examining her, pronounced her to be still a virgin. The husband, on the contrary, claimed that the marriage had been consummated.

The pope ordered that the girl be returned to the convent which she had entered, and that she remain there until the trial was completed. While she was securely in the convent, her husband's proofs were to be heard, as well as any other proofs which she might have to offer. Finally, because *"saepe fallit tactus et oculus obstetricum,"* Honorius commanded that the judge appoint another set of midwives to determine whether the girl still retained her virginity.[37]

Note that the Supreme Pontiff recognized the right to each party to employ experts. When, however, the testimony of the experts was not harmonious, the court was

[35] C. 7, X, *de frigidis et maleficiatis et de impotentia coeundi,* IV, 15, s.v. *septima manu.*

[36] Potthast, n. 7756 (Persutti).

[37] C. 14, X, *de probationibus,* II, 19.

to appoint more skilled experts, and to abide by their decision.

Article III. The Expert after the Decretals of Gregory IX until the Council of Trent

From the time of the Decretals of Gregory until the year 1840 there was no legislation concerned with experts, with the exception of two canons in the *Liber Sextus* of Boniface VIII. Because, however, the Decretals of Gregory were given the force of law, it was quite natural that there should have been much commentary on them. As the teaching of the many commentators on the Decretals is substantially the same in the matter of experts, the writer will attempt to synthesize their writings. For the sake of convenience the commentators will be divided into two groups, those who wrote prior to the time of the Council of Trent (1545-1563), and those who wrote after that time.

Section 1. Cases in which Experts were Used

Most frequently used were midwives and physicians to perform the physical examination of the spouses in causes of non-consummation and impotence.[38] Not only were men to be inspected by men, and women by women, but some canonists held that, when sufficient proof could not otherwise be obtained, it was permissible for male physicians and surgeons to perform the physical inspection of women. Francis de Aretio (also called Aretinus; Francis de Accoltis, 1418-1486) seemed to be the first to mention this. Men physicians could be employed when no midwives were available, he wrote, and the woman could not object to the inspection on the grounds of embarrassment, because too much was at stake to neglect any proofs. (The inspection

[38] Baldus de Ubaldis (1327-1400), *Super Decretalibus* ad cc. 4, 14, X, *de probationibus,* II, 19. Cf. also Henricus Boich († ca. 1350), *In Quinque Libros Commentaria,* (Venetiis, 1576), ad c. *Continebatur,* X, *de desponsatione impuberum,* IV. Hostiensis, *Summa Aurea,* Lib. IV, p. 315, *de frigid, et malef. et impot. coeundi,* (14); *Commentaria,* ad c. 6, X, *de frigid, et malef. et impot. coeundi,* IV, 15, s.v. *pleniorem.*

was performed with a view to the dissolution of the marriage bond, and perhaps also with the hope of obtaining permission to contract a new marriage.)[39]

Philippus Decius (1454-1537) followed the opinion of Aretinus, and reasoned that, since the Decretals demanded the use of a surgical remedy for impotence in women when that was possible without grave danger of death,[40] accordingly the law certainly contemplated and expected the prior inspection of women by the male doctor or surgeon.[41]

Andreas Tiraquellus (Tiraqueau; 1479-1559) referred to the teaching of Aretinus and Decius, but was himself inclined to disagree with them.[42]

Other uses of the expert were indicated by Durantis (1237-1296). His mention of the various uses of experts is more valuable when one recalls that he was a teacher and an auditor of what was later to become the Roman Rota. In this double capacity he ably reflected the practice of this century. He wrote that *"medico creditur de sua medicina . . . fabro de fabrica . . . doctori de discipulo . . . mensori de officio suo . . . et generaliter unicuique in arte sua experto credendum est."*

Durantis then related an interesting example of the use of physicians as experts. A student had asked a money-changer for the payment of some money that was owed him. Instead of giving him the money, the money-changer hit the student with a heavy iron hook, killing him. Brought to trial, the money-changer denied that he had hit the boy, claiming rather that a mule had kicked the boy, killing him! The prosecutor brought in surgeons to inspect the

[39] Farnciscus de Aretio, *Consilia* (1546), Consilia 142, nn. 14, 16, 17.

[40] C. 7, X, *de frigidis et maleficiatis et de impotentia coeundi,* IV, 15,.

[41] Philippus Decius, *Super Decretalibus,* additae sunt ad calcem singulorum capitum, annotationes omnes clarissimorum Iurisconsultorum Hieronymi Gigantis, Silvestri Aldobrandini, Caroli Molinaei, et aliorum quorundam, (Lugduni, 1559), ad c. *Proposuisti,* ij.

[42] Andreas Tiraquellus, *De Legibus Connubialibus, et Iure Maritali* (Lugduni, 1569), Lex 4, n. 28, s.v. *Proinde.*

corpse, and they reported that the fatal wound was caused not by the kick of a mule, but by the blow of a heavy iron hook. Sentence was pronounced in conformity with the judgment of the experts.[43]

The *Liber Sextus* reveals still another use of experts, namely, that of skilled theologians, canon and civil lawyers in the trials of heretics.[44] These experts, as advisors and counsellors to the court, were to ascertain whether or not the statement of the accused was necessarily to be construed as heretical. Their use was recommended not only by Pope Boniface VIII (1294-1303), but also by his predecessors, Innocent, Alexander, and Clement.[45]

From this information one may be assured that, whenever the interest of truth dictated that experts be consulted, regardless of the type of controversy, they were consulted.

SECTION 2. QUALITIES REQUIRED OF EXPERTS

No definite norms were established. It was rather spelled out in general terms that experts were to be skilled in their profession and worthy of belief.[46]

As regards experts in non-consummation causes, Hostiensis was more specific. Such experts were to be chosen from the neighborhood, or at least from the same city, and they were to be neither too young (therefore lacking experience) nor too old (perhaps defective in sight).[47]

[43] Gulielmus Durandus (or Durantis), *Speculum Iuris* (Venetiis, 1577), Lib. II, partic. 2, § 3, nn. 26, 27.

[44] C. 12, *de haereticis,* V, 2, in VI°. Cf. also Guido a Baiiso, *In Sextum Decretalium Commentaria* (Venetiis, 1577), ad. c. 12, *de haereticis,* V, 2, in VI°, s.v. *peritos.*

[45] C. 20, *de haereticis,* V, 2, in VI°.

[46] Baldus de Ubaldis, *Super Decretalibus,* ad c. 14, X, *de probationibus,* II, 19, at § 3. Cf. also Hostiensis, *Summa Aurea,* Lib. II, *de probationibus,* 6, "*Et quot,*" K, *octavo;* cf. also Innocentius IV (Sinibaldus Fliscus), *Commentaria in V Libros Decertalium* (Venetiis, 1570), ad c. 6, X, *de frigid. et malef. et impot. coeundi,* IV, 15, s.v. *providas* (hereafter cited *Commentaria*); Panormitanus, ad c. 4, X, *de probationibus,* II, 19, at n. 2.

[47] *Commentaria,* ad c. 6, X, *de frigid. et malef. et impot. coeundi,* IV, 15, s.v. *parochiae.*

SECTION 3. THE NUMBER OF EXPERTS REQUIRED

The required number of experts was greatly disputed. The Decretal legislation seemed occasionally to assimilate the *septimae manus* witnesses and the *matronae*. Generally, however, these were evidently distinct offices, and, rather than that a specific number was stated, only the plural number was used, e.g., *peritae, matronae, obstetrices, periti.* Most of the canonists were, therefore, satisfied with at least two experts, and thought that in exceptional circumstances one outstanding expert might suffice.[48]

SECTION 4. THE APPOINTMENT OF EXPERTS

The judge appointed the experts either at the instance of the parties or on his own initiative, i.e., *ex officio*. Experts chosen *ex officio* were preferred to those selected by the parties.[49]

SECTION 5. THE OATH OF EXPERTS

Were experts required to take an oath? An unreserved "yes" to this question cannot be given. The most common opinion was that, since experts were not witnesses in the strict sense, they were not required to swear *de veritate,* but were required to swear only *de credulitate.*[50] Panormitanus sometimes seemed to require no oath at all of the experts. The writer, however, is of the opinion that Panormitanus always demanded at least the oath *de credulitate.*[51]

[48] Sandeus, Vol. III, column 1041; Cf. also Innocent IV, ad c. 6, X, *de frigid. et malef. et impot. coeundi,* IV, 15, s.v. *providas;* cf. also Baldus, ad c. 14, X, *de probationibus,* II, 19, at § 4 of "*Causam*"; Panormitanus, ad c. 4, X, *de probationibus,* II, 19, § 4.

[49] Sandeus, Vol. III, column 1041, ad c. 18, *de homicidio voluntario vel casuali,* V, 12; cf. also Baldus de Ubaldis, *Super Decretalibus,* ad c. 14, X, *de probationibus,* II, 19, on "*Causam,*" § 1, p. CLXXVI; Panormitanus, *Commentaria,* ad c. 4, X, *de probationibus,* II, 19, at § 10.

[50] Cf. pp. 12, 13, in this dissertation for the distinction between the oath *de veritate* and *de credulitate.*

[51] Panormitanus, *Commentaria,* ad c. 4, X, *de probationibus,* II, 19, at §§ 4, 5.

In one place the Abbot of Sicily asked whether experts were to be believed without an oath, and he wrote, "The reason for doubting is that they (the experts) do not testify concerning that which they perceive by the corporeal sense, but by a judgment of the intellect according to the skill of their art. Hence, since they may err, they might easily perjure themselves if they should swear." He admits a divided opinion among the glossators of civil law on the same question and informs us that Joannes Andreae and Hostiensis required the oath *de credulitate,* but forbade the oath *de veritate* from experts, for fear of error and perjury.

Abbas' personal conclusion is *"in dubio credo, quod debent iurare."* Thus he demanded that they swear, but surely he means only *de credulitate.*[52]

SECTION 6. PROBATIVE VALUE OF EXPERT TESTIMONY

The testimony of experts was of greater value than the sworn testimony of the parties. Although a gloss stated that it was preferred to *all* other proof, one knows that it was possible to repudiate the testimony of experts by more learned experts' testimony. These more learned experts were chosen either by the opposing party or by the judge himself.

And though it is true that the judge was bound to pronounce sentence according to the testimony of the more skilled experts, it was the judge himself who decided which was the sounder testimony and who were the more skilled experts. Obviously, then, the opinion of experts chosen by the judge was considered of greater worth than the opinion of those chosen by the parties.[53]

[52] Panormitanus, *Commentaria,* ad c. 4, X, *de probationibus,* II, 19, at § 11.

[53] Sandeus, Vol. III, column 1041, ad c. 18, X, *de homicidio voluntario vel casuali,* V, 12. Cf. also Baldus de Ubaldis, *Super Decretalibus,* ad c. 4 (*Proposuisti*), X, *de probationibus,* II, 19; Panormitanus, *Commentaria,* ad c. 4, X, *de probationibus,* II, 19, at § 3.

CHAPTER III

THE EXPERT FROM THE COUNCIL OF TRENT UNTIL THE *CUM MONEAT GLOSSA* (1840)

ARTICLE I. THE CANONICAL WRITERS OF THAT PERIOD (1563-1840)

Although the Council of Trent did not enact any legislation concerning the expert, the writer has divided his material into pre- and post-Trent periods for reasons of convenience. It will be seen that with reference to the matter of experts there was very little difference in the teaching which emanated from canonists before or after the Council of Trent (1545-1563).

SECTION 1. THE NATURE AND TYPES OF EXPERTS

Experts partake of the nature of a witness and of a judge: a witness, in that they give testimony; a judge, in that their testimony is based on a judgment which they make in accord with the rules of their particular skill.[1]

Following this twofold nature of the expert, Cardinal John Baptist de Luca (1614-1683), in his excellent treatment of this subject, distinguished various types of experts. The primary divisions are the *periti testes* and *periti arbitri.*

Periti testes are witnesses *de iure* rather than *de facto,* because the testimony they give depends more upon the judgment of their intellect than upon the perception of their senses, although there is an admixture of both in many cases.

Periti arbitri, on the other hand, reflect a species of experts who are employed by the court for giving their judgment rather than for testifying. These are used more fre-

[1] Thomas Sanchez (1550-1610), *De Sancto Matrimonii Sacramento Disputationum Libri decem* (Tomi tres, Venetiis, 1726), Lib. 7, disp. 113, n. 1 (hereafter cited Sanchez).

quently upon a choice made *ex offiicio* by the judge than upon the instance of the disputing parties. This rule obtained, so wrote the Cardinal, because...

> Upon the judge, although he is otherwise learned and intelligent in the law, but nonetheless unskilled in that art or ministry by means of which knowledge and light is had of unknown and obscure truth, is incumbent the obligation to employ an expert in that work, as an assessor, or counsellor to him in the matter.[2]

Periti testes were governed by the same rules as witnesses in the ordinary sense, in whatever regarded their examination by the judge, the value afforded to their testimony, and the exceptions raised against them.[3]

Periti arbitri were further distinguished as those who, through the parties, were nominated by the judge, and as those who were employed by the judge himself, *ex officio.* If the parties agreed on the selection of one expert or set of experts, or if each chose his own experts, with the simultaneous consent of the opposing party, then this expert was more accurately named an *arbiter.* If the parties each chose men favorable to themselves, without the consent of the adversary, such experts were properly called *sapientes,* since they represented a species of advocates or procurators deputed by the party to inform the judge of the party's rights. The expert who was appointed *ex officio* by the judge was given the title of assessor or counsellor.[4]

With these distinctions made, the rule of law, "*quod iudicio peritorum in arte est deferendum,*" could properly be applied. As defined, the *sapientes* as experts indeed testified, but in their *relationes* no solemnities were required, such as were called for in the case of the *arbitri* (chosen with the mutual consent of the parties) and the *assessores*

[2] Jo. Baptista de Luca (1614-1683), *Theatrum Veritatis et Justitiae* (16 vols., Venetiis, 1734), Lib. 15 Pars I (*de iudiciis et de praxi Curiae Romanae*), Disc. 33, n. 20 (hereafter cited *Theatrum*).

[3] *Theatrum,* Lib. 15, Pars I, Disc. 33, n. 22.

[4] *Ibid.,* n. 23.

(chosen *ex officio* by the judge). Hence the rules governing experts did not apply to the *sapientes,* who as favorable to a party were chosen apart from the consent of the adversary.[5]

Mention may be made here of an unofficial or extrajudicial expert. As a man skilled in some art or science he was consulted by the judge only for the purpose of informing himself. This consultation took place secretly, without citing the parties, and was not considered part of the process. The judge employed this extrajudicial expert not because the law required it, but solely for becoming more fully qualified to judge the case before him.[6]

SECTION 2. CASES IN WHICH EXPERTS WERE USED; REQUISITE QUALITIES

The writers on canon law in this period wrote profusely of the uses of experts in the ecclesiastical courts. They informed their readers again and again that experts could be used in any matter when the truth would more readily be obtained by means of such a use.[7] The examples most frequently given involved surveyors in boundary disputes; the artist or sculptor in judging an art work; surgeons, "*de vulnere*" and physicians, "*de morbo*"; midwives, to determine virginity; architects and builders, to determine the value of buildings.[8]

[5] *Loc. cit.*

[6] Ludovicus Engel (ca. 1634-1674), *Collegium Universi Juris Canonici* (editio nona, a Gaspare Barthel, Beneventi, 1760; prostat Venetiis), Lib. II, tit. 19, § III, nn. 10, 11 (hereafter cited Engel); cf. also Franciscus Schmalzgruber (1663-1735), *Ius Ecclesiasticum Universum, seu Lucubrationes Canonicae in Quinque Libros Decretalium Gregorii IX Pontificis Maximi* (5 vols. in 12, Romae, 1843-1845), Lib. II, tit. 19, n. 18 (hereafter cited Schmalzgrueber).

[7] De Luca, *Theatrum,* Lib. 15, Pars I, d. 33, n. 20.

[8] Cf. e.g., De Luca, *Theatrum,* Lib. 15, Pars I,, d. 33, n. 20; Emmanuel Gonzalez-Tellez (d. after 1673), *Commentaria perpetua in singulos textus quinque Librorum Decretalium Gregorii IX* (4 vols., Lugduni, 1673), Lib. II, tit. 19, c. 4, n. 7 (hereafter cited Gonzalez-Tellez); Cajetanus Felix Verano (1648-1713), *Iuris Canonici Universi Commentarius Paratitularis* (5 vols. Monachii, 1703-1708), Lib.

Experts were to be truly skilled in their field, and truthful. If they were of bad reputation, they were not to be employed; and if somehow the unqualified were used, exceptions could be brought against them.[9]

In performing the corporal inspection of women, the *matronae* who were called for were understood to be midwives (*obstetrices*), since they were ordinarily more qualified for the task. It was not necessary, however, that midwives be used, since the law did not require this.[10] The requirement that this examination be performed *"a matronis fidei bonae, et expertis in opere nuptiali"* could be fulfilled by women who were not midwives, but who were otherwise qualified as matrons, in that they had borne children and understood what was demanded in the inspection.[11] It was not necessary for the matrons to be of the nobility, as some had thought. There was no law requiring such persons.[12]

If there was some hesitation in earlier times about allowing male doctors and surgeons to perform the inspection of women in the more difficult cases, such hesitation disappeared almost entirely in this period. Following Aretinus and Decius, Thomas Sanchez wrote that when a higher quality of *peritia* was desired (for establishing proof of impotence) than could be found in women, then expert physicians could perform the corporal examination of women. The importance of the matter in question demanded that such proof be obtained even at the expense of some natural embarrassment on the woman's part. The reason-

II, tit. 19, nn. 2, 3 (hereafter cited Verano); Anacletus Reiffenstuel (1642-1703), *Jus Canonicum Universum* (5 vols. in 7, Parisiis, 1864-1870), Lib. II, tit. 19, n. 21 (hereafter cited Reiffenstuel); Franciscus Schmier (1680-1728), *Iurisprudentia Canonico-Civilis, seu Ius Canonicum Universum, iuxta V libros decretalium* (2 vols. Venetiis, 1754), Lib. II, tract. III, cap. IX, sectio 2, nn. 26-53 (hereafter cited Schmier).

[9] Cf. Reiffenstuel, Lib. IV, tit. 15, n. 35.

[10] C. 14, X, *de probationibus*, II, 19.

[11] Reiffenstuel, Lib. IV, tit. 15, n. 37.

[12] Sanchez, Lib. 7, d. 113, n. 3.

ing of Sanchez, like that of his predecessors, was presented thus: Inasmuch as the decretals *"Ex litteris"* and *"Fraternitatis"* demanded that a remedy be afforded by doctors and surgeons in cases wherein impotence could be cured without grave danger to the woman, then surely these same decretals supposed that the doctors and surgeons would previously inspect the woman to determine whether the impotence were remediable. If in such a case a doctor's or surgeon's inspection was to be employed, then, so Sanchez reasoned, it was also to be employed in cases where a dissolution of the bond was asked on grounds of impotence or non-consummation.[13] Qualified midwives, whenever they were available, were of course preferred to male doctors. Among the authors who subscribed to this same argument were Gonzalez-Tellez and Reiffenstuel.[14]

SECTION 3. THE APPOINTMENT AND EXCLUSION OF EXPERTS

Experts were appointed by the judge either *ad instantiam partium* or *ex officio,* regardless of the kind of expert they might be, whether what Cardinal de Luca termed *periti testes, periti arbitri, sapientes,* or *assessores.*

The Cardinal mentioned that in many curiae it was the practice to allow the parties to nominate their own *"peritum benevolum,"* and thereupon the judge would appoint him. In practically every case these experts acted almost as attorneys for their parties, and were discordant in their testimony. Then the judge would have to appoint a *tertius peritus* acceptable to both parties. The testimony of this third expert was to be received without any allowance for a fourth or fifth expert to be chosen, lest the trial continue *ad infinitum.*

To avoid innumerable delays, the Cardinal suggested that the practice of the Rota be followed. In line with it each party could present a list of experts in whom he had confidence, and a list of those in whom he did not have con-

[13] Sanchez, Lib. 7, d. 113, n. 21.

[14] Gonzalez-Tellez, Lib. II, tit. 19, c. 4, n. 7; cf. also Reiffenstuel, Lib. IV, tit. 15, n. 41.

fidence. From this list of experts the judge was to select, from the very start of the *peritia,* an expert who was acceptable to both parties.[15]

The parties needed to be cited and had to be present at the election of the experts by the judge.[16] If the judge wished secretly to inform himself through an extrajudicial expert, even though he was not bound by law to do so, he could unofficially consult the expert without the knowledge or presence of the parties.[17]

Experts could be rejected for the same reasons for which witnesses could be rejected.[18] The expert whom the judge had chosen *ex officio* as his assistant could be rejected on the grounds of suspicion alleged by one of the parties and confirmed with that party's oath. The mere sworn accusation of suspicion, however, did not suffice for rejecting an expert who had been chosen by the parties as mutually agreeable to them.[19]

SECTION 4. THE NUMBER OF EXPERTS REQUIRED

As in the earlier centuries, the number of needed experts was disputed, at least when the corporal inspection was concerned. It may be safely said, however, to have been by far the more probable opinion to demand two experts, at least in matters of such supreme importance as matrimonial causes. Sanchez was extremely clear in this matter:

> Duae matronae sunt necessariae et sufficiunt ut de virginitate deponant; et idem in aliis artis peritis. Quia a regula generali, dictanti in ore duorum vel trium stare omne verbum . . . res haec non excipitur.[20]

He admitted the external authority of certain authors

[15] Cf. De Luca, *Theatrum,* Lib. 15, Pars I, d. 33, nn. 24, 30.

[16] Cf. Sanchez, Lib. 7, disp. 113, n. 14.

[17] Cf. Engel, Lib. II, tit. 19, n. 12; De Luca, *Theatrum,* Lib, 15, Pars I, d. 33, n. 29; Schmalzgrueber, Lib. II, tit. 19, n. 19.

[18] Cf. De Luca, *Theatrum,* Lib. 15, Pars I, d. 33, n. 22.

[19] Cf. Sanchez, Lib. 7, disp. 113, n. 8; De Luca, *Theatrum,* Lib. 15, Pars I, d. 33, n. 24.

[20] Sanchez, Lib. 7, disp. 113, n. 16.

before him who were satisfied with only one expert if that was the only one in the town, or who were content even in the more difficult causes with one expert, provided he was *peritissimus*. He did not, however, agree with them, least of all *in causa conjugali,* for there was too much at stake to be satisfied with only one matron, even the most qualified. He was satisfied with one expert in matters of lesser importance, however, if more than one expert could not be found in the same city.[21] Gonzalez-Tellez taught that no more than two or three midwives should be used for the corporal inspection of women. Verano and Reiffenstuel likewise were satisfied with two experts in this matter.[22]

SECTION 5. THE OATH REQUIRED OF EXPERTS

The phrase *de credulitate* was no longer used in designation of the kind of oath that was required of experts, but the doctrine remained the same. It is to be noted that, although the ordinary witnesses swore *de veritate,* experts swore to the *probability* of things, since by means of their science they arrived not at absolute certitude, but only at indications of what was true; at most, they ordinarily attained only to moral certitude, and hence were not to swear *de veritate.* On this, Sanchez was quite lucid:

> Matronae, ac caeteri artis periti non tenentur cum omnimoda certitudine testificari, sed tantum *versisimiliter, iuxta aestimationem,* quam ex artis peritia assequuti sunt; quando peritia versatur circa illas artes, quae non constant certis et indubitatis disciplinae regulis. Quare in hoc distant ab aliis testibus qui regulariter *de veritate absoluta* debent testificari.

The parties were required to be present for the taking of this oath.[23]

21 Sanchez, Lib. 7, disp. 113, n. 16.

22 Gonzalez-Tellez, Lib. II, tit. 19, c. 4, n. 4; Verano, Lib. II, tit. 19, n. 18; Reiffenstuel, Lib. IV, tit. 15, n. 36 and n. 40. Reiffenstuel (*loc. cit.*) stated that at least two "*medici aut chirurgi*" were to examine the man if he was suspected of impotence.

23 Cf. Sanchez, Lib. 7, disp. 113, nn. 13, 14, 15.

The oath was not demanded if the experts had already been required to take an oath upon the acceptance of their particular office.[24] Explaining more precisely the nature of the expert's oath, Reiffenstuel said that by reason of this oath the expert was to favor neither side, but was to speak the truth faithfully, in accord with the measure in which his conscience perceived it.[25]

SECTION 6. JUDICIAL DUTIES OF EXPERTS

After being properly appointed and sworn, the experts received instructions from the judge on the manner in which they were to perform their duties, and on the time allotted for their performance. It was found necessary for the judge to be minutely specific in his instructions to the experts, both as to the manner of performing their duties, and also as to the way in which their reports were to be given, because often the experts acted more in the capacity of judges than of witnesses. Even the Rota was forced to remind experts of their proper sphere of activity.[26]

As regards the *matronae* appointed for the corporal inspection of women, they were not to begin their examination until they had subjected the woman to the warm water bath for a time sufficient to insure against any deception on her part. The bath was to be given in the matrons' presence. This was merely a repetition of what had been taught by the earlier canonists. Sanchez wrote:

> Hinc deducitur, sanum consilium esse, ut iudex districte praecipiat matronis, ut antequam feminam inspiciant quo de eius virginitate deponant, faciant ipsis praesentibus eam in balneo aquae competenter calidae lavari, et tanto tempore mo-

[24] Cf. Verano, Lib. II, tit. 19, n. 3. It is to be noted that this previous oath of office was of customary observance (*"moris est"*). Cf. also Schmier, Lib. II, tr. III, cap. IX, sec. II, n. 47.

[25] Reiffenstuel, Lib. II, tit. 19, n. 22; also Lib. IV, tit. 15, n. 39; Schmalzgrueber, Lib. II, tit. 19, n. 20, at 6.

[26] Cf. De Luca, *Theatrum*, Lib. 15, Pars I, d. 33, nn. 31, 32, 33, 35; Schmalzgrueber, Lib. II, tit. 19, n. 7.

> ram in eo trahere, quantum necessarium fuerit, ut si forte glutino apposito verenda mulieris compressa sint, atque coarcta, ut virgo appareat, id liquefieri possit. Quia in valore matrimonii investigando quaecumque probationes possibiles adhibendae sunt, et potius debent esse superfluae, quam diminutae.[27]

After this precaution had been observed, it was not sufficient to be satisfied with a mere ocular inspection of the woman; a tactile examination was required as a final safeguard.[28]

SECTION 7. THE REPORT OF EXPERTS

If for a sufficient reason the experts were unable to complete their examination and to make their report within the time allotted, the judge could grant an extension of time, so that their testimony might be admitted after the publication of the acts, or after the conclusion of the cause, "*. . . imo, etiam post rem iudicatam,*" wrote Schmalzgrueber.[29]

The writer is of the opinion that Schmalzgrueber actually meant that "after the pronouncement of sentence" the testimony could be admitted. Surely he did not mean after the cause had become a *res iudicata* in the technical sense, for it was commonly held that testimony could not be given after the cause had passed into a *res iudicata.* The fact was that a marriage cause involving alleged non-consummation (one of the most frequent sources for information concerning experts) never became a *res iudicata.* Hence Thomas Sanchez wrote that the testimony of experts could be admitted after the publication of the acts in causes wherein the issue even after a sentence did not become a *res iudicata,* but that their testimony could not be admitted after

[27] Sanchez, Lib. 7, disp. 113, n. 11.

[28] *Ibidem,* n. 10. Cf. also Reiffenstuel, Lib. IV, tit. 15, n. 38, where mention was made of the required tactile investigation, but no mention was made of the *balneum.*

[29] Schmalzgrueber, Lib. II, tit. 19, n. 7.

such publication in causes wherein the issue after a sentence did become a *res iudicata.*[30]

The experts were to be diligently interrogated by the judge upon their report. Inasmuch as their testimony was not *de veritate,* but only *de verisimili,* the experts were to give not only their findings and their conclusions, but also the reasons for these conclusions.[31]

The parties to the dispute were to be cited for the deposition of the *sapientes,* who favored the party that appointed them, but they were not required to be present for it.[32] The judge, even without the petition of one of the parties, could *ex officio* correct the testimony of the experts.[33]

Despite the rule that the testimony of a third expert was to be received (when these *sapientes* had been discordant in their testimony), lest the process continue *ad infinitum,* a fourth expert could be appointed only when it became apparent from the testimony of the third expert that he was in error, or that he was suspect on some other grounds.[34] If, however, the third expert was favorably received, it was asked whether he had to side with one or the other of the decisions rendered by the parties' experts. The answer was that he was not so bound, but could render his own specific judgment independently of the other experts. Of course, he was required to give the reasons for his conclusions. This was the more common opinion and practice in Cardinal De Luca's time.[35]

When the expert had been chosen *ex officio* with the consent of both parties (whether this was done from the very beginning or only as the selection of a *tertius peritus*), it was not necessary for the parties to be cited for the ex-

[30] Sanchez, Lib. 7, disp. 113, n. 23.

[31] Cf. *Ibidem,* n. 12; cf. also De Luca, *Theatrum,* Lib. 15, Pars I, d. 33, n. 34.

[32] Sanchez, Lib. 7, disp. 113, n. 14.

[33] *Ibidem,* n. 26.

[34] Cf. De Luca, *Theatrum,* Lib. 15, Pars I, d. 33, n. 25.

[35] *Ibidem,* n. 26.

pert's deposition. This as the more probable opinion could safely be followed in places where it was not definitely adverse to the local *stylus tribunalis.* When the parties were not cited, it sufficed for the expert to give his complete report (*relatio*) to the judge, who then added it to, combined it with, and sealed it in, the acts. If it was of interest to one of the parties to examine the report, the latter could do so, but was required to inform the opposing party of his action, so that he, too, could investigate the testimony and lodge any complaints against it that he deemed necessary.[36]

SECTION 8. PROBATIVE VALUE OF EXPERT TESTIMONY

Verano considered ocular inspection of secondary importance among the types of proof admissible in court, giving to the confession of the parties the primary place.[37] Ocular inspection was so important for proving impotence in marriage causes that Reiffenstuel regarded the *inspectio corporum* to be absolutely necessary.[38] Ordinarily the inspection of experts produced only probable conclusions, for it established merely indications of truth. Experts, however, could sometimes be employed in a matrimonial cause wherein their investigation afforded physical certitude. Reiffenstuel thus pointed out the varying degrees of value that could attach to the testimony of experts:

> Si habita inspectione corporum appareant signa *certa* impotentiae, quia, v.g., apparet virum carere utroque testiculo, aut habere abscissa virilia; aut foeminam esse ita arctam, ut absque vitae periculo incidi non possit, matrimonium *illico* annullandum, nec ullum tempus ad probandum concedendum est; nec requiritur iuramentum propinquorum, nec coniugum, quod se invicem nunquam carnaliter cognoverint... nec desideratur iuramentum coniugum aut propinquorum, utpote superfluum in casu, in quo per depositionem iuratam peritorum

36 *Ibidem,* n. 27.

37 Verano, Lib. II, tit. 19, n. 2.

38 Reiffenstuel, Lib. IV, tit. 15, n. 35.

res manifesta est. Possunt tamen cohabitare ut frater et soror.[39]

When the inspection revealed no physically certain evidence of impotence, although there was present *"quasi moraliter certa"* evidence of such impotence, the marriage could be, and indeed was required to be, pronounced null. In this event the oath of the parties and of the *septimae manus* witnesses was required before the declaration of nullity was to be granted. It is worthy of note that the so-called "triennial experiment" was not necessary.[40] If after the inspection there appeared only dubious signs of perpetual impotence, *"prout plerumque fit in frigidis, et maleficiatis,"* then the triennial experiment was required, in addition to the oath of the parties and the *septimae manus* witnesses, before a pronouncement of nullity was to be made.[41]

If from the acts it was not apparent that the experts had been diligently questioned by the judge upon their depositions, their testimony proved nothing; their testimony was of no value if the reasons for the experts' opinions did not appear.[42] Although negative proofs were more difficult, and greater credence was given to a few affirming than to many denying, still, with reference to the testimony of the experts, the same measure of credence could obtain for the one who deemed that the woman was not a virgin, as obtained for the one who deemed that she was a virgin. A few *"peritiores,"* however, prevailed over many experts of ordinary qualifications.[43]

It should be remembered that experts were then, as now, considered only a subsidiary help in discovering the truth, and were not to be employed when the truth could readily be obtained in some other fashion.[44]

[39] *Ibidem*, n. 42.
[40] *Ibidem*, n. 43.
[41] Reiffenstuel, Lib. IV, tit. 15, n. 44.
[42] Sanchez, Lib. 7, disp. 113, n. 12.
[43] *Ibidem*, nn. 18, 19.
[44] Cf. De Luca, *Theatrum*, Lib. 15, Pars I, d. 33, n. 37.

If it was sometimes said that proof obtained through experts was the strongest of all proofs, one must understand that as true only in those rather rare cases in which the inspection of the experts brought to light signs that evinced physical certitude. It was more often true that the value of the experts lay not in their discovery of absolute certitude, but in their finding *"indicia veritatis."*[45] Accordingly the judge was not obliged to follow the opinion of the experts in issuing his sentence.[46]

Article II. Decisions of the Roman Curia

Section 1. The Roman Rota

"At the very same time that the great canonists were developing *peritia* as a type of proof, the Roman Rota was giving it very practical approbation. For the decisions of the Rota are replete with instances of proof by expert witnesses; and written into those decisions is much discussion of the proper rôle of the expert in the judicial process. From those oft-repeated discussions came norms to guide the future deliberations of the Rota, to shape the procedure of other tribunals, and to mold subsequent legislation by the Church."[47]

The Sacred Roman Rota "... at first took cognizance of only those cases which by special commission of the Sovereign Pontiff were assigned to it. Afterwards two classes of cases became the customary matter of its jurisdiction, viz., litigious cases of a spiritual character, such as benefices, and civil cases arising within the Pontifical Territory.... After the institution of the Roman Congregations, the labors of the Sacred Rota, which had reached their climax in the fifteenth century, began to diminish notably. The chief reason for this diminution of its functions was that the Roman Congregations acquired authority to decide questions upon matters which had previously belonged to the

[45] Schmalzgrueber, Lib. II, tit. 19, n. 21.

[46] Cf. Engel, in the *Annotationes* to Lib. II, tit. 19, n. 12, *ad fin.*

[47] Arthur, *Expert Witnesses,* p. 24.

competence of the Rota. Then, since 1870, when the Roman Pontiff was robbed of all his temporal possessions, there were no longer any purely civil cases to be tried by this tribunal."[48]

From this information it is seen why the expert most often employed by the old Rota was the expert assayer of value. He was used to determine the worth of buildings in civil cases; of property of various kinds belonging to benefices. Other experts, of course, were employed by the Rota. The index of any volume of Decisions of that tribunal will contain many references to cases involving the terms *"Peritia," "Peritior," "Peritus."* The writer will point out some of the principles drawn from these cases.

Consonant testimony of the experts was said to offer the greatest argument of truth.[49] If, however, either or both of the litigants made a judicial confession, and if both accepted the sentence imposed, then any contrary testimony by the experts was considered erroneous and of no moment.[50]

The judge could employ an expert extrajudicially in order the better to inform himself on an issue, and could even reverse an earlier decision in reliance on this expert's testimony.[51] The choice of an expert by the party extrajudicially and without a citation of the opposing party was of no juridical value.[52] The attestations of experts were considered extrajudicial, without any degree of proof, if they

[48] Michael Martin, *The Roman Curia as It now Exists* (London: R. & T. Washbourne, Ltd., Paternoster Row, 1913), pp. 138-139 (hereafter cited *The Roman Curia*).

[49] S. R. Rota, *Sutrina Dotis*, 14 martii, 1698—*Sacrae Rotae Romanae Decisiones Nuperrimae*, (1684-1706). (10 tomes, Romae, 1751-1763), Tom. V, Pars II, decis. 438, n. 3 (hereafter cited *Decisiones Nuperrimae*).

[50] Cf. S. R. Rota, *Bononien. Dotis*, 28 iunii, 1700—*Decisiones Nuperrimae*, Tom. VI, decis, 369, nn. 1, 5.

[51] S. R. Rota,, *Romana Pecuniaria*, 3 iulii, 1684—*Decisiones Nuperrimae*, Tom. I, decis. 101, introd.

[52] S. R. Rota, *Neapolitana Fabricae*, 22 ian. 1700—*Decisiones Nuperrimae*, Tom. VI, decis. 234, n. 7.

contained improbable statements, and if no good reasons were given for the statements.[53]

No one could impugn the testimony of experts chosen by himself.[54] Moreover, special value was attributed to the testimony of an expert who testified contrary to the interest of the litigant who had hired him.[55] The *peritia* could not be impugned if it had already been judicially approved.[56] If no appeal had been brought against it, the *peritia* was considered judicially approved.[57] The testimony of an expert could not be impugned unless real proof of error could be shown.[58]

In determining the assets and liabilities of a partnership, an expert was used, and the decision was to be rendered, *"attenta... iustitia resultante ex relatione Periti...."*[59] Expert assayers of value who disagreed in their estimates were considered concurrent on the smallest indicated sum.[60] Very slight difference in estimates and measurements as related by the experts were to be reputed by the judge as unimportant and as agreeing in substance.[61] When experts concurred substantially, great weight was to be afforded their testimony, especially if among them was a *peritior* elected with the consent of the parties, and from whose *relatio* no appeal had been made.[62]

[53] S. R. Rota, *Camerinen. Concursus,* 26 nov. 1691—*Decisiones Nuperrimae,* Tom. III, decis.134, nn. 15, 16.

[54] S. R. Rota, *Callien. Bonorum,* 26 aprilis 1697—*Decisiones Nuperrimae,* Tom. V, decis. 250, n. 1.

[55] S. R. Rota, *Mediolanen. Fructuum,* 26 aprilis 1706—*Decisiones Nuperrimae,* Tom. IX, decis. 244, n. 3.

[56] S. R. Rota, *Romana Pretii Palatii,* 21 iunii 1686—*Decisiones Nuperrimae,* Tom. I, decis. 314, n. 5.

[57] S. R. Rota, *Romana Societatis Stagni,* 29 ian. 1685—*Decisiones Nuperrimae,* Tom. I, decis. 136, n. 2.

[58] *Ibidem,* n. 3. [59] *Ibidem,* n. 1.

[60] S. R. Rota, *Romana Incisionis Arborum,* 1 iulii 1695—*Decisiones Nuperrimae,* Tom. IV, decis. 27, nn. 2, 3.

[61] S. R. Rota, *Bononien. Pecuniaria,* 27 ian. 1687—*Decisiones Nuperrimae,* Tom. I, decis. 5, n. 8.

[62] S. R. Rota, *Camerinen. Redditionis Rationis,* 23 aprilis 1700—*Decisiones Nuperrimae,* Tom. VI, decis. 301, n. 1.

Hence, when there was no discord between experts and no suspicion raised against them, it was not allowed to employ a *tertius peritus* lest the trial go on endlessly.[63] When it became necessary, the judge was to appoint as the *tertius peritus* one agreed upon by both parties. Only when they could not agree was he to elect and appoint the *tertius* contrary to their wishes.[64] When the testimony of the earlier employed experts was discordant, the later appointed *peritior* was not bound to side with either of the earlier employed experts, for he was to reach a decision that was in line with his own judgment.[65] This judge-appointed *peritior* was accorded a preferred rating over the other experts though he disagreed with them.[66]

When several assayers of value had presented estimates considerably different one from another, the judge was to employ the *Theoria Saliceti* in arriving at the judicially just appraisal of value. This "theory" amounted to nothing more or less than the average estimate, as arrived at by dividing the total sum of the estimates by the number of estimates submitted. Thus if three experts submitted estimates of $300, $450, and $625, the total of $1375 was divided by three, and the resulting $458.33 would have been adjudged the just price, or estimate of value.[67]

Peritia reflected a type of ocular inspection, which in judicial *"accessus"* was considered superior to all other proofs.[68] It should be noted here that many of the authors

[63] S. R. Rota, *Romana Mercedis,* 1 iulii 1697— *Decisiones Nuperrimae,* Tom. V, decis. 358, nn. 1, 3.

[64] S. R. Rota, *Neapolitana Campanilis,* 23 febr. 1685—*Decisiones Nuperrimae,* Tom. I, decis. 148, n. 8.

[65] S. R. Rota, *Bononien. Pecuniaria,* 27 iunii 1685—*Decisiones Nuperrimae,* Tom. I, decis. 230, n. 1.

[66] S. R. Rota, *Bononien. Pecuniaria,* 27 ian. 1687—*Decisiones Nuperrimae,* Tom. II, decis. 5, n. 2.

[67] S. R. Rota, *Verulana Laesionis,* iunii 1773—*Decisiones Sacrae Rotae Romanae coram Olivatio* (Romae, 1785), Tom. IV, decis. 380, nn. 1, 3.

[68] S. R. Rota, *Romana Emphyteusis,* 11 martii 1699—*Decisiones Nuperrimae,* Tom. VI, decis. 41, nn. 17, 22.

treated of the expert under the indexed heading of *"Ocularis inspectio."*

Despite the great importance accorded to experts, the judge was not bound to use experts if he could reach a warranted decision in the cause on his own judgment and knowledge.[69] In all these decisions there was no positive command that the judge follow the opinion of the experts in rendering his verdict. Rather, the rule seems to have been as before, namely, that *peritia* constituted simply one species of proof, and the judge was to consider *all* the proofs submitted before rendering his verdict.

SECTION 2. THE SACRED CONGREGATION OF THE COUNCIL

"The Sacred Congregation of the Council was instituted on August 2, 1564, by Pope Pius IV, and in the order of time was the second of the Roman Congregations, the first, that of the Holy Office, having been established in 1542.

"Its original purpose, as may be surmised from its title, was to urge the execution and observance of the Decrees of the Council of Trent; subsequently it obtained from Pius V authority to interpret these decrees, so that it received the title of Congregation of the Cardinals, Interpreters of the Council of Trent."[70]

Sixtus V, reserving to himself the decision on whatever related to matters of faith, limited the Congregation's powers to an interpretation of the disciplinary decrees of the Council, so that for the issuing of decrees the Congregation still needed to consult the Pope.

"To its province belonged various cases which were explicitly or implicitly contained in the Tridentine decrees, such as the rights and obligations of bishops, chapters, parish priests, benefices, the validity of ordination and of solemn profession, *sponsalia,* and matrimony."[71]

This explanation makes its clear why no mention of the

[69] S. R. Rota, *Romana Census,* 3 dec. 1694—*Decisiones Nuperrimae,* Tom. IV, decis. 304, n. 9.

[70] Martin, *The Roman Curia,* p. 45.

[71] Martin, *The Roman Curia,* p. 46.

expert physician or midwife employed in matrimonial causes of impotence or non-consummation was found in the decisions of the early Rota.

A consultation of Salvatore Pallottini's excellent work,[72] under section thirteen of the thirteenth volume, will reveal a multitude of references to decisions of the Sacred Congregation of the Council when experts were employed for the corporal examination of men and women as demanded in causes of alleged impotence in marriage.[73] It will suffice here to point out a few decisions which over the span of years are typical of the Congregation's attitude toward experts.

After three years of marriage a couple claimed that their marriage was invalid because of the man's impotence. In the court of first instance the woman was inspected by midwives, and "*medici magni nominis*" physically examined the man, declaring him to be perpetually and incurably impotent. When the cause was brought before the Congregation of the Council, another expert was employed by that high tribunal.[74]

In a cause wherein impotence of the husband was alleged, the bishop's court had employed four experts to examine the man, two physicians and two surgeons. The wife had been inspected by three midwives after the use of the *balneum*. These procedures, it was related, were the customary safeguards in such a cause.[75]

[72] *Collectio Omnium Conclusionum et Resolutionum quae in Causis Propositis apud Sacram Congregationem Cardinalium, S. Concilii Tridentini Interpretum, prodierunt ab eius institutione anno 1564 ad 1860, distinctis titulis alphabetico ordine per materias digesta,* cura et studio Salvatoris Pallottini (17 vols. Romae, Typis S. Congregationis de Propaganda Fide, 1868-1893).

[73] Cf. esp. paragraphs 11, 12, 15, 17, 23, 24, 25, 26 in sec. 13, Vol. XIII.

[74] *Arimien. Nullitatis Matrimonii,* 16 mart. 1720—*Thesaurus Resolutionum Sacrae Congregationis Concilii* (167 vols., 1718-1908. Vols. I-V, Urbini, 1739-1740; Vols. VI-CLXVII, Romae, 1741-1909), I, 273 (hereafter cited *Thesaurus*).

[75] S.C.C., *Anconitana,* 19 ian.; 16 mart. 1793—*Codicis Iuris Cano-*

In a later cause brought before the Sacred Congregation of the Council, the *Defensor Matrimonii* claimed that proof of non-consummation had not been established in the lower tribunal, because the sacred canons were violated, since only one midwife had inspected the woman, and indeed without the precaution of the previous *balneum;* moreover, neither the midwife, nor the matrons, nor the expert physicians had been interrogated by the judge according to the questionnaire submitted by the *Defensor Matrimonii.*[76]

Just four years prior to the time of the first enacted legislation (in 1840) on judicial experts since the Decretals of Gregory IX, a cause was brought to the Sacred Congregation of the Council at the command of the pope. The marriage was attacked on the grounds of the impotence of the husband. In the course of the trial in first instance, the woman was examined and declared to be a virgin; but the husband refused to be examined, claiming that an already sufficient proof was derived from the inspection of his wife. The pope, when consulted, commanded the man to submit to an inspection by experts. The pope added that, when the inspection was completed, the acts of the entire process were to be forwarded to the Congregation of the Council. Through this papal intervention one can note quite clearly the Sacred Pontiff's regard for the value of proof derivable through experts.[77]

nici Fontes, cura Eñi Petri Card. Gasparri editi, 9 vols., Romae (postea Civitate Vaticana): Typis Polyglottis Vaticanis, 1923-1939 (Vols. VII-IX ed. cura et studio Eñi Iustiniani Card. Serédi), n. 3884 (hereafter cited *Fontes*).

[76] S.C.C., *Panormitana Matrimonii,* 25 ian. 1817—*Thesaurus,* LXXVII, 5.

[77] S.C.C., 30 ian. 1836—*Thesaurus,* XCVI, 16.

CHAPTER IV

LEGISLATION GOVERNING THE EXPERT FROM 1840 UNTIL THE CODE OF CANON LAW (1918)

"After the time of the *Corpus Iuris Canonici* there occurs a gap of five centuries, for it was not until the nineteenth century that there appeared new legislation relative to the use of experts in ecclesiastical tribunals."[1]

An investigation of this "new" legislation will show to what a great extent it was influenced by the teaching of the canonical writers and the writers of the Roman Curia.

Article I. The Instruction "Cum moneat Glossa" of 1840

On the 22nd of August, 1840, the Sacred Congregation of the Council issued an Instruction which contained rules to be employed in the conducting of formal matrimonial causes.[2] In the opening words of the Instruction reference is made to a gloss on a decretal in the Gregorian Collection wherein it was stated that in matrimonial causes every precaution was to be used *"proper periculum animarum."* The wonderful teaching of Sanchez was also referred to.[3] The Constitution *Dei miseratione* (1741) of Benedict XIV, which contained many procedural reglations, was likewise mentioned.[4]

Thereupon the new procedural rules to be used in matrimonial trials were set forth. It is the norms for the causes of alleged impotency that are of interest for this study.

First to be interrogated in a cause of alleged impotence were the *periti physici* whom the spouses had already consulted.[5] Besides these previously consulted doctors, other

[1] Arthur, *Expert Witnesses*, p. 20.

[2] *Fontes*, n. 4069.

[3] Sanchez, Lib. 7, disp. 107.

[4] *Fontes*, n. 318.

[5] *Fontes*, n. 4069, at paragraph *Si querela*.

experts, especially at the instance of the *defensor matrimonii,* were to be employed in an official capacity when it was petitioned that the marriage be dissolved because of the resultant non-consummation of the union.

The judge was to determine a time limit within which both spouses were to submit a list of doctors and surgeons approved by them and the *defensor* for the performance of the physical inspection of both husband and wife. A similar list of those in whom they had no confidence was also to be presented.

From this list the judge was to select three doctors and two surgeons who were "more celebrated in the city" because of their knowledge, religion, and probity. These five, whom the judge was to appoint to perform the inspection of the husband, were to use none but upright means for determining his potency. In the decree of appointment the day, the hour, and the place for the examination were to be stated, and to the experts there was to be given authorization whereby they could re-examine the husband, if necessary.

At the designated time the judge, the *defensor,* the chancellor, and the experts were to go to the place appointed for the inspection of the husband. One at a time the experts were to examine the man, using whatever decent and honorable means they thought useful. They were to determine from this examination whether the man was potent, and, if not potent, whether his impotence was physically or morally certain, and what were the causes of the impotence; whether it was perpetual or temporary, curable or incurable, antecedent or consequent to the marriage.

Having performed the examination, each doctor and surgeon was to submit in writing his findings, conclusions, and reasons for the conclusions. This report (*relatio*) was to be drawn up in the vernancular.[6] In accord with a sealed interrogatory prepared by the *defensor matrimonii* each of the experts was to be questioned concern-

[6] *Fontes,* n. 4069, introductory paragraphs.

ing his report. If not all of the experts could be questioned in one day, then another day was to be designated for the completion of the interrogations.

It is noteworthy that each of the experts was required to take an oath *"de veritate dicenda"* before the questioning, and a confirmatory oath *"de veritate dicta"* after the questioning. The completed interrogatory was then to be signed by the expert, the judge, the *defensor,* and the chancellor.

For the physical inspection of the wife, the judge was to appoint at least three midwives. He was to follow the same method of procedure as in the appointment of the expert doctors and surgeons. These midwives were to be carefully instructed by at least two of the aforesaid experts (*"uno medico et altero chirurgo"*) on the manner of performing the ocular and tactile inspection of the woman.

On the stated day of the inspection, the woman was to be brought to the home of an upright matron appointed by the judge. There, in the presence of the matron and the three midwives, the wife was to remain in the warm-water bath (tested beforehand by the experts to be sure that it was "pure water") for at least three-quarters of an hour. Then, lest there be any temporal occasion for fraud on the woman's part, she was immediately to be examined by the midwives. Each midwife was individually to inspect the woman, during which inspection the court-appointed matron was always to be present. The inspection could not be performed at night, but only during the day, in a well-lighted room.

The judge, the *defensor*, and the chancellor, with the expert doctor and surgeon, were to proceed to the matron's house where the inspection had taken place. There they were to receive the reports of the midwives, given individually, concerning the indications of the woman's virginity or non-virginity, as determined by them in their investigation. The midwives were then to respond more precisely to questions concerning their reports, which questions were to be submitted by the *defensor*. Next the doctor and surgeon were to be asked their judgment, based upon the reports and depositions of the midwives. Lastly, the "*honesta matrona*" was to be questioned regarding her constant presence during the entire time of the "*balneum*" and the inspections, and regarding the proper conduct of the midwives during the examination.[7]

From this Instruction one notes how the earlier teaching of the canonical writers and the practice of the Roman Curia were adopted almost in their entirety. Except for being more specific in certain matters (e.g., regarding the number of the experts; regarding the length of time for the *balneum*), the Instruction did not differ from the earlier teaching and practice.

Article II. The Instruction of the Holy Office in 1858

Only eighteen years after the *Cum moneat Glossa,* the Holy Office issued an Instruction dealing with a special process permitted only with papal intervention. When the pope had dispensed from the accurate observance of the provisions of the *Dei miseratione* of Benedict XIV in a cause involving the impotence of the husband, along with the consequent non-consummation of the marriage (and only in such an event), the Instruction of the Holy Office could be used.

First the Instruction[8] treated of the examination of the parties, then of the witnesses, and finally of the employment of experts to perform the corporal inspection.

In the main, this Instruction prescribed what was already demanded by the *Cum moneat Glossa.* These differences, however, may be quoted:

1. Only two "*ex celebrioribus civitatis physici medicinam et chirurgiam callentes seligantur*" to determine the man's potency, as compared with the three *medici* and two *chirurgi*

[7] *Fontes,* n. 4069.

[8] S.C.S. Off. instr. a. 1858—*Fontes,* n. 946.

of the previous Instruction. The physician or surgeon, however, who had previously been consulted by the husband could not be employed as the court expert.

2. More specific instructions were given in this later document regarding what precisely was to be discerned in the inspection.[9]

3. Instead of the previously required three, two midwives were considered sufficient for the physical examination of the woman under this shortened process.

4. The *balneum* was not deemed irremissibly necessary; it was mandatory only when the male physicians and the midwives deemed it advisable.

5. As in the examination of men, so in the inspection of women under this new Instruction more specific advice was given the midwives in respect of the proper performance of their duties.[10]

6. In the earlier Instruction it was not clearly stated whether the midwives had to report their findings orally or in writing, but this shortened process permitted them to offer oral testimony, which was then to be faithfully recorded by the notary (*cancellarius*).

7. These written depositions were then to be given to the two male physicians, who could, if some doubt remained, examine the midwives again. If the doctors were still undecided, they themselves could inspect the woman in the presence of a *"matrona antiquae virtutis"* designated by the ordinary. It seems that the *matrona* was not

[9] *Fontes,* n. 946, at paragraph *Singulorum.*

E.g., "... Animadvertendum autem, ut mediis utantur licitis et honestis, et perscrutandum praecipue utrum illius virilia sint iuxta naturae leges accurate conformata; nimirum an penis naturalem habeat dimensionem, promptamque erectionem ad coeundum necessario duraturam; an aliquo morbo fuerit affectus, a quanto tempore ..." etc.

[10] Cf. *Fontes,* n. 946, at paragraph *Corpus insuper.*

E.g.: "Accurate observabunt signa integritatem mulieris constituentia, nimirum conformationem partium, iuncturam, duritiem, rugositatem, et colorem; an hymen sit integrum, vel confractum in totum vel in parte ..." etc.

necessary when the midwives performed the examination. The physicians were then, individually, to give to the judge their conclusions and the reasons upon which they based them.

Article III. The Instruction of the Holy Office in 1883

In the year 1883, the Holy Office directed an Instruction to the Bishops of the Oriental Rites.[11] This Instruction contained procedural rules to be observed in matrimonial causes of various kinds. Of interest to this study is Article Five, *De impedimento impotentiae,* which falls within the second part of the Instruction.[12] In this article were treated the rules governing the examination of the parties, and of the witnesses, and then mention was made of the experts involved in the cause. Basically the rules for the inspection of husband and wife remained the same. Some points, however, should be observed.

Two experts sufficed for the examination of the husband, though they were to be, as before, *"ex celebrioribus medicinae et chirurgiae peritis."* Before they undertook the inspection they were required to swear to fulfill their office diligently, and to testify afterwards without partiality to either side. This seemed to be a new requirement, for no mention of this oath had been made previously; rather, simply the oath which immediately preceded the taking of the testimony was demanded.

The expert physicians were required to submit to the court a written report of their findings, conclusions, and reasons for the conclusions. They were to state in their report (*relatio*) whether they thought the man was impotent; whether the impotence was congenital or acquired, absolute or relative. Their report, confirmed with an oath, was to be given to the notary (*cancellarius*), who incorporated it with the other acts of the cause.

[11] *Fontes,* n. 1076; cf. also *Acta Sanctae Sedis* (41 vols., Romae, 1865-1908), XVIII (1885), 344-368 (hereafter cited *ASS*).

[12] *Fontes,* n. 1076—Pars II, Tit. VI, Art. 5, n. 46.

Again two midwives were sufficient for the inspection of the woman. They, too, were required to take an oath faithfully to fulfill their office. Then they were to be instructed by at least two experts, *"uno medico, altero chirurgo,"* upon the physical inspection to be performed.

After the inspection the midwives were singly and separately to report openly to the tribunal their findings regarding the woman's physical integrity and her capability of rendering the marital debt. This report was to be made under oath, either in writing or orally. The midwives, however, were not subjected to an examination by the two male experts. Instead, their reports were studied by the doctor and the surgeon, who in their turn reported their judgment of the midwives' reports, namely, whether the midwives from what they observed were justified in the conclusions they presented.

In this article, beginning with the paragraph, *"Quod si in aliquibus locis,"* several concessions were made. They hark back to the more lenient opinions of canonists in earlier times.

If the requirement that there be two *medici periti* to examine the man, and two midwives to examine the woman, be impossible or very difficult to meet in view of the circumstances of the place, then it was *tolerated* that only one *medicus* and one midwife be used. In this unusual event it was necessary that the report of the doctor or of the midwife be sent to two other persons learned in the science of medicine or surgery, whether these learned people lived in the same locality or elsewhere. The ones thus consulted were to study the report submitted to them, and were to offer their sworn judgment upon it, namely, whether credence should be given it, and whether the conclusions in the report were justified by the findings of the inspection.

According to this Instruction of the Holy Office, the inspection was to be omitted entirely if the woman in question was a widow, or if it became evident that she had had sexual relations with another man either before or after separation from her husband, with whom she was now in legal controversy.

Lastly, a ruling was made explicit for the first time. This ruling evidently must have been implied in all the previous legislation in this matter. Insofar as it could be done, the physicians and the midwives chosen were to be Catholics; but if that could not be done, then it could be *tolerated* that non-Catholics be employed, provided that they certainly were honest and upright, and not imbued with an anti-Catholic spirit.

Although this Instruction was addressed to the Bishops of the Oriental Rites, its rules were safe norms for use in the Western Rites. In fact, in the Instruction as contained in the *Acta Sanctae Sedis,* there appeared a *"monitum"*[13] to the effect that the Instruction should be used also by non-Oriental bishops, in due accommodation, wherever necessary, to their own tribunals.

This same idea was adopted by the Sacred Congregation for the Propagation of the Faith, for in 1883 (the very year that this Instruction of the Holy Office to the Oriental Bishops was issued) there was directed to the ordinaries of the United States an Instruction concerning Ecclesiastical Trials in Matrimonial Causes. This Instruction is very similar to the Holy Office's Instruction.[14]

In the section dealing with the impediment of impotence, the Instruction to the Bishops of the United States directed that to determine if impotence was present, and, if so, whether it was antecedent and perpetual, absolute or relative, the earlier Instruction of the Holy Office was to be followed.[15]

[13] *ASS,* XVIII (1885), 344, s.v. *Monitum.*

[14] Thus in the *Acta Sanctae Sedis,* Vol. XVIII, p. 369, the Instruction to the Ordinaries of the U.S. follows immediately the Instruction to the Oriental Bishops, and in relation to it *"fere ad verbum concordat,"* according to a footnote on p. 369.

[15] *"Hunc in finem prae oculis habenda erit instructio Supremae Congregationis S. Officii."*—*Fontes,* n. 4901, § 46. A footnote in the *Fontes* at this point refers to both n. 946 (process used with papal dispensation) and n. 1076 (the Instruction to the Oriental Bishops).

Article IV. The *Regulae Servandae* of the Rota in 1910

On June 29, 1908, in his Apostolic Constitution, *Sapienti Consilio,*[16] Pope St. Pius X reorganized the Roman Curia. It was this Constitution which exempted the United States from the jurisdiction of the Sacred Congregation for the Propagation of the Faith, and committed it to follow the common law of the Church.[17]

In reorganizing the Roman Curia, St. Pius X accorded to the Roman Rota a new importance, recalling its former glory. It was to be *the* Tribunal of the Church. Its competence was outlined in four canons of the *Lex Propria,* also issued on June 29, 1908.[18]

The Rota was to decide in the first instance the causes committed to it by the Roman Pontiff, acting either *motu proprio,* or at the petition of the contesting parties; it was to handle causes which had been tried judicially by ordinaries in the first and second instance and thereupon were appealed legitimately to the Holy See. As a court of last instance it was to settle the causes already decided in the first or second instance by ordinaries or by any other tribunal, when the causes had not yet become *res iudicatae* and had been appealed to the Holy See.

If the *Lex Propria* established general rules for the Roman Rota, particular rules concerning judicial acts of that tribunal were set forth in the *Regulae Servandae in Iudiciis apud Romanae Rotae Tribunal* on August 4, 1910.[19] These *Regulae* contained a chapter devoted entirely to the subject of judicial experts.[20] Although the rules were originally meant to govern only the Roman Rota, many of them were later adopted into the Code of Canon Law of 1918.[21]

[16] *Acta Apostolic Sedis, Commentarium Offiiale* (Romae: Typis Polyglottae Vaticanis, 1909—) I, 7 (hereafter cited *AAS*).

[17] Const. *Sapienti Consilio,* I, 6°, 2—*AAS,* I (1909), 12.

[18] Canons 14-17—*AAS,* I (1909), 23-24.

[19] *Fontes,* n. 6461; also *AAS,* II (1910), 783-850.

[20] Titulus IV, Caput III, §§ 120-136—*AAS,* II (1910), 822-826.

[21] *Codex Iuris Canonici,* Pii X Pontificis Maximi Iussu Digestus, Be-

Hence, it will be of value to consider in detail the entire chapter of the *Regulae* on experts.

If the panel of auditors (*turnus*) had prescribed proof by *peritia*, the *Iudex Instructor* was empowered to choose the experts from among the ones presented by the parties, unless the *turnus* had reserved the nomination to itself.[22] If the experts were not chosen by the judge *ex officio*, they could be chosen by one of the parties, upon due citation of his adversary. On the day appointed, both parties had the right to present experts who were more qualified and worthy; thereupon the *Iudex Instructor* was to select the experts to whom neither party had raised reasonable grounds of suspicion. If, however, after the experts were already chosen, one of the parties persisted in his exception against them, and the *Iudex Instructor*, having heard the opposite party, was unwilling to reject the experts, then the question was to be submitted to the *turnus* to be decided according to the rules of procedure for handling incidental questions.[23] Unless it had been already determined by law, the number of experts was left to the discretion of the *turnus* or the *Instructor*, to be decided in consideration of the petition of the parties and the nature of the question involved.[24]

In causes concerning the validity of matrimony, Sacred Ordination, and religious profession, *"pro illustrandis quaestionibus quae S. Theologiam attingunt,"* one or more *periti-consultores* were to be deputed *ex officio*, in abstraction from the petitions and designations of the parties. When the judge assigned such an expert-consultor, he was bound to assign a *defensor* to the party who had no *defensor* and otherwise was unable to defend himself. If there was need

nedicti Papae XV Auctoritate Promulgatus, Praefatione, Fontium Annotatione et Indice Analytico-Alphabetico ab Emo Petro Card. Gasparri auctus (Reprint, Westminster, Md., The Newman Press, 1949). Cf. especially the footnotes to canons 1792-1811.

[22] Rota, *Regulae* of 1910, § 121—*AAS*, II (1910), 823.

[23] Rota, *Regulae* of 1910, § 121—*AAS*, II (1910), 823.

[24] Rota, *Regulae* of 1910, § 122—*AAS*, II (1910), 823.

of this, the court-appointed *defensor* was to be given to the party gratuitously.[25]

This was the first time that the question of payment to the experts employed in judicial processes received mention. The casual way, however, in which *"gratuitum patrocinium,"* to be furnished by the expert was given mention indicates that it must have been common to give some payment to the expert, in a way similar to the indemnification accorded to witnesses.

The decree appointing the experts was to contain mention of the object of the *peritia* with all necessary instructions concerning the duties of the experts and the manner in which they were to make their written report.[26] This decree of appointment was to designate one of the two possible ways in which the report could be drawn up, namely:

1. there could be an individual report, written and signed by each expert, or

2. there could be simply one report, in which the majority opinion of the experts was to be explained, with an indication of the dissenting opinions, but without any identification of the ones who held these opinions. This common report was to be signed by all the experts, regardless of their agreement or disagreement with the majority opinion.[27]

The parties had a right to know the object of the *peritia* before it was performed, unless it concerned a criminal cause or a serious matter of public order, under which circumstances it was expedient not to inform the parties beforehand of the object of the *peritia,* but rather to communicate to them only the result of the *peritia* or the opinion of the experts.[28]

After the parties learned the object of the *peritia,* they could make opportune suggestions, even asking for changes

[25] Rota, *Regulae* of 1910, § 123, nn. 1, 2—*AAS, II* (1910), 823.

[26] Rota, *Regulae* of 1910, § 124—*AAS,* II (1910), 823.

[27] Rota, *Regulae* of 1910, § 125, n. 2; n. 1—*AAS,* II (1910), 823-824.

[28] Rota, *Regulae* of 1910, § 126, n. 1—*AAS,* II (1910), 824.

in the rescript of deputation. It was allowable for the parties to make these suggestions orally to the expert in the same session in which they learned the object of the *peritia,* and in which the expert took his oath.[29]

The notary was to keep the acts of the session in which the expert appeared, and these acts were to be signed by himself, the judge, and the expert.[30]

The judge, if he wished, could omit the administration of an oath to the expert, especially if the expert was to render an opinion concerning juridical-theological questions, rather than concerning a certain question of fact. Nevertheless it was left to the prudent discretion of the judge to administer the oath to an expert even when he made his report, especially if the report revealed new circumstances of fact.[31]

The *Regulae* explicitly mentioned the indemnification of the experts, for they required that the decree of appointment should fix a fitting sum of money to be paid the experts, and should specify which party was to make the payment. Ordinarily the expert was to be paid by the party who had asked for the *peritia,* or in favor of whom the *peritia* was ordered to be performed.[32]

In causes wherein the nullity of a marriage was alleged on the claim of impotence, the Instruction *Cum moneat Glossa* of 1840 was to be observed both for the election of the experts and for the performance of the experts' duties. In the event that the aforesaid Instruction was not completely observed, it was left to the *turnus* to decide whether the substance of the proof through *peritia* had been preserved, or whether something that was omitted needed to be supplied.[33]

For the expediting of exceptions proposed against instruments or public or private acts, when there was need to

[29] Rota, *Regulae* of 1910, § 126, nn. 2, 3—*AAS,* II (1910), 824.
[30] Rota, *Regulae* of 1910, § 128—*AAS,* II (1910), 824.
[31] Rota, *Regulae* of 1910, § 129, nn. 1, 2—*AAS,* II (1910), 824.
[32] Rota, *Regulae* of 1910, § 130, nn. 1, 2—*AAS,* II (1910), 824-825.
[33] Rota, *Regulae* of 1910, § 131, nn. 1, 2—*AAS,* II (1910), 825.

prove whether these instruments were genuine or not, and if sufficient proof had not been obtained through witnesses, handwriting experts were to be used. These experts were, if possible, to be such as were also approved by the public authority.[34] The handwriting expert was to establish his proof by comparing the handwriting certainly attributable to a definite author with the handwriting doubtfully attributable to the same author.[35]

If one of the experts died before completing his duty, or resigned the office after receiving it, or was legitimately repudiated, or on the contrary was dispensed from fufilling his office, then another expert was to be substituted by the *Iudex Instructor*, the *turnus*, or the *Ponens*, after a hearing was granted the other interested parties.[36]

If the facts which concerned the object of the *peritia* were not sufficiently clarified for the judges of the *turnus*, they could demand of the experts further declarations, and could also prescribe that a new *peritia* be performed by other experts appointed even *ex officio*.[37]

The opinion of the experts (*votum peritorum*) was then to be given to the judge who had decreed the *peritia*. This judge was to examine the report to see whether it reflected a compliance with all the prescriptions in the experts' mandate of appointment; he was to receive the oath of the experts (if, according to § 129, n. 2, he deemed this expedient), and to have their *votum* incorporated with the other acts. The *votum* was to be relayed to the parties, "*per intimationem*," either at the instance of the more diligent party, or *ex officio*.[38]

The judges were not bound to conform their judgment to the opinions of the experts, if that proved contrary to their own persuasion.[39]

[34] Rota, *Regulae* of 1910, § 132, n. 1—*AAS*, II (1910), 825.
[35] Rota, *Regulae* of 1910, § 132, n. 2—*AAS*, II (1910), 825.
[36] Rota, *Regulae* of 1910, § 133—*AAS*, II (1910), 825.
[37] Rota, *Regulae* of 1910, § 134—*AAS*, II (1910), 825.
[38] Rota, *Regulae* of 1910, § 135, nn. 1, 2—*AAS*, II (1910), 825-826.
[39] Rota, *Regulae* of 1910, § 136—*AAS*, II (1910), 826.

This chapter on the experts is the most complete pre-Code legislation on the subject. In a different chapter of the *Regulae,* mention is made of the expert assayer employed by the *Ponens* or *Iudex Instructor* as often as it was useful to have an expert on value.[40] This type of expert was very frequently employed by the early Rota, as has been described in an earlier section of this treatise.[41]

ADDENDUM

INSANITY CASES

All of the pre-Code teaching which the writer could consult revealed absolutely nothing concerning the importance of experts in matrimonial causes wherein invalidity was claimed on the grounds of insanity at the time of the marriage. Rather, it seemed to be the expected thing that the judge was to hear the testimony of person acquainted with the party allegedly insane, and to judge the case on these proofs, without seeking the advice of expert physicians or psychiatrists.

This, however, should not be so surprising, when the rather recent birth of psychiatry as a distinct science is considered.

Only two pertinent decisions were found, and these will be related briefly.

A girl had been in a mental asylum previous to her marriage. She was released at the insistence of her parents, although the doctors were unfavorable. Marriage followed shortly thereafter, but within a few months the girl, hopelessly insane, was re-committed to the institution. In the course of the trial in which the validity of the marriage was impugned, the doctors who had treated the girl while she was in the asylum before and after the marriage were called upon to testify. They seemed, however, to testify

[40] Rota, *Regulae* of 1910, Tit. IV, Cap. V, Art. III (*De iuramento litis aestimatorio*), § 164—*AAS,* II (1910), 831.

[41] See pp. 36-38 of this dissertation.

only in the capacity of eye-witnesses, not as experts in the technical sense.[42]

In another cause wherein the marriage was claimed to be invalid because of the insanity of one of the parties at the time of the marriage, the *Defensor Matrimonii* claimed that the decision given in the court of first instance was invalid, since no *peritia* had been employed. The *ponens* of the *turnus* in the Sacred Roman Rota replied that although the use of experts in such a cause could serve a useful purpose for detecting the reason of insanity and for indicating its remedies, nevertheless there were many common signs which the ordinary witness could recognize as indications of insanity. Further, so wrote the *Ponens*: *"Nec ulla lex canonica peritiam requirit, ad probandum impedimentum amentiae."*[43]

This statement surely serves to explain why the writer discovered no more indications regarding the use of experts in insanity causes!

[42] S. R. Rota, *Nullitatis matrimonii, 23 dec. 1909, coram R.P.D. Seraphino Many*, dec. XIX.—*S. Romanae Rotae Decisiones seu Sententiae quae . . . prodierunt ab anno 1909*—(Romae, Typis Vaticanis, 1912—), I (1909), 164 (hereafter cited *S.R.R. Decisiones*).

[43] S. R. Rota, *Nullitatis Matrimonii, 27 iun. 1916, coram R.P.D. Seraphino Many—AAS*, IX (1917), 250. Cf. also *S.R.R. Decisiones*, VIII (1916), 121.

PART II

CANONICAL COMMENTARY

CHAPTER V

NOTION AND DIVISION

ARTICLE I. NOTION OF THE EXPERT

From the wording of canon 1792[1] may be deduced the following definition of an expert:

> A judicial expert is a person endowed with a particular skill or knowledge, who is legitimately called into a judicial process in order that he may help the judge to establish some fact or to determine the true nature of a thing by conducting an examination and giving a report in accord with the principles of his art or profession.

This definition makes it clear that the expert is employed as a means for obtaining judicial proof. The proof established through experts is called *peritia,* and is a proof distinct from that afforded by the confession of the parties, the testimony of witnesses, judicial access and inspection, documents, or the oath of the parties themselves.[2] Despite the fact that *peritia* is a proof distinct from the others, it bears a great deal of resemblance to the proof established by witnesses. It is for this reason that some commentators define the expert as reflecting a type of witness.[3] Other

[1] "Peritorum opera utendum est quoties ex iuris vel iudicis praescripto eorum examen et votum requiritur ad factum aliquod comprobandum vel ad veram alicuius rei naturam dignoscendam."

[2] These are the seven types of proof enumerated by the Code in Book IV, Title X, *de probationibus.*

[3] J. Noval, *Commentarium Codicis Iuris Canonici,* Liber IV, *De Processibus,* Pars I, *De Iudiciis* (Augustae Taurinorum, Romae: Marietti, 1920), n. 513 (hereafter cited *De Iudiciis*). Cf. also F. X. Wernz, *Ius Canonicum, ad Codicis Normam Exactum* opera P. Vidal (7 vols. in 8, Vol. VI, *De Processibus,* editio altera, a Felice Cappello recognita, Romae: Apud Aedes Universitatis Gregorianae, 1949), VI, n. 489 (hereafter cited Wernz-Vidal, *De Processibus*); M. Lega, *Commentarius in Iudicia Ecclesiastica iuxta Codicem Iuris Canonici* (2. ed., 3. vols., ed. V. Bartoccetti, Romae: Azienda Libraria Cattolica Italiana, 1950), II, 744, n. 1 (hereafter cited Lega [ed. Bart.], *Iudicia Ecclesiastica*).

commentators readily admit that the expect functions to a great degree as a witness, but they refrain from regarding the expert as reflecting any special type of witness.[4] The writer agrees with the latter commentators in refusing to regard the expert as reflecting a special type of witness, or an "expert witness," but prefers to term him simply "the expert."

It is true that until the year 1910 experts were always considered under the *witness* heading of the several types of proof. They were, however, always clearly distinguished from the ordinary witness, both as to the object of their testimony and with reference to the oath which they pronounced.[5] Because of this distinction from the ordinary witness, the experts were given separate treatment in an entire chapter of the new Procedural Rules of the Sacred Roman Rota which were issued in August of 1910.[6] The Code of Canon Law, which became binding law eight years later, retained this separate treatment of experts as reflecting a species of proof different from that established by witnesses.[7]

[4] Goyeneche, *De Processibus*, Breves Adnotationes ad Lib. IV Codicis Iuris Canonici (1 vol., 2 parts, Romae: ad S. Ioannis Lat., 1947), I, pars 2 (fasciculus alter), n. 51 (hereafter cited *De Processibus*). Cf. also E. F. Regatillo, *Institutiones Iuris Canonici* (4. ed., 2 vols., Santander: Sal Terrae, 1951), II, n. 545 (hereafter cited *Institutiones*); M. Conte a Coronata, *Institutiones Iuris Canonici*, (5 vols., Vol. III, *De Processibus* 4. ed., Romae, Taurini: Marietti, 1956), III, n. 1324 (hereafter cited *De Processibus*); U. Beste, *Introductio in Codicem* (3. ed., Collegeville, Minn., St. John's Abbey Press, 1946), p. 821, at can. 1792; W. J. Doheny, *Canonical Procedure in Matrimonial Cases*, (2 vols. Vol. I, *Formal Judicial Procedure*, 2. ed., 1948; Vol. II, *Informal Procedure*, 2. printing, 1948, (Milwaukee: Bruce Publ. Co.), I, 382 (hereafter cited *Canonical Procedure*); L. Miguélez Dominguez-S. Alonso Morán-M. Cabreros de Anta, *Código de Derecho Canónico y Legislación Complementaria* (5. ed., Madrid: *La Editorial Católica*, 1954), commentary on can. 1792 (hereafter cited *Código y Comentarios*).

[5] Cf. *supra*, pp.12, 13.

[6] Rota, *Regulae* of 1910, Caput III, §§ 120-136. Cf. pp. 50-55 of this dissertation.

[7] C.I.C., Lib. IV, Title X, Caput III, *De Peritis*, canons 1792-1805.

The use of the term *expert* rather than the use of the expression *expert witness* also seems preferable in view of the fact that in some circumstances a professionally qualified person who is debarred from acting as a judicial expert must be cited as a witness.[8]

SECTION 1. FUNCTION OF EXPERT AS WITNESS AND JUDGE

Besides acting in the function of witnesses, experts also act as judges, but to a much lesser degree.[9] Roberti states that "the office of an expert stands midway between that of a witness and that of a judge."[10] Similar to a witness, the expert gives judicial testimony; similar to the judge, he draws conclusions and gives his opinion. The witness testifies only to a fact perceived through his senses. The expert does more, employing his specialized skill or art to determine the precise nature of the fact, and through his reasoning process, based on principles of his profession or art, arrives at a conclusion which he declares in his judicial report. This judgment of the expert, however, has not judicial, but only scientific, value.[11]

Some legislations give predominance to the function of the experts as judges, while others give predominance to their function as witnesses. According to the Code of Canon Law, predominance is given to the operation of the expert as a witness rather than as a judge. Thus the Code usually considers *peritia* more as the work of an individual than as

[8] Can. 1982. S.C. de Sacramentis, decr., *De processibus in causis dispensationis super matrimonio rato et non consummato,* 7 maii 1923—*AAS,* XV (1923), 389-391; and *Regulae Servandae, ibid.,* pp. 392-413, Rule 88 (hereafter cited by the opening words of the decree, *Catholica Doctrina*); S.C. de Sacramentis, *Instructio servanda a tribunalibus dioecesanis in pertractandis causis de nullitate matrimoniorum,* 15 aug. 1936—*AAS,* XXVIII (1936), 313-361; at Article 143 (hereafter cited *Instructio "Provida"*).

[9] Sanchez, Lib. 7, disp. 113, n. 1.

[10] F. Roberti, *De Processibus* (2 vols., Romae, 1926), Vol. II, pars I, n. 357.

[11] L. Quintana Reynés, *La Prueba en el Procédimiento Canónico* (Barcelona: Bosch, 1942), p. 131 (hereafter cited *La Prueba*).

that of a collegiate body.[12] It directs that experts can be rejected for the same reason that witnesses can be rejected.[13] When the Code determines the number of experts[14] and states the probative value of their testimony,[15] it indicates that the faculty of judging remains that of the *iudex,* and is not relinquished to the expert.

SECTION 2. THE EXPERT, DISTINCT FROM THE WITNESS

"An expert is one whose knowledge and experience make him an authoritative specialist in some art or science." Thus Doheny defines the expert,[16] and from his definition one realizes that in most cases the experts will be men of culture and erudition. There may, however, arise causes, infrequently to be sure, in which an otherwise uneducated person may serve as the expert, provided he has a practical and specialized knowledge of the matter under discussion, and is able to apply this knowledge to the concrete matter in hand. Thus an unschooled farmer could be cited as the expert in an imaginary cause wherein agricultural matters are controverted.[17]

Of the witnesses, on the other hand, no specialized skill, knowledge, or art is required. Honesty and the proper functioning of the senses suffices, for the witness testifies only to what he has seen, heard, or learned through the ordinary use of his faculties. No opinion or judgment is asked of him, nor is any accepted if it is voluntarily given. He is to state facts of which he has personal knowledge, and is not allowed to testify with reference to his reasoned conclusion or his inference from the fact of which he has knowledge.[18]

[12] Can. 1802.

[13] Can. 1796, § 1.

[14] Can. 1793, § 3.

[15] Can. 1804, § 1.

[16] *Canonical Procedure,* I. 382.

[17] Regatillo, *Institutiones,* II, n. 545.

[18] S. Woywod, *A Practical Commentary on the Code of Canon Law,* revised by C. Smith (2 vols., revised and enlarged edition, New York: Jos. F. Wagner, Inc., London: B. Herder, 1948), II, p. 311, n. 1740.

When the expert is employed, these restrictions of the witness do not bind him. Rather, it is precisely to testify concerning his reasoned opinion that he is utilized by the court. An example may clarify this distinction between the witness and the expert.

John, as a witness, may testify that he personally saw Peter strike Ralph with a hammer. This is the fact as he saw it. A physician who was not present at the time may be called upon to examine the wounded Ralph, and may testify that he judges from the size and the form of the wound that it was caused by the blow of a hammer. The doctor, as an expert, has applied his professional knowledge and skill to pronounce his opinion upon the cause of a still visible effect.

This example will serve as an illustration of the distinction made by some authors, namely, that the witness testifies concerning a *transitory fact,* while the expert offers to the judge his knowledge regarding a *permanent fact.* Such permanency, however, can only be understood, in some events, in the sense of the actual existence of the fact at the time the *peritus* performed his examination.[19]

SECTION 3. OBJECT OF EXPERT EXAMINATION AND TESTIMONY

The formal object of the *peritia* is the examination and opinion of the experts in accord with the dictates of their art or science. The material object of *peritia* is 1) some fact, whether natural or juridical (e.g., a wound, and its actual seriousness with reference to a possibly perpetrated delict), and 2) the nature of something, in its causes, effects, etc. This indicates the final object, or end, of the *peritia,* which is 1) the proof of a fact, or 2) the determination of the nature of a thing.[20]

Generally the expert examines a fact already known or proved through other means, giving his scientific or artistic opinion upon the cause of a certain effect. At other times

[19] Wernz-Vidal, *De Processibus,* pp. 445-446, n. 489, note 3.
[20] Goyeneche, *De Processibus,* I, fasc. alter, n. 51.

he is required only to give his opinion upon the nature of a fact, e.g., the authenticity and date of a writing which is subjected to his examination. Clearly, these things the unskilled witness would be unqualified to do, or could do only with great difficulty.

De facto, the expert is often employed by the ecclesiastical court to act after the manner of an eyewitness in order to discover a still unknown or unproved fact, when there are no other witnesses who could be employed with propriety. Such would be the case, for example, when corporal inspection is necessary in causes of impotence or nonconsumation of matrimony. Besides acting as witnesses *de visu,* however, such experts must render an opinion concerning a fact and its nature, cause, or effect, e.g., in causes of impotence or non-consummation, as discovered by them in the physicial examination of the parties.[21]

On repeated occasions the judge, while he reserves the right to obtain through other means the knowledge of a past fact, or having already obtained such knowledge through other means, even to the point that he has formed his own opinion, will nonetheless solicit the solution or answer of an expert upon determined questions related to the known fact. This fact the expert presupposes, and for this reason he will not have to investigate the same fact or circumstance already known through his instruction from others, but he will admit the existence of that fact as the foundation for his answers and scientific conclusions.

It is not at all rare that experts are required to give their opinion concerning facts or circumstances not directly controverted in the judgment between the parties.[22]

SECTION 4. *Peritia,* AN EXTRAORDINARY PROOF

The establishment of proof through the use of experts, inasmuch as it is not easy, is often expensive, and necessitates a delay in the process, is considered as an extra-

[21] Wernz-Vidal, *De Processibus,* pp. 445-446, n. 489, note 3.
[22] Quintana Reynés, *La Prueba,* p. 310.

ordinary means.[23] Nonetheless it is in some events commanded by the law itself.[24]

ARTICLE II. DIVISIONS OF *Peritia*

A) The proof through the use of experts may be judicial or extrajudicial. Judicial proof is that which is spoken of in canon 1792, and is used whenever the law or the judge deems it necessary or opportune. There are detailed procedural rules for this judicial type of *peritia*,[25] while the extrajudicial *peritia* has no legal rules to govern it.

The judicial *peritia* embraces that expert examination which is made precisely with a view to giving testimony in a judicial process, and hence has all of the probative value that is afforded to the *peritia* in the Code. The extrajudicial examination of a person, fact, or effect, with no immediate view to giving testimony in a trial, and without being requested by the judge, lacks the judicial probative value of a true judicially requested *peritia*. It is not altogether without value, however, and may be confirmatory of other proofs, thus aiding the judge in his arrival at moral certitude. The testimony of extrajudicial experts is of recognized importance in the Code, for sometimes physicians and experts who have previously examined a party (with no view to or thought of giving testimony in an ecclesiastical trial) may be called to testify at least in the capacity of witnesses.[26]

Although an extrajudicial *peritia* is not valueless, nonetheless it cannot substitute for a judicial *peritia*, for it lacks the legal safeguards of a judicial *peritia*. These legal safeguards are:

1) the reservation of appointment of experts to the judge (c. 1793, § 1);

[23] Lega (ed. Bart.), *Iudicia Ecclesiastica*, II, p. 747, n. 4.

[24] Cf. canons 1976, 1982, concerning matrimonial processes of impotence, non-consummation, and lack of consent due to insanity.

[25] Canons 1792-1805.

[26] Cf. canons 1978 and 1982.

2) the right of excluding the unqualified or suspect (c. 1795, § 2);
3) the right of parties to repudiate the person of the expert (c. 1796, § 1);
4) the oath required of the expert (c. 1797, § 1);
5) the threat of penalties for an improper performance of duty (c. 1794), and
6) the payment of damages by the expert if he delays unduly (c. 1798).[27]

Cardinal De Luca mentioned what seems to have been a still different type of extrajudicial expert. The judge, he said, in order to understand more correctly all the facts attending the cause, could secretly appoint a skilled person to investigate and report personally and privately to the judge the result of his examination.[28] Somewhat similar in our day would be the demand of a preliminary physical examination and report by a physician when a petition for a dissolution of the bond is sought for the reason of a claimed non-consummation of the marriage. Though extrajudicial, and not among the requirements of the special process for causes of non-consummation, it is evident that there is much practical wisdom in recommending such an extrajudicial *peritia* before forwarding the petition to the Holy See for permission to construct the case *super rato et non-consummato*.[29]

B) A *peritia* by reason of its object may be personal (if a person is examined), local (if a place is investigated), or material (if some material object is studied).

C) If a *peritia* is ordered by the judge not *ex officio*, nor because of a positive precept of law, but simply upon the instance of one of the parties in the cause, it is called a *voluntary "peritia."* Otherwise it is called *necessary*.

D) A preventive or conservative *peritia* may occasionally be of use. Such a *peritia* may be defined as the expert

[27] Cf. Roberti, *De Processibus*, II, Pars I, n. 357.

[28] *Theatrum*, Lib. 15, Pars I, disc. 33, n. 29.

[29] Hickey, "De Processu super matrimonio rato et non consummato," *The Jurist*, I (1941), 215; cf. *infra*, pp. 176-177, footnote 38.

examination and testimony of some fact which might not otherwise be available, or which might perish before the regular time for the employment of experts. Thus, for example, the extrajudicial examination of the woman who is a party to a marriage cause of alleged non-consummation might serve "as a protection, so to speak, of the evidence derived through the *argumentum physicum,* for in the interval between the sending to Rome of the petition and the formal construction of the process, many things may happen to affect the condition of the petitioner. Accidents may occur, or serious illness may develop, the treatment of which may require various sorts of remedies or even operations impairing the probative value of the canonical inspection."[30]

The object of a judicial process can be: (1) the prosecution or vindication of the rights of physical or moral persons, or the declaration of the juridical facts concerning such persons (e.g., the validity of an ordination, or of a marriage). Such matters are called *contentious* causes; (2) offenses with a view to inflicting or declaring a penalty; and these are *criminal* causes.[31] Ordinarily, regardless of the object of the trial, proof is not admitted until after the joinder of issues (*litis contestatio*). Provision is made, however, for the eventuality in which proof might be lost by such a delay, so that the judge may admit the proofs concerned even before the joinder of issues.[32]

Arguing from the foregoing two canons, Vidal (1867-1938) stated that a *preventive peritia* is not foreign to canon law. He continued substantially as follows:

> A juridical fact concerning some physical or moral person can also be the object of judgment, and it can happen that such a juridical fact would de-

[30] Hickey, *The Jurist,* I (1941), 215.

[31] Canon 1552, § 2.

[32] "Antequam litis contestatio locum habuerit, iudex ad testium *aliarumve probationum* receptionem ne procedat, nisi in casu contumaciae, aut nisi testium depositionem recipere oporteat, ne ipsa ob probabilem testis mortem, ob discessum eiusdem vel *ob aliam iustam causam* recipi postea nequeat, aut *difficulter* possit."—Can. 1730 (Italics inserted.)

pend upon a transitory fact which leaves no traces, for the perfect knowledge of which fact there is required the help of experts in order that they may give their opinion. The absence of this early examination of the transient fact might cause the total loss of the proof, e.g., concerning damage suffered, when it is not certain immediately if the damage was accidental, or if it was due to the guilt or negligence of someone; and the estimate of the amount or the value of the damage might not later be possible in consequence of the passage of time. An identical case could arise relative to the judicial actions *"ex novi operis nuntiatione et damno infecto,"*[33] or in the inspection of a deed or document, or in the division of an inheritance.

In such cases, if it is feared that a dispute would arise in case the estimate and the *peritia* were entrusted to experts in a private or particular manner, a *peritia* can be sought through an appeal to the judge in the same form as for the introduction of a cause. Receiving such a request, the judge will summarily examine it to see if there is a well-founded right in virtue of which the judgment of the expert is sought concerning the thing or fact which is mentioned in the petition. It is sufficient if the judge discover what is juridically called a *fumus boni iuris,* i.e., an indication of a good right. He must also consider whether the petitioned *peritia* is truly necessary to prevent the lost of evidence. Should the judge discover both the *"fumus boni iuris"* and the necessity of the *peritia* for the avoidance of the loss of evidence, he will decree the *peritia* as a means to conserve the truth, of the same type as the examination of a witness who may later be unobtainable. Naturally the opposing party will retain the right to impugn even the *peritia* itself during the regular process of the trial.[34]

E) Is arbitration in law or in equity a division of *peritia?* Although such office would be fulfilled by a man truly

[33] Canons 1676-1678.

[34] Wernz-Vidal, *De Processibus,* n. 490, and note 4 under that number.

skilled in some art or science, it is not properly called *peritia*, nor should the men who arbitrate be called experts, but rather arbitrators.[35] The Code sets up regulations concerning the use, the appointment, and the procedure of arbitrators, and these norms must be followed.[36]

[35] Coronata, *De Processibus*, n. 1324; cf. also Lega (ed. Bart.) *Iudicia Ecclesiastica*, II, p. 746, n. 3.
[36] Canons 1929-1932.

CHAPTER VI

NECESSITY AND UTILITY OF *PERITIA*

ARTICLE I. NECESSITY AND UTILITY

Canon 1792 states that experts are to be used as often as, from the prescription of law or of the judge, their examination and expert opinion is required to prove some fact or to determine the true nature of a thing. From this one sees that the proof obtained by means of the expert is sometimes necessarily to be employed, and sometimes left to the discretion of the judge. Whether required by law or by the judge, however, experts are employed with increasing frequency in ecclesiastical courts.

SECTION 1. NECESSITY

The Code itself demands the use of experts in matrimonial causes of impotence and non-consummation,[1] as well as in causes of alleged lack of consent due to insanity.[2] Experts are demanded in causes alleging the nullity of sacred orders or of the obligations attached thereto, if the cause of nullity is claimed to be a defective intention due to insanity.[3]

Handwriting experts must be employed in any cause wherein there is doubt as to who is the true author of some writing brought to the attention of the tribunal.[4] Finally,

[1] Can. 1976; *Catholica Doctrina,* Rules 64, 84; *Instructio "Provida,"* Art. 139.

[2] Can. 1982; also *Instructio "Provida,"* Art. 139.

[3] Cf. can. 1995 with can. 1982. Cf. also S.C. de Sacramentis, Decretum, *Regulae Servandae in processibus super nullitate sacrae ordinationis, vel onerum sacris ordinibus inhaerentium,* 9 iun., 1931, n. 68—*AAS,* XXIII (1931), 457-473, esp. 471; (hereafter cited *Regulae super Nullitate S. Ordinationis*); cf. *Appendix, seu Formulae*—*AAS,* XXIII (1931), 473-492.

[4] Can. 1800, § 1; *Instructio "Provida,"* Art. 140, § 1.

in the process of beatification or canonization, medical experts must be called upon to determine the nature of the disease and to report upon allegedly miraculous cures.[5]

These are the only cases in law demanding the use of experts. Is the law which requires their use a law that looks simply to the licitness, or does it also look to the validity, of the trial and the ensuing sentence? There is not one recorded case in the Rota wherein a plea of nullity of the sentence was upheld because of the failure to employ experts when the law commanded it.[6] Indeed, decisions of that body make it quite clear that the *peritia* is required not as a requisite for validity, but as a condition for licitness.[7]

The same conclusion is deduced from canon 1869, which states that the judge must have moral certitude about the matter to be defined in the sentence before pronouncing that sentence. He arrives at this certitude by examining the acts and proofs, which he must evaluate according to his own conscience, unless the law explicitly makes some specific demand for the efficacy of some particular proof. If he cannot arrive at this certitude after a diligent examination of the cause, he must decide, (in marriage causes, for example) *Non constare de nullitate in casu.* Ordinarily the opinion of experts is only one of the many means employed for arriving at moral certitude. If the judge in an exceptional case inadvertently or unknowingly omits the examination of the party, with the help of experts, and fails to secure their opinions, but does in some other fashion attain to moral certitude, his decision is valid, though perhaps gravely illicit.[8]

[5] Cf. cans. 2088, § 3; 2118; 2119; 2122, §§ 2, 3, 4; 2031; 2036, § 1; 2037, § 3; 2093, §2. The writer reminds the reader of his intention to exclude in this dissertation any detailed treatment of experts in beatification or canonization processes.

[6] J. Torre, *Processus Matrimonialis* (3. ed., Neapoli: M. d'Auria, 1956), p. 288, at article 139.

[7] S. R. Rota, *Decisiones,* VIII (1915), p. 211, n. 12.

[8] Doheny, *Canonical Procedure,* I, 383-384.

SECTION 2. UTILITY

Besides the cases enumerated above, there are many cases in which the use of experts will be found helpful, so many, in fact, that Cardinal Lega (1860-1935) wrote that "the law does not consider, nor *could* it consider, every case in which the use of an expert would be useful."[9] Hence, it is left to the judge to decide when a *peritia* should be utilized.

The judge can accept or demand a *peritia* whenever, in order to establish some fact or to explain it, there is required some technical or professional knowledge or skill (not necessarily difficult) which men generally do not possess, e.g., for an appraisal.[10] Undoubtedly there will arise many cases in which the testimony of witnesses will not be sufficient to establish sufficient proof without the aid of experts. The simple witness is unable fully to appraise the facts which he observes, and the judge himself has no obligation to know all of the sciences which may be necessary for bringing to light the pertinent facts and the legitimate deductions therefrom.[11]

Experts may be employed in both public and private causes.[12]

A list of the causes in which a *peritia* could reflect a useful type of proof here follows:

1. Causes with which a judicial access and inspection are connected.[13]

[9] Lega (ed. Bart.) *Iudicia Ecclesiastica,* II, p. 747, n. 6.

[10] T. Muñiz, *Procédimientos Eclésiasticos* (2. ed., 3 vols., Barcelona, 1925), III, n. 343 (hereafter cited *Procedimientos*). Cf. also Roberti, *De Processibus,* II, pars I, p. 81, n. 357.

[11] Quintana Reynés, *La Prueba,* p. 131.

[12] Noval, *De Iudiciis,* n. 515, at can. 1792: "Quod facere potest etiam in causis privatis, quia canon non distinguit, et merito, nam iudex non potest quidem facta seu argumenta probatoria quaerere in his causis, sed tenetur eadem facta ipsi exhibita perpendere, adhibitis mediis suo iudicio necessariis ad veritatem detegendam."

[13] Can. 1808, § 1—Iudex, rem vel locum recognoscens, peritos adhibere potest, si ipsorum opera necessaria vel utilis videatur.

Can. 1808, § 2—Si periti adhibeantur, serventur, quantum fieri potest, quae praescripta sunt can. 1793-1805.

2. Judicial actions which seek to halt the erection of new buildings, or notable alterations in old ones, to the prejudice of third parties, and to avert threatened injury to one's land or house through the dilapidated condition of a neighboring house, or from old and tottering trees or any other object that endangers the adjacent property. These actions at court are in the Code treated under the heading, *"de actionibus ex novi operis nuntiatione et damno infecto."*[14]

3. Judicial controversies concerning parish and diocesan boundaries.[15]

4. Causes looking to the dividing, the alienating, or the assigning of goods or of territory to a parish or a diocese.[16]

5. Criminal causes in which the court must, e.g., determine the value of a thing stolen, established the gravity of a wound, or detect a forgery.

6. Causes in which a specialized knowledge is needed for the reading of a difficult document.[17]

7. Causes which look to a determination of the just indemnification of judicial witnesses.[18]

8. Marriage causes other than those which involve impotence, non-consummation, and insanity (for in these causes *peritia* is compulsory). Thus in "a case of nullity tried in four instances the expert testimony of physicians was called upon to ascertain whether the woman in question was afflicted with the disease called ozena. The husband having suspected the presence of this disease had given his marital consent under the express stipulation that the woman did not have this disease. The first, third, and

[14] Cans. 1676-1678.

[15] Lega (ed. Bart.), *Iudicia Eccelsiastica,* II, p. 748, n. 4.

[16] Cans. 1427, § 3; 1530, § 1, 1°.

[17] C. Augustine, *A Commentary on the New Code of Canon Law* (8 vols., Vol. VII, 2. ed., St. Louis: Herder, 1923), VII, 242 (hereafter cited *A Commentary*).

[18] Can. 1787, § 2; *Instructio "Provida,"* Art. 127, § 3.

fourth instances of trial gave sentence for nullity based on expert testimony."[19]

In a cause wherein a woman was alleged to be the illegitimate daughter of the man she sought to marry, there was employed an expert who testified concerning the unmistakable dissimilarity between the woman and the legitimate children of her contemplated spouse in voice, in appearance, in personality, etc.[20]

9. Procedures wherein the matter of separation from bed and board claims attention and calls for a solution.[21]

ARTICLE II. THE DECISION TO ADMIT *Peritia*

SECTION 1. WHEN THE LAW DEMANDS THE USE OF EXPERTS

In the causes wherein the law demands the use of experts, the judge must *ex officio* admit the employment of experts, unless the *peritia* is obviously useless.[22] If the futility of this legally required *peritia* is clearly and immediately apparent, the judge, without need of consulting the defender of the bond need not order the use of experts. Indeed, he should not order it,[23] for it represents a dilatory and expensive type of proof.[24]

If the judge has only a slight suspicion that the *peritia* may be useless, then he is commanded by law to employ experts, and need consult no one. He is left no discretionary power in such a case, for the wording of canon 1976, "...*nisi ex adiunctis evidenter appareat*" obviously cannot be interpreted to mean that a mere suspicion of the uselessness of the proof suffices for debarring the experts. Should there be serious reason, however, to doubt the utility of

[19] F. Wanenmacher, *Canonical Evidence in Marriage Cases* (Philadelphia: The Dolphin Press, 1935), n. 285 (hereafter cited *Canonical Evidence*).

[20] S.R. Rota, *Decisiones*, II (1910), p. 104, n. 19.

[21] Wanenmacher, *Canonical Evidence*, n. 285.

[22] *Instructio "Provida,"* Art. 139; Canon 1976. Cf. also *Catholica Doctrina*, Rules 64, § 1; 84, §§ 1, 2.

[23] *Catholica Doctrina*, Rule 86; canon 1749.

[24] Lega (ed. Bart.), *Iudicia Ecclesiastica*, II, p. 747, n. 4.

the corporal examination in causes of non-consummation, the judge should discuss the matter with the *defensor vinculi,* and only then is he to decide whether to admit the proof through experts.[25] In marriage causes of impotence and insanity, the *suffragium peritorum* is always required,[26] whereas the corporal or psychiatric examination of the party may not always be necessary.[27] When the futility of such a physical examination is not immediately evident, but there is serious doubt regarding its utility, then it seems that the judge is not immediately to demand the expert inspection, but should first consult the parties and the *defensor vinculi* before deciding.[28]

SECTION 2. WHEN *Peritia* IS NOT DEMANDED BY THE LAW

In marriage causes other than those of impotence, non-consummation, or defective consent due to insanity, the auditing judge (*iudex instructor*) upon the instance of one of the parties, or even *ex officio,* decides whether or not to admit the *peritia.* In either case, he must consult the *defensor vinculi.* If the parties disagree on the need of the *peritia,* the judge refers the matter to the collegiate tribunal.[29]

Likewise in all other causes involving the public good, if the *peritia* is not already commanded by law,[30] the judge must decide whether or not to admit the use of experts. This he will do either *ex officio,* or at the instance of the parties, consulting previously with the promoter of justice or the defender of the bond of sacred ordination.[31]

[25] *Catholica Doctrina,* Rule 85.

[26] *Instructio "Provida,"* Art. 139; canon 1982.

[27] Canons 1976; 1982.

[28] By analogy with *Catholica Doctrina,* Rule 85. Cf. also canon 1749; *Instructio "Provida,"* Art. 95, § 2.

[29] *Instructio "Provida,"* Art. 140, § 2.

[30] As it is commanded in the cause of nullity of Sacred Orders or the obligations attached thereto, which nullity is allegedly due to the mental defect of the petitioner.—*Regulae Super Nullitate S. Ordinationis,* n. 68, with canons 1995, 1982.

[31] Cf. canons 1839; 1586; 1996.

Causes concerning purely private matters require the decision of the judge alone regarding the utility of the *peritia,*[32] and then always at the instance of the parties.[33]

The party who petitions the use of experts may do so either in his introductory *libellus,* or at any time during the process, as an incidental question, e.g., when some suspected document is submitted by his opponent in litigation.[34] In the petition for a *peritia* should be indicated the thing which or the person who is to be the object of the expert examination and report, as well as the precise subject matter of the investigation.[35]

Though the judge should not lightly disregard the petition of a party for the use of experts, he is in no way forced by that petition to admit it. For the *peritia* is conceded not only for the benefit of the parties,[36] but also for the benefit of the judge, that he may the more readily arrive at the moral certitude required for his pronouncement of sentence.[37] If he already has sufficient proof without the use of experts, there is no need to admit the petitioned *peritia.*[38]

The petition of the party, made orally or in writing,[39] is to be examined by the judge, and will ordinarily be admitted or rejected by him in a decree[40] wherein he must state the reason for admitting or rejecting the petition.[41] He could, however, choose to render his decision by means

[32] Cf. canon 1792.

[33] Canon 1793, § 2, permits the party to suggest the designation of experts. Since the party is allowed to petition that certain experts be appointed, it is evidently implied that he also can petition the use of a *peritia.* Cf. also canon 1618.

[34] Wernz-Vidal, *De Processibus,* n. 492.

[35] Muñiz, *Procédimientos,* III, p. 276, n. 344. Cf. canon 1799, § 1.

[36] Cf. canons 1793, § 2; 1618 with 1619, § 1; 1748, § 1.

[37] Canon 1869, §§ 1, 2.

[38] Cf. canons 1860, § 2; 1749. Goyeneche, *De Processibus, I* pars 2, n. 52, I.

[39] Cf. canons 1709; 1838.

[40] Cf. canon 1839; *Instructio "Provida,"* Art. 188, § 1.

[41] Canon 1840, § 3.

of an interlocutory sentence.[42] If the judge detects no fraud in the petition, nor any attempt to delay the process, he must admit the *peritia,* provided that there be even a simple indication of the party's right so to petition, i.e., provided that a *fumus boni iuris*[43] militate in the petitioning party's favor. If there is no such indication of a good right, the petition is to be rejected. *Peritia* should also be rejected in private causes when the disputed material object is of slight value, and the parties make no effort to reach an accord on the estimate. Then the judge himself, to avoid added expense and delay, is to act as arbiter by deciding the value.[44]

The promoter of justice, the defender of the bond, or the party who feels himself aggrieved by the judge's decree admitting or rejecting the petition for a *peritia* must within ten days[45] request the judge who issued the decree either to revoke or to amend it. If no such request is made, the parties are considered to acquiesce in the decree.[46]

If the judge, upon the redress sought by the parties, does not revoke his decree in marriage causes, he must send it at once to the collegiate tribunal for a decision.[47] Should he fail to do this, it appears that the party may seek redress with the collegiate tribunal after waiting five days.[48]

[42] Cf. canon 1840, § 1; *Instructio "Provida,"* Art. 190.

[43] Canons 1839; 1749; *Instructio "Provida,"* Art. 95, § 2.

[44] Cf. Quintana Reynés, *La Prueba,* pp. 136-137; Wernz-Vidal, *De Processibus,* n. 495.

[45] *Instructio "Provida,"* Art. 188, § 2.

[46] Canon 1841; *Instructio "Provida,"* Articles 140, § 2; 188, § 3; *Catholica Doctrina,* Rule 22, § 2.

[47] *Instructio "Provida,"* Art. 188, § 3.

[48] Doheny (*Canonical Procedure,* I, 457) bases his opinion on the analogy that exists with reference to canon 1710 and Article 67 of the *Instructio "Provida."*

CHAPTER VII

THE APPOINTMENT OF EXPERTS

Article I. Appointment by the Tribunal

The actual appointment of experts is reserved to the judge.[1] In marriage causes the appointment of experts is reserved to the presiding judge, and not to the auditing judge (*iudex instructor*), even though the latter, or the collegiate tribunal itself, has decided that the matter under consideration requires experts.[2] Bottoms, however, thinks that in one case the auditor himself may appoint the experts:

> In view of the fact that the auditor can determine that an expert is required, it seems that he could also designate an expert who has been previously recognized by the court as a qualified expert, or is permanently employed as such by the court, without reference to the presiding judge.[3]

The present writer cannot agree with him, since the expression *"designandi sunt"* in Article 141 of the *Instructio "Provida"* seems to exclude any appointment of experts without the action of the *praeses*.[4] The mentioned article

[1] Can. 1793, § 1: "Iudicis est peritos eligere vel designare."

[2] *Instructio "Provida,"* Art. 141 "Periti designandi sunt, audito vinculi defensore, a praeside, cuius est eorum numerum praefinire (cf. can. 1793); salvo praescripto art. 150." Cf. also Art. 140, § 2, with Art. 141.

[3] Archibald M. Bottoms, *The Discretionary Authority of the Ecclesiastical Judge in Matrimonial Trials of the First Instance*, (The Catholic University of America Canon Law Studies, n. 349 (Washington, D.C.: The Catholic University of America Press, 1955) pp. 129-130 (hereafter cited as *Discretionary Authority of the Judge*).

[4] It is true that according to Article 96, § 1, the words *praeses*, *instructor*, and *auditor* are used indiscriminately in Articles 93-174. But *"generi per speciem derogatur,"* and Article 68, § 2, mentions only the *praeses* as the one who can choose experts when the collegiate tribunal has not reserved this action to itself.

seems purposely to reserve the appointment to the presiding judge (*praeses*), rather than to the auditing judge (*instructor*), in order to lend greater authority to the appointment. In this same vein, only the ordinary himself, with the consent of the woman party, is to appoint men physicians for the physical inspection of the wife in causes involving impotence or non-consummation.[5]

Lega[6] and Roberti[7] distinguished between the *eligere* and *designare* of canon 1793, § 1. To them, the *eligere* means the appointment of experts without any previous presentation by the parties, while the *designare* signifies the appointment of experts from among those whom the parties have suggested to the judge. This seems a further argument that the ruling of "*Provida*" in Article 141 intends to give only the presiding judge the power to appoint experts, even though these should have been previously presented by the parties, or even approved by the court in some earlier session, for the aforesaid article does not employ the word *eligere*, or any form thereof, but has merely *designandi sunt a praeside*.

The selection of the experts, says Roberti, may be made by the parties or by the judge.[8] The experts selected by the parties receive greater confidence from the parties, while those who are selected by the judge are more independent. Practically then, so continues Roberti, it is impossible to leave the parties complete freedom in their choice of experts, for everyone would be inclined to appoint those who are favorable to himself. For this reason the civil law of

[5] Suprema Sacra Congregatio S. Officii Decretum, *De Quibusdam Cautelis Adhibendis in Causis Matrimonialibus Impotentiae et Inconsummationis*, n. 3. See S.C.S. Off., decr. 12 iunii, 1942—*AAS*, XXXIV (1942), 200-202 (hereafter cited with the opening words, *Qua singulari* of 1942). English translation appears in Bouscaren's *Digest*, II, 549-551.

[6] *Iudicia Ecclesiastica*, (ed. Bart.), II, p. 749, n. 2.

[7] *De Processibus*, II, pars I, n. 358.

[8] *Loc cit.*

nearly all nations empowers the judge to select and appoint the experts.[9]

The Code of Canon Law allows the judge personally to select and appoint the experts *ex officio,* or to appoint them from the ones already presented by both of the parties or only by one of them, with the consent of the other party.[10]

In purely private causes the judge can designate the experts *ex officio* or at the request of both parties, or of one of them, provided the other party consents.[11] In such cases the judge may, when he decrees the admission of a *peritia,* set a date within which the parties are to submit a list of approved experts.[12] When he has received this list, however, the judge is not bound to employ the experts suggested by the parties, even though they should agree on the same approved experts.[13] Rather, he is free to proceed *ex officio,* appointing experts of his own choice, just as he

[9] The German (§§ 404, 405) and Austrian (§ 351) Codes assign to the judge absolute power in appointing the experts. The Italian Penal Code (art. 253) allows the parties to appoint experts upon whom they agree; should they disagree, the judge decides who is to be appointed. In the United States the parties to the suit generally select their own experts, with the result that quite often one can read of causes wherein experts for the defense testify contradictorily to the experts for the prosecution. In illustration of this one may quote from an editorial that appeared in the Washington, D.C., *Sunday Star,* Oct. 30, 1955, under the title "Insanity Acquittal":

> This case presented the familiar spectacle of two Government psychiatrists, one hired by the prosecution and the other by the defense, testifying in direct conflict. One said Mrs. Haynes was sane at the time of the killing; the other swore that she was of unsound mind on July 19, when Nancy Penton was shot to death. As time goes on, what is going to be the public reaction to this kind of "expert" testimony? What is going to be the effect on public confidence in, and respect for, the judicial process?

[10] Can. 1793, § 2; Rota, *Regulae* of 1910, § 120: "Peritos eligere Iudici Instructori competit *ad praesentationem partium* si peritiam turnus praescribat, quin sibi peritorum nominationem reservaverit."

[11] Noval, *De Iudiciis,* n. 516, at word *potest* of can. 1793, § 2.

[12] Rota, *Regulae* of 1910, §§ 120; 121, n.2—*AAS,* II (1910), 823.

[13] Cf. the word *potest* of can. 1793, § 2, contrary to the earlier *debet* of the *Regulae* of 1910, § 121, n. 3. Cf. also Goyeneche, *De Processibus,* I, pars 2, n. 52, II.

would in the event the parties should disagree on the experts suggested,[14] or should fail to submit any names at all.[15] It would seem wiser, however, to appoint the ones agreed upon by the parties, in order to avoid later exceptions which might be brought by the parties against experts chosen *ex officio.*[16]

In matters involving the public good, even in those causes wherein a *peritia* is demanded by law, the parties can present to the judge the names of those experts whom they would like the court to employ.[17] Whether he does or does not choose those who have been suggested by the parties, the judge must consult the *defensor vinculi* for his advice and suggestions in marriage causes, and in causes concerning sacred orders, just as he must hear the *Promotor Justitiae* in criminal causes.[18] Muñiz (1874-1948) remarks that the designation of the experts is of no efficacy or validity if the judge does not consult the *defensor* or *promotor* in causes relating to the public good.[19] In view, however, of the word *audito* of canon 1793, § 2, and Article 141 of "*Provida,*" it seems that a failure to consult the *defensor* or the *promotor* would not invalidate the appointment of the experts, but would simply render it illicit.[20]

The actual appointment of the experts must be made by means of a decree, in which will be incorporated:

a) the names of those experts chosen;

[14] Muñiz, *Procédimientos* III, n. 344.

[51] Coronata, *De Processibus,* n. 1326.

[16] Coronata, *De Processibus,* n. 1325. This seems but a reflection of Cardinal De Luca's earlier advice. Cf. historical section, *supra,* pp. 27-28.

[17] Lega (ed. Bart.), *Iudicia Ecclesiastica,* II, p. 749, n. 2.

[18] Canons 1793, § 2; 1586. The *Instructio "Provida,"* Art. 141, mentions only the *defensor vinculi,* although sometimes the intervention of the *promotor* may be required.—Cf. Art. 190, § 2; Doheny, *Canonical Procedure,* I, 459.

[19] *Procédimientos,* III, n. 344.

[20] Cf. Regatillo, *Institutiones,* I, pp. 159, 160, n. 210, at canon 105, for the two opinions on the interpretation of the word *audito.*

b) the individual points with which the *peritia* is concerned;[21]

c) the interval of time allowed[22] and, if necessary, the place in which the examination is to take place.[23]

This decree is then sent to the experts and to the parties, in order that the latter may file objections, if they wish, against the experts appointed.[24]

Article II. Number of Experts Appointed

It is left to the prudent discretion of the judge to appoint one or more experts, according to the nature of the cause and the difficulty of the matter, unless the law itself determines the number.[25]

Section 1. Number not Determined in Law

When the law itself has not determined the number of experts, the judge is free to appoint as many experts as he deems necessary or useful, but he is obliged not to appoint too many,[26] lest he delay the trial and add unnecessary expenses. In determining the number to be appointed, the judge in causes concerning the public good should consult the *defensor* or the *promotor*,[27] and should consider the reasonable petition of the parties.[28]

Uneven Number not Required

There is no requirement of canon law which demands that the judge appoint an uneven number of experts when he is given discretionary power to determine the number.

[21] Canon 1799, § 1.

[22] Canons 1798; 1799, § 2.

[23] *Catholica Doctrina,* Rule 92.

[24] Canon 1796, § 1; *Instructio "Provida,"* Art. 145.

[25] Canon 1793, § 3.

[26] By analogy with canon 1762; *Instructio "Provida,"* Art. 123, § 2.

[27] Though canon 1793, § 3, does not mention this, it seems of sufficient importance to hear these officials.

[28] Rota, *Regulae* of 1910, § 122—*AAS,* II (1910), 823.

There are, however, several authors who call it "expedient" that the judge appoint an uneven number. Thus, Lega held it expedient—in order, namely, that there could readily be a majority—to appoint three, or an uneven number of experts, at least in the cause wherein, according to canon 1802, a joint report is to be given by a plural number of experts.[29] Noval recommended that in every cause wherein more than one expert is to be appointed, and the law does not specify the number, there should be appointed "an uneven number, lest a majority opinion be lacking; but not more than five, lest there be confusion."[30]

It is true that those civil laws which consider the *peritia* as the work of a collegiate group (*opus collegiale*) could scarcely do otherwise than command an uneven number of experts.[31] In canon law, however, the number of experts can be even or uneven, since in canon law the office of expert is considered individually (*opus individuale*) rather than collectively. Wernz-Vidal point out, in this regard, that generally separate reports are demanded of the several experts, and that even when the judge orders a joint report the opinion of each expert is to be noted, so that the judge can interrogate each separately.[32] Since the *peritia* is clearly an *opus individuale,* so says Roberti, and since the office of the expert is prevalently that a witness, two experts will generally suffice when a plural number of experts is to be appointed.[33]

Muñiz not only agreed that there is no necessity in law to employ an uneven number of experts, but he actually preferred an even number, should a plurality be appointed. The appointment of an even number of experts, he said,

[29] Lega (ed. Bart.), *Iudicia Ecclesiastica,* II, p. 750, n. 3, b.

[30] Noval, *De Iudiciis,* n. 516; cf. also Coronata, *De Processibus,* n. 1326.

[31] Roberti, *De Processibus,* II, pars I, n. 357, citing the Italian Penal Code, article 253, which requires one or three experts.

[32] Wernz-Vidal, *De Processibus,* p. 450, n. 493, note 17. Cf. canons 1802, 1801, §§ 2, 3.

[33] Roberti, *De Processibus, loc. cit.*

leaves the judge greater freedom for properly evaluating each report, for thus he will not be tempted to surrender his faculty of judgment to the majority opinion of the experts.[34] Further, he pointed as a norm to the fact that the Code itself asks for an even number of experts in the only two causes where the number is specified.[35]

Lega appears to have offered the best solution for causes wherein the number of experts is not specified by law. In such causes, he said, the judge should appoint only one expert, if he thinks that one will suffice for the matter. If he discovers, upon the report of the first expert, that the question is not clearly resolved, then, and only then, should he appoint a second expert. In this way he will keep expenses at a minimum and will avoid the unnecessary delay so readily occasioned by the employment of superfluous experts. Besides, the discordant opinions of the experts bring more complication than clarification to the issue. Hence, the judge is not to appoint even two experts unless the gravity of the matter truly demands it. The very fact that the law is satisfied with two experts in the gravest of causes (matrimonial causes, and processes of beatification and canonization) should clearly indicate the mind of the legislator as regards the number of experts necessary.[36]

Contrary, however, to the view of Lega,[37] who requested an uneven number of experts when a joint report is to be rendered, it seems better to hold that not even then should there be appointed three or an uneven number of experts. If two experts will suffice, there is no need to appoint a third simply for the sake of a resultant majority opinion.

SECTION 2. NUMBER DETERMINED IN LAW

When the law defines the number of experts to be appointed, the judge is left no personal discretion in the mat-

[34] Muñiz, *Procédimientos,* III, p. 275, n. 342.

[35] Muñiz, *op. cit.,* III, p. 277, n. 345.

[36] Lega (ed. Bart.), *Iudicia Ecclesiastica,* II, pp. 749, 750, n. 3, a.

[37] Lega (ed. Bart.), *Iudicia Ecclesiastica,* II, p. 750, n. 3, b.

ter.[38] He must fundamentally (*per se*) choose the precise number specified by law, neither a greater nor a smaller number. He is forbidden to appoint more than the number specified because of the resultant added expense and delay; he is forbidden to appoint fewer because of the gravity of the matter involved.

The law itself determines the number of experts required for the corporal inspection in causes of impotence or non-consummation. It demands that two skilled medical doctors be appointed *ex officio* for the examination of the man, and that two licensed midwives (or, if possible, and by preference in law, two women physicians, and in special circumstances, even male gynecologists) be appointed to examine the woman.[39]

These are the only causes in law, outside of the beatification, and canonization process,[40] in which the number of experts is specified. Not even in causes involving defective matrimonial consent due to insanity is a definite number of experts required.[41]

When the number of experts is defined, the judge is fundamentally (*per se*) not allowed to increase or decrease that number. Contingently (*per accidens*), however, causes may arise which excuse from the strict observance of the law. Thus one physician and one midwife will suffice for the corporal examination of the woman party in a non-consummation case, if it becomes impossible or very difficult to obtain the two physicians or the two licensed midwives specified in law.[42] This ruling may serve as the *stylus curiae* in similar causes when it becomes morally impossible to obtain the required number of experts, for it was

[38] Canon 1793, § 3.

[39] Canon 1979, §§ 1, 2; *Catholica Doctrina,* Rules 89, § 1; 95; *Qua Singulari* of 1942, nn. 2, 3. Cf. also *Instructio "Provida,"* Art. 150.

[40] Canon 2031, n. 1.

[41] Canon 1982; *Instructio "Provida,"* Art. 151, "*. . . unus, vel, pro casus gravitate, duo medici deputentur. . . .*"

[42] *Catholica Doctrina,* Rule 89, § 2. For detailed commentary see this dissertation, *infra,* pp. 147-148.

originally contained in an Instruction of the Holy Office concerning both impotence and non-consummation,[43] and has been upheld in practice by the Rota.[44]

On the other hand, it may sometimes be necessary to employ more than the number defined in law. Thus if the two chosen in impotence and non-consummation causes[45] are discordant in their reports, the judge may appoint a third, a more skillful expert (*peritior*), to pronounce his professional opinion upon their report, or he may even appoint different experts to repeat the *peritia* entirely.[46] The judge may do the same, i.e., appoint a *peritior* or employ experts distinct from the ones originally chosen, whenever after their appointment the experts become suspect, or are found to be unequal to or unqualified for fulfilling the office of expert.[47]

By virtue of canon 1803, then, the judge is allowed to employ additional experts, but only when he realizes, *after* their appointment, that the first experts chosen are unable to provide him with satisfactory expert evidence.

Could it even happen that the judge might *ab initio* appoint more than the number of experts specified in law? It seems that an affirmative answer can be given to the question. It may happen that the judge reasonably anticipates an unsatisfactory report as contemplated in canon 1803 if he employs only the legally specified number of experts. Foreseeing this unsatisfactory outcome, the judge could *ab initio* employ more than the defined number of experts, thereby avoiding the delay occasioned by a later appointment of a *peritior*. E.g., in a small town the judge may *ab initio* appoint the only three available physicians

[43] S.C.S. Off., instr. (ad Ep. Rituum Orient.), a. 1883, tit. VI, art. 5, at paragraph *Quod si.—Fontes*, n. 1076. Cf. *supra*, p. 48.

[44] S.R.R. *Decisiones*, X (1918), 1.

[45] Canon 1979, §§ 1, 2.

[46] Canon 1803, § 1.

[47] Canon 1803, § 2. For further commentary, see pp. 103-105 of this dissertation.

if he foresees that because of their rather mediocre ability he will not be satisfied with the report of only two of them, and would be required in any event to appoint the third as an expert.

One may conclude, then, that the judge in non-consummation causes (or the *praeses* in impotence causes concerning the validity of marriage) is bound ordinarily to appoint two, and only two experts for the examination of each party. Sometimes, however, he may be forced by moral impossibility to employ only one in place of the two experts specified; and sometimes he may find himself constrained to employ more than two experts in order to attain a satisfactory expert examination and report.

What is to be thought of those many respected authors[48] who state that the judge is prohibited from appointing a smaller number of experts than that defined in law, but that he is not prohibited from appointing a greater number of experts than that defined in law? It seems to the writer that these authors, although they did not state it, were simply contemplating the reasons which could compel the judge, with a view to obtaining a satisfactory report, to employ a greater number of experts than the number defined in law.[49] Moreover, these authors did not state whether this *surplus* appointment is to be made *ab initio* or only after the appointment of the legally required number of experts.

[48] Wernz-Vidal, *De Processibus*, p. 450, n. 493; Lega (ed. Bart.), *Iudicia Ecclesiastica*, II, p. 750, n. 3, c; Dominguez-Morán-De Anta, *Código y Comentarios*, at canon 1793; Quintana Reynés, *La Prueba*, p. 135; Goyeneche, *De Processibus*, I, pars 2, n. 52, III; Coronata, *De Processibus*, p. 269, n. 1326.

[49] The authors, in this supposition, relied on canon 1803, §§ 1, 2, which enables the judge to increase the number of the experts. Cf. also Litterae Apostolicae *Sollicitudinem Nostram*, 6 ian. 1950—*AAS*, XLII (1950), 5-120, and in particular can. 316, § 3 (hereafter cited: Oriental Code, *De Iudiciis*). Canon 316, § 3, of this new Oriental Code, *De Iudiciis*, has evidently adopted the view of the cited authors, for it reads: "Prudenti iudiciis arbitrio relinquitur unum pluresve peritos eligere pro causae natura et rei difficultate, *dummodo ne sint pauciores numero ipsa lege constituto*." (Italics supplied.)

If the judge feels himself compelled, by virtue of canon 1803, to appoint additional experts, he must consult the *defensor vinculi.*[50] He should, likewise, in order to forestall any later possible objection,[51] consult the interested parties, and also the *promotor iustitiae,* if the latter has part in the trial.[52]

ARTICLE III. QUALIFICATIONS OF EXPERTS

All other things being equal, there are to be appointed to the office of expert those who have been approved as qualified by the competent authority.[53] Who is this competent authority? Noval contended that there must be a public or an official approbation, written or unwritten; and if unwritten, the approbation may be either express or tacit, "for those who have degrees (*titulum peritiae*) or can present official (written) approbation cannot always be obtained."[54] Generally, the competent authority would be some college, university, or association empowered by the civil government to issue academic degrees or certificates of fitness in a particular art or science.[55]

In apparent contradiction to this, however, is Coronata, who says that the competent authority for approving the qualifications of the experts is "certainly the judge or some other ecclesiastical magistrate, e.g., the ordinary."[56] In view, however, of the rest of his commentary on the relevant canons it is clear that Coronata does not deny the fact that ordinarily the experts should have a degree from some public civil authority; indeed, he explicitly admits this, saying that in temporal matters nothing prohibits the judge

[50] Cf. can. 1803 along with *Instructio "Provida,"* Arts. 144, 141.

[51] Canon 1796, § 1.

[52] Rota, *Regulae* of 1910, § 122; Lega (ed. Bart.), *Iudicia Ecclesiastica,* II p. 750, n. 3, c.

[53] Canon 1795, § 1. Ad periti munus, ceteris paribus, deligantur, qui competentis magistratus auctoritate idonei fuerint comprobati.

[54] Noval, *De Iudiciis,* n. 518, at can. 1795, § 1 (Parentheses supplied.)

[55] Cf. Lega (ed. Bart.), *Iudicia Ecclesiastica,* II, p. 751, n. 6.

[56] Coronata, *De Processibus,* p. 270, n. 1326.

from using experts with degrees and approved by the public civil authority.[57] He likewise indicates that sometimes the law itself prescribes that those precisely who possess degrees should be appointed as experts.[58] Coronata, however, emphasizes the *ceteris paribus* of canon 1795, § 1, stating that the precept to appoint such as are already approved by the public authority binds only in the rare case when those who might be chosen as experts are entirely equal in all other qualifications, scientific as well as moral.[59] It is indisputably the office of the ecclesiastical judge to determine whether the ones to be chosen are equal in all qualities other than the possession of an academic degree. Besides, as Roberti says, an academic degree furnishes simply a presumption of capability.[60] The thought of Coronata, then seems to be that it is the office of the ecclesiastical judge or ordinary to determine whether this presumption of capability, derived from an academic degree or civil attestation of fitness, stands or falls.

In marriage causes, those who are to be chosen as experts must, in addition to having a diploma or a certificate of capability, be experienced and outstanding in their proper art or science, and commendable for their religious and upright lives.[61]

[57] Coronata, *De Processibus, loc. cit.*

[58] Coronata, *De Processibus*, p. 269, n. 1326, citing canon 1979.

[59] Coronata, *De Processibus*, p. 269, n. 1326: "Praeceptum eligendi qui sunt publica auctoritate idonei comprobati non urget, nisi in casu quo eligendi sint prorsus aequales in omnibus qualitatibus sive moralibus sive scientificis, nempe in moralitate seu honestate, in scientia vel arte, in experientia, in fama, etc., quod non facile accidere solet." Cf. also Muñiz, *Procédimientos*, III, n. 345.

[60] Roberti, *De Processibus*, II, pars I, p. 82, n. 358. Cf. also Goyeneche, *De Processibus*, I, pars, 2, p. 70, n. 52, IV. Augustine agrees with this presumption, "for generally speaking—except where the evil of 'graft' is deeply rooted and widely spread, and where bigotry is rampant—diplomas are a safe indication of one's skill and experience."—*A Commentary*, VII, can. 1796, p. 243.

[61] Cf. canon 1979, §§ 1, 2. Also *Catholica Doctrina*, Rules 87, 89; the *Instructio "Provida,"* Articles 142, § 1; 150, n. 2; 151; *Qua singulari* of 1942, nn. 2, 3, 5; *Regulae Super Nullitate S. Ordina-*

While for private causes the requirements of the expert would not be so stringent as for causes involving the public good, nonetheless the requirements of the *Instructio "Provida"* and the *Catholica Doctrina* may serve as norms even in private causes. Love of truth and of justice, a good reputation both for his professional ability and for his morally decent conduct—these are things the judge should seek in persons to be chosen as experts, whether for causes involving the public, or for causes involving the private good. In causes, however, which involve the validity of marriage or of sacred orders, it is understandable that the judge should demand a higher degree of professional skill than for merely private causes.

In marriage causes especially,

> the experience of the Sacred Roman Rota and diocesan tribunals has emphasized the necessity of these more stringent requirements. Hence, in case of impotency not any medical practitioner may be designated as an expert, but only those who are truly and eminently specialists in gynecology, urology, and similar branches of medical science. Likewise in cases of insanity only medical experts who are eminently versed in psychiatry and mental diseases should be appointed.[62]

Must the experts be Catholics? Preferably, yes; that is, *ceteris paribus,* the experts should be Catholics.[63] What is important is that the experts be outstandingly capable in their profession, and that they be religious, upright men.[64]

tionis, n. 68. For further consideration, see this dissertation, pp. 142-148, on experts for non-consummation and impotence causes; pp. 160-169 on experts in insanity causes.

[62] Doheny, *Canonical Procedure,* I, 386. Cf. pp. 142-148, 160-169, for detailed information concerning the requirements of experts in causes of impotence, non-consummation, and lack of marital consent in consequence of insanity.

[63] Cf. Wanenmacher, *Canonical Evidence,* p. 181, n. 293; Augustine, *A Commentary,* VII, 243, at canon 1796.

[64] Instruction *Cum moneat Glossa* of the S.C. Council on Aug. 22, 1840, at paragraph *Exhibitis—Fontes,* n. 4069 (hereafter cited: *Cum moneat Glossa*). Cf. also S.C.S. Off., Instruction of 1858, at para-

Hence, if these qualities exist in the expert, even though he is not a Catholic, he may be chosen, if an equally competent Catholic specialist cannot be found.[65] To the writer it appears unacceptable to say that "even with but mediocre ability, a soundly religious physician is preferable to a greater scientist in whom there is no religious conscience to direct his actions and opinions."[66] This lack of religious conscience does not necessarily and seriously taint the expert in his actions and opinions. Moreover, a good Catholic but one of only mediocre ability, can certainly not perform the office of expert so well as the more proficient non-Catholic. If, however, a man is actively anti-Catholic, he should not be chosen, for his judgment will most assuredly be influenced by this enmity to the Church.[67] Nor could a non-Catholic psychiatrist, or even a Catholic one, be accepted as the expert if he held psychological principles and theories evidently adverse to Catholic doctrine.[68]

graph *Corpus insuper—Fontes*, n. 946; *Catholica Doctrina*, Rule 87; *Instructio "Provida,"* Arts. 142, § 1; 151; S.C.S. Officii, *Qua singulari* of 1942, nn. 3, 5, 6.

[65] S.C.S. Off., instr. (ad Ep. Rituum Orient.), a. 1883, tit. VI, art. 5, last paragraph, "Medici et obstetrices, quantum fieri poterit, *inter catholicos*, eligantur; si vero ex his haberi nequeant, *tolerari* poterit, ut acatholici adhibeantur, dummodo tamen aliunde constet, eos esse probos et honestos, neque a spiritu catholicae religioni infenso duci."—*Fontes*, n. 1076. (Italics inserted.)

[66] Wanenmacher, *Canonical Evidence*, p. 181, n. 293, as cited by Pickett, *Mental Affliction and Church Law*, Series canonica—Tomus 25 (Ottawa: University of Ottawa Press, 1952), p. 158 (hereafter cited *Mental Affliction*).

[67] Cf. Lega, (ed. Bart.), *Iudicia Ecclesiastica*, II, p. 751, n. 6; also S.C.S. Off., instr. (ad Ep Rituum Orient.), a. 1883, tit. VI, art. 5, last paragraph, *Medici—Fontes*, n. 1076.

[68] *Instructio "Provida,"* art. 151: "In causis amentiae unus vel, pro casus gravitate, duo medici deputentur, qui in scientia psychiatrica peculiariter sint versati, cauto tamen ut excludantur qui sanam (catholicam) doctrinam hac in re non profiteantur." Since there is no distinct body of knowledge known as "Catholic" psychiatry, one must conclude that the canon intends to speak negatively, i.e., it excludes from the office of expert those who profess theories obviously contrary to Catholic teaching, e.g., those who deny the fredom of the

Article IV. Disqualifications of Experts

There must be excluded from the office of expert all who are excluded from serving as witnesses, according to the norm of canon 1757.[69] The ones thus excluded are:

As unsuited (*non idonei*):[70]

1) Those who have not reached puberty, and
2) persons who are feeble-minded.

As suspect:[71]

1) Excommunicated persons, perjurers, and infamous persons, after a declaratory or condemnatory sentence;
2) persons of such debased morals as to be regarded unworthy of credence, and
3) public and implacable enemies of the party.

As incapacitated:[72]

1) Parties to the cause, or those who take their place, such as a guardian in the cause of his ward, the judge or his assistants, the advocate, and others who are assisting or who have assisted the parties in the same cause;
2) priests, with reference to any knowledge they may have obtained through sacramental confession, even if they have been released from the obligation of the seal; further, persons with reference to anything overheard by them in any way on the occasion of confession, for such matter cannot be accepted as even an indication of the truth, and
3) the consort in a cause of his spouse; blood-relations and relations by marriage in the cause of persons related to them in any degree of the direct line and in the first degree of the collateral line, except in the causes which deal with the civil or religious state of

will, and those who deny the existence of the spiritual soul of man.—cf. S.R.R. *Decisiones*, I (1909), 87, 88.

[69] Canon 1795, § 2: *Instructio "Provida,"* Art. 142, § 2; *Catholica Doctrina*, Rule 87.

[70] Canon 1757, § 1. [71] Canon 1757, § 2. [72] Canon 1757, § 3.

the person, the knowledge of which cannot be had from other sources, and when the public welfare demands that the truth be ascertained.

Since the public good and the religious state of the parties are involved in marriage causes, canon 1974 permits relatives to testify as witnesses. Such a concession cannot be granted in favor of experts, because of the difference between the office of expert and that of witness. The witness testifies only to what he has learned through his senses, and hence necessity may rule that testimony be received from parents or close relatives, who are more likely to be first-hand witnesses. This is not true on the part of the expert, who from a scientific examination and in accord with the rules of his profession reasons to the conclusion which he reports judicially. Hence any qualified expert may perform the *peritia;* there is no need to employ a relative or a first-hand witness as expert. In fact, the close association with the party which usually exists in first-hand witnesses is an obstacle to objective judgment on the part of the expert. Therefore the exception afforded to relatives and spouses in canons 1757, § 3, n. 3, and 1974, is applicable only when such persons are to act as witnesses, and not when they are to act as experts.[73] Lega was willing to admit such relatives as experts only when absolutely no other qualified expert could be obtained.[74]

Again, because of the difference between the office of expert and that of witness, neither the unsuited nor the suspect may be received as lending some sort of supporting or additional *expert* testimony, though persons who are suspect may in this limited measure be received as witnesses.[75] In an attempt further to guarantee the objective honesty of the *peritia* in non-consummation causes, the decree *Catholica Doctrina* extends the disqualifications of experts. Hence,

[73] Cf. Lega (ed. Bart.), *Iudicia Ecclesiastica,* II, pp. 751, 752, n. 7.

[74] *Loc. cit.*

[75] Cf. can. 1758; Wernz-Vidal, *De Processibus,* p. 452, n. 493; Roberti, *De Processibus,* II, pars I, p. 82, n. 358; Qunitana Reynés, *La Prueba,* p. 136.

not to be selected are those who can be identified or linked with the circumstances mentioned in canon 1613, § 1, namely, if on account of consanguinity or affinity to the parties (even to the second degree in the collateral line), or because of friendship or antipathy toward the parties, or even because of advantage or disadvantage that might result from the decision in the causes, suspicion could arise as to the probity of their expert judgment or opinion in the cause.[76]

The wording of the *Instructio "Provida,"* governing other marriage causes, is essentially the same as that of *Catholica Doctrina,* though not so specific.[77] It calls for the exclusion of all from the office of expert who may be connected by any bond of intimacy with either party.

The purpose of these disqualifications is to secure an expert opinion which is completely objective, free from all bias, prejudice, or favoritism.[78] Such an opinion could not readily be obtained when the expert stands to gain considerable advantage should a favorable decision be rendered, or when he will suffer a great loss in the event of an unfavorable decision. Moreover, the dispassionate quality required of experts could hardly be looked for when there exists an intimate friendship with one of the parties. This could particularly obtain when an expert psychiatrist might be inclined to view the manifestations of insanity in his friend as mere idiosyncracies.[79]

The rules of exclusion thus far refer directly only to the spouse or the relatives of the expert, with no direct reference made to interested third parties who may be keeping company with one of the consorts. Nevertheless the judge must not appoint as expert one whose friend or relative is an interested third party, e.g., a nephew or a niece who would like to marry one of the parties in the litigation. Such

[76] *Catholica Doctrina,* Rule 87.

[77] *Instructio "Provida,"* Art. 142, § 3: "Excluduntur quoque a periti munere qui quemlibet cum alterutra parte necessitudinis nexum habeant."

[78] Doheny, *Canonical Procedure,* II, 444.

[79] Cf. Doheny, *Canonical Procedure,* I, 387.

an expert would surely be considered as unduly interested in the outcome of the cause.[80]

Likewise unacceptable as experts are those who have privately inspected the parties in reference to the fact upon which is based their petition for a declaration of nullity, namely the plea of impotence or of defective matrimonial consent in consequence of insanity.[81] Equally excluded are those who have privately examined the consorts in connection with the fact upon which the petition for the declaration of non-consummation is based.[82]

The reason for excluding as experts those who have previously examined the parties in the same matter which is the foundation of the matrimonial cause is that they will likely have fixed opinions, based upon their previous examination. They may also have formed bonds of friendship with their client, and thereby be led to judge, even unconsciously, in a manner favorable to their client.[83]

In the causes of a non-consummated marriage, in the event that the *peritia canonica* becomes impossible or useless, the Sacred Congregation of the Sacraments is accustomed to grant an indult, dispensation, or sanation admitting the expert testimony obtained from a previous non-canonical examination of the woman party in the cause. It then, however commands that the experts be questioned by means of formal interrogatories concerning the previous inspection, and that they confirm with an oath the earlier *peritia* they may have performed at the injunction of some civil tribunal. This previous *peritia* may also be subjected to the examination and judgment of other experts selected by the Sacred Congregation itself. With such an indult it is possible in many causes, otherwise despaired of, to obtain moral certitude, and a juridical declaration of non-consummation.[84]

80 Doheny, *Canonical Procedure,* II, 445.

81 Canons 1978; 1982; *Instructio "Provida,"* Art. 143.

82 Canon 1978; *Catholica Doctrina,* Rule 88.

83 Cf. Wernz-Vidal, *De Processibus*, pp. 451-452, n. 493.

84 Wernz-Vidal, *De Processibus*, p. 451, n. 493, note 18, in which

Although an indult is required for the acceptance of testimony from experts, *qua* experts, if they previously examined the party, the law itself permits the acceptance of testimony from these experts, *qua* witnesses, in causes of non-consummation and nullity of marriage;[85] the law *commands* it in causes of defective consent in consequence of insanity.[86] It is obvious that such physicians and psychiatrists will at times be very important and valuable witnesses. This would be especially true when the party to be examined cannot be reached for the examination, or refuses to undergo the judicial inspection out of hatred for his spouse, or because he (or she) dislikes being submitted again to a physical examination.[87] The decree *Catholica Doctrina,* in emphasizing the worth of the testimony obtainable in causes of non-consummation from physicians who earlier had subjected a party to a physical examination, stated: "It is permitted, however, and proper that these [previously examining experts] be introduced as witnesses; and the inclusion of their written attestations, in so far as this can be done, among the documents relating to the cause should never be omitted."[88]

It may prove very helpful in causes of non-consummation, impotence and insanity to have a complete case history of the party. To ascertain the precise nature of a mental disorder, reports on the different phenomena manifested at divers stages of the derangement aid materially.[89] Because, however, the expediting of insanity causes generally proves more difficult than that of impotence or non-consummation causes, doctors who have examined the party extrajudicially *must* be heard as witnesses. Their testimony as witnesses

reference is made to Bassibey, *Procédure Matrimoniale,* nn. 392 ff., for many such cases of indults.

[85] Canon 1978; *Catholica Doctrina,* Rule 88; *Instructio "Provida,"* Art. 143.

[86] Canon 1982; *Instructio "Provida,"* Art. 143.

[87] Torre, *Processus Matrimonialis,* p. 295, at Article 143.

[88] *Catholica Doctrina,* Rule 88.

[89] Doheny, *Canonical Procedure,* I, 387, 388.

will especially be of great weight if their previous examination was made under non-questionable circumstances (*tempore non suspecto*). Information obtained when there was no serious thought of impugning the marriage is more likely to reflect the truth of things than information obtained after the initiation of the judicial process.[90]

It must be remembered, however, that those who have examined the party privately may not testify as witnesses before they are released by the party from the obligation of professional secrecy. Furthermore, they must prudently feel that they can testify. If they decide they cannot, in conscience, prudently reveal what they have learned professionally, the court cannot force them to testify.[91] It is obvious that an insane person cannot act for himself in releasing the psychiatrist from professional secrecy; in this his guardian must act for him.[92]

Torre explains that, when there has been a judicial and an extrajudicial *peritia,* the tribunal can arrange a meeting of the experts employed in the examinations.[93] This indeed seems to provide an excellent aid to the judge in arriving at certitude, especially in the more difficult causes, when the judge is not fully satisfied with the judicial *peritia.*[94]

[90] Torre, *Processus Martimonialis,* p. 295, at Article 143.

[91] Canon 1755, § 2, n. 1; *Instructio "Provida,"* Art. 121, § 2, n. 1.

[92] Doheny, *Canonical Procedure,* I, 388. Cf. also *Instructio "Provida,"* Art. 77; can. 1650.

[93] Torre, *Processus Matrimonialis,* p. 295, at Article 143.

[94] Reasoning from canon 1803; *Catholica Doctrina,* Rule 93, §2.

CHAPTER VIII

OBJECTIONS TO AND SUBSTITUTION OF EXPERTS

Article I. Legal Objections

SECTION 1. REASONS FOR OBJECTIONS

Objections may be lodged against experts for the same reasons that exceptions may be lodged against witnesses.[1] Witnesses may be challenged by means of an exception (*reprobatio personae testis*) whenever there is any just reason for their exclusion,[2] even if that reason is not explicitly determined by law.[3] Similarly, any just reason for the exclusion of the expert would also afford sufficient grounds for bringing an exception against him.[4]

Among the reasons designated by law for the exclusion of witnesses and experts[5] are impuberty, mental debility,[6] declaratory or condemnatory excommunication, perjury, legal infamy, base immorality, grave enmity toward one of the parties.[7] Experts may be objected to if they are suspected of partiality toward one or both of the parties,[8] whether the basis of that partiality be professional ties, friendship, or close blood relationship.[9] They may be chal-

[1] Canon 1796, § 1; *Instructio "Provida,"* Art. 145. Although in the decree *Catholica Doctrina* there is no express provision for the raising of an objection to experts, this principle of the Code obtains even in the administrative procedure that deals with a ratified but non-consummated marriage.—Doheny, *Canonical Procedure,* II, 466.

[2] Canon 1764, § 2.

[3] *Instructio "Provida,"* Art. 131, § 2.

[4] Cf. canon 1796, § 1, with 1764, § 2. Cf. also canon 319, § 1, of Oriental Code, *De Iudiciis,* applicable here by force of canon 20, C.I.C. "... a legibus latis in similibus. ..."

[5] Canon 1795, § 2.

[6] Canon 1757, § 1.

[7] Canon 1757, § 2.

[8] *Instructio "Provida,"* Art. 145.

[9] Canon 1757, § 3; *Catholica Doctrina,* Rule 87.

lenged if they do not possess the requisite moral and professional qualifications demanded of experts by law.[10] Finally, a legal objection may be brought against the person of the expert who previously examined the party in reference to the fact which later became the object of the expert examination.[11]

Whereas, however, the raising of an objection to the person of the expert is permitted, there can be no reprobation of the conclusions to which he testifies. The reason for not permitting the raising of an objection to the conclusions of the expert upon the facts observed derives from the intent to allow the expert greater freedom in his office. He is not merely to testify to the facts examined and discovered, but is also to give his professional opinion concerning those facts. An objection can be raised, however, against the manner in which the *peritia* was performed, e.g., inasmuch as the requirements of law or of the judge were not properly observed in the examination or the report, or inasmuch as the expert showed himself to be incapable, unqualified, or suspect in the performance of his duties. Likewise, in the event that the judge does not act *ex officio,* the parties may point out to the judge the faulty reasoning of the expert in arriving at his conclusions from the facts reported, or his failure to consider certain important factors in making his report. Contradictory statements in the report of a single expert may be called to the attention of the judge, just as discrepancies in the reports of two or more experts may be adverted to. Accordingly the judge may be asked to appoint one or more new experts, or at least a *peritior,* to give his opinion upon the challenged reports.[12] In these ways the opinion of the experts about the fact is challenged, not indeed directly, but rather indirectly.

[10] Cf. *supra,* p. 28.

[11] Canons 1978; 1982; *Catholica Doctrina,* Rule 88; *Instructio "Provida,"* Art. 143.

[12] Arguing from canons 1783, § 2; 1803, § 1. Cf. Wernz-Vidal, *De Processibus,* pp. 452-453, n. 494.

SECTION 2. WHO MAY RAISE THE OBJECTIONS

These objections may be raised by either or both of the parties,[13] or by the *promotor* or *defensor*, if they have part in the trial.[14] If, however, the parties presented the expert who then became appointed, or if they consented in his appointment even though they did not present him,[15] they cannot raise an exception against the expert unless they prove, or at least swear, that the reason for the exception arose only after the appointment of the expert, or until that time was unknown.[16] On the other hand, if the parties neither presented the expert, nor consented in his appointment by the judge, they may raise exceptions against the expert even for reasons which existed and were known before the appointment.

SECTION 3. TIME FOR PRESENTING THE OBJECTIONS

Objections may be lodged a) between the appointment of and the acceptance by the experts; b) after the expert has already undertaken his task; c) upon the completion of the *peritia*,[17] or d) even after the publication of the experts' report (*publication peritiae*), if the reason for the objection was non-existent or unknown earlier.[18]

This right of the parties to raise exceptions at any time may have been renounced by them, however, in consequence of their implicit or explicit acceptance of the expert when he was appointed, e.g., by their failure to raise exceptions against the expert even though they could easily have done so when they were invited and were actually present at the swearing-in of the expert, or even during his execution

[13] *Instructio "Provida,"* Art. 145.

[14] Cf. can. 1667; Lega (ed. Bart.), *Iudicia Ecclesiastica*, II, p. 753, n. 8.

[15] Roberti, *De Processibus*, II, pars I, p. 82, n. 359.

[16] By analogy with can. 1764, §§ 3, 4; *Instructio "Provida,"* Art. 131, § 1.

[17] Wernz-Vidal, *De Processibus*, p. 452, n. 494; Lega (ed. Bart.), *Iudicia Ecclesiastica*, II, 752, n. 8.

[18] Canons 1783, § 1; 1764, § 4.

of the *peritia*. It is the intention of the law that the parties be present when the expert takes his oath of office, and even when he performs his examination (subject matter permitting),[19] in order that they may immediately propose their exceptions, if they have reason to do so.[20]

Doheny,[21] by analogy with the law regarding objections against witnesses,[22] states that known exceptions against the expert must be brought by the parties within three days after their notification regarding the persons who were appointed as experts. This three-day limit serves as a good norm, but it cannot strictly be demanded, for the law does not determine the precise time limit for proposing exceptions against the expert.[23] It does, however, demand that dilatory exceptions be raised as soon as possible by the party after he has learned of the unacceptable qualifications of the appointed expert.[24] A late proposal of a known reason for the raising of an objection is quite naturally suspect, and accordingly the judge must take care that the exception is not raised simply for the purpose of retarding the process.[25] It may well happen, however, that the expert becomes suspect only after his appointment, or is only then seen to be incompetent or unqualified for this particular judicial cause. In this event the parties, or the *defensor*, could petition the judge to remove the suspect expert, even though he may be in the midst of his examination, or even when he has finished it.[26]

If the party knew of the unacceptable qualification of the expert from the very time of the appointment, but through

[19] Can. 1797, § 2.

[20] Lega (ed. Bart.), *Iudicia Ecclesiastica*, II, p. 752, n. 8.

[21] *Canonical Procedure*, I, 385.

[22] Cf. can. 1764, § 4; *Instructio "Provida,"* Art. 131, § 1.

[23] Cf. can. 1796, § 1; *Instructio "Provida,"* Art. 145.

[24] Cf. can. 1628, § 1.

[25] Wernz-Vidal, *De Processibus*, p. 452, n. 494, arguing from canon 1749.

[26] Cf. can. 1803, § 2; if the judge can act *ex officio*, then he may also act at the instance of the parties. Cf. also can. 1764, § 4; *Instructio "Provida,"* Arts. 144; 131, § 1.

his own neglect failed to lodge an exception against the expert until after the completion of the *peritia,* he may lodge his exception. Exceptions are of their very nature perpetual.[27] If the party can prove that the expert is canonically unqualified to serve as an expert,[28] the judge must disregard as uncanonical the *peritia* of the disqualified expert, and appoint a new qualified expert.[29] Nonetheless, the party who raised the tardy exception must pay the expenses of the disqualified expert, as well as the needlessly incurred court expenses. He by his guilty silence occasioned the futile *peritia.*[30]

SECTION 4. OBJECTION ADMITTED OR REJECTED BY DECREE

When the judge has received the objection (*recusatio*) against the person of the expert, he should immediately inform the expert not to begin his examination, or, if he has already begun it, then to suspend it until the petition for his removal is decided.[31] Thereupon the judge is to consider the objection, and either admit or reject it by means of a decree,[32] in which he should briefly state the reasons for his admission or rejection.[33]

There is no need for such a formal treatment and consideration of the matter as would be required were an interlocutory sentence to be given. Rather the judge, considering the reasons and proofs adduced by the party who lodged the exception,[34] needs only to determine whether or not the allegation has any foundation. He should, of course, consult the *defensor* or *promotor,* if they have part in the trial.[35] If the challenge is without foundation, the judge

[27] Can. 1667.

[28] Cf. canons 1795, 1796.

[29] Can. 1803, § 2.

[30] Arguing from can. 1910, § 2, and canonical equity. Cf. also *Instructio "Provida,"* Art. 234, 2°.

[31] Wernz-Vidal, *De Processibus*, p. 452, n. 494.

[32] Canon 1796, § 2; *Instructio "Provida,"* Art. 146.

[33] Canon 1840, § 3; *Instructio "Provida,"* Art. 193.

[34] Canon 1748, § 1; *Instructio "Provida,"* Art. 94.

[35] *Instructio "Provida,"* Art. 69.

is to reject it, and inform the expert to proceed with his examination and report.

In marriage causes, if the parties still feel that they have a legitimate objection to the expert, they are permitted to have recourse to the collegiate tribunal against the decree of the auditing judge (*auditor*) or presiding judge (*praeses*).[36] If recourse is made, the expert again must suspend his examination until the matter is finally settled.

Should the objection of the parties be well founded, and supported by convincing proofs at least to the extent that doubt is cast upon the expert's professional and moral qualifications as demanded by the Code,[37] then the judge must sustain the objection, and will duly appoint a substitute to supplant the debarred expert.[38]

Article II. Substitution of Experts

When the judge has sustained the objection of the parties, of the *defensor,* or of the *promotor,* against the personal or professional qualifications of the expert, he must substitute another expert in his place,[39] observing the same procedure as for the original appointment.[40]

Sometimes the judge himself must appoint substitute experts, even though no objection has been raised by the parties, by the *defensor,* or by the *promotor.* He may make the substitution for the same reasons which entitle the parties to bring exceptions against the expert, as well as for whatever reason renders the examination or report of the expert unsatisfactory.[41]

Section 1. Incompetent Experts

The judge, then, must *ex officio* substitute qualified experts for those who, after their appointment, become sus-

[36] *Instructio "Provida,"* Arts. 69; 188, § 2.
[37] Cf. cans. 1795, 1796.
[38] Can. 1796, § 2; *Instructio "Provida,"* Art. 146.
[39] Can. 1796, § 2; *Instructio "Provida,"* Art. 145.
[40] Cf. this dissertation, pp. 78-82.
[41] Cans. 1795, § 2; 1803, § 2; *Instructio "Provida,"* Art. 144.

pect, or are discovered by him to be in any way unequal to or unqualified for the office of expert in the particular cause under question. Should one of the appointed experts die before completing his *peritia,* or resign his office, or be excused by the judge from performing it, the judge must appoint a substitute.[42]

These regulations provide for the practical situations which may arise to prevent the appointed experts from performing their duties. Sometimes the appointed expert may be only temporarily unable to pursue his examination, as for example if he should become ill, or have to make an emergency trip, or suddenly have an unforeseen increase in his other professional activities. In such cases, the judge, hearing the parties, can extend the time limit set for the completion of the expert examination and report.[43] If, however, the expert will be unable to perform his duties for a long time, the judge should graciously inform him that another expert will be substituted in his stead, so that the process will not be unduly delayed.

SECTION 2. UNSATISFACTORY REPORTS

The judge may appoint substitute experts even after the originally chosen experts have completed the judicial report of their examination. If their reports are discordant, revealing a disagreement among the experts, the judge at his discretion may appoint another more qualified expert (*peritior*) to give his opinion upon the discordant reports, even conducting another physical examination, if need be; or he may substitute other experts to perform the examination anew and to report their findings to the court.[44]

When a substitute expert is appointed, whether that substitution was made at the request of the party or at the

[42] Rota, *Regulae* of 1910, § 133.

[43] Canon 1799, § 2; *Instructio "Provida,"* Art. 147, § 4.

[44] Canon 1803, § 1; *Catholica Doctrina,* Rule 93, § 2; *Instructio "Provida,"* Art. 153. Cf. pp. 120-121; 182-185 of this dissertation for further details.

initiative of the judge, and regardless of the reason for the substitution, the judge must observe the same procedure that attended the appointment of the first expert, i.e., he must hear the parties in private causes, and the *defensor vinculi* or the *promotor iustitiae* in causes involving the public good.[45]

[45] Canon 1793, §§ 1, 2. Cf. this dissertation, pp. 78-82.

CHAPTER IX

PRELIMINARIES OF THE EXPERT EXAMINATION

Article I. Appointment

SECTION 1. INFORMAL INVITATION

A very important part of the procedure in appointing experts is the initial, informal contact which the tribunal makes with the doctors or other professional men. While this preliminary extra-judicial discussion with the expert is nowhere demanded by law, it is certainly demanded by practicality.

The person designated as expert is to be invited, not obliged, to accept the office. He has no obligation to lend his assistance to the tribunal, except in the rare and scarcely practical case in which the public good requires *peritia* and there is no other qualified expert available.[1] He should not, then, be officially appointed as expert until he has signified his intention to accept the office. Merely to appoint the expert, citing him to appear for an oath of office, and then to proceed to the examination and report would only antagonize the professional man whose cooperation the court needs.

For the sake of an example, to serve as a model even in other cases, the writer submits what he thinks should be included in the preliminary discussion with the doctor to be appointed as expert in a *ratum, non-consummatum* marriage cause. This informal conversation with the doctor will embrace practically all of the legislation pertinent to the *peritus* and *peritia*. Therefore many things only touched on here will receive detailed commentary in their proper place in the formal steps of procedure.

[1] Wernz-Vidal, *De Processibus*, p. 453; n. 490; Lega (ed. Bart.), *Iudicia Ecclesiastica*, II, p. 750, nn. 4, 5; Muñiz, *Procédimientos*, III, p. 277, n. 344.

When the judge has properly determined whom he wishes to serve as the expert, he should discuss the matter with him, mentioning the fact that the tribunal finds it necessary to obtain the services of a specialist in a particular case wherein the parties claim that their marriage has not been consummated. He should tell the doctor that, because of his outstanding moral and professional qualifications, the court would appreciate his aid. Then the judge should explain, if necessary, the canonical concept of consummation, and should briefly outline the object and subject matter of the *peritia*.[2] He should assure the doctor that if he agrees to perform the corporal inspection, the court will obtain from the party to be inspected a signed release of the doctor from his obligation of professional secrecy, thereby allowing him to submit a detailed report to the court, and to testify concerning that report.[3]

The judge should tell the doctor of the legal requirement which demands the oath of office and secrecy before undertaking the physical examination, and should ask the doctor to indicate the time when he could more conveniently appear for this oath.[4]

The doctor must be told how he may recognize the party to be examined, in order that any substitution of parties may be obviated.[5] The manner of conducting the physical

[2] Canon 1799, § 1.

[3] Question n. 25 of a sample questionnaire used in the judicial interrogation of the woman party in non-consummation causes.—Formula XIX, pp. 424-427, in the Appendix to the Decree *Catholica Doctrina* of 1923—*AAS*, XV (1923). (Hereafter referred to as: Appendix, *Catholica Doctrina*.) Cf. Doheny for English translation of this questionnaire. *Canonical Procedure*, II, 458-460.

[4] Formula XXIX, used by the appointed experts, Appendix, *Catholica Doctrina, AAS*, XV (1923), 432. English translation in Doheny, *Canonical Procedure*, II, 454. Cf. p. 210, this dissertation.

[5] *Normae Observandae in Processibus super Matrimonio Rato et non Consummato ad Praecavendam Dolosam Personarum Substitutionem*, n. 4, § 1.—S.C. de Sacramentis, March 27, 1929; (*AAS*, XXI (1929), 490-493). English translations in Doheny, *Canonical Procedure*, II, 316-320; Bouscaren, *Canon Law Digest*, I, 792-796. (Hereafter cited: S.C. de Sacr., *Normae* of 1929).

examination should be stated,[6] and the expert should be informed that any further details will be sent in a decree accompanying the official appointment of the expert. Even the acts of the cause, which in the opinion of the judge seem necessary or useful, should be sent to the expert.[7]

The matter of the doctor's fee is to be mentioned, and there should be determined, in accord with the acknowledged local custom,[8] the amount and the method of payment.

Finally, the doctor's convenience should be considered[9] for the fixing of the place, the day, and the hour for the physical examination,[10] and the time within which the written reports are to be submitted.[11]

SECTION 2. FORMAL APPOINTMENT

After the preliminary, informal discussion, in which the person desired as the expert has signified his intention to accept the office, the judge should officially decree his appointment. This decree of appointment will indicate the purpose of the *peritia,* the place of the expert examination,[12] and the time within which the examination must be performed and the reports submitted.[13] There should be a statement to the effect that the examination is to be performed according to the norms of law and the prescriptions of the judge, and with a due observance of the rules of Christian propriety and modesty.[14]

[6] *Catholica Doctrina,* Rules 90, 92.

[7] By analogy with the *Instructio "Provida,"* Art. 147, § 2.

[8] Canon 1805.

[9] George R. Evans, "*Ratum et non-Consummatum* Procedure: Regulations Concerning Corporal Examination," *The Jurist,* XVI (1956), p. 175, n. 7.

[10] *Catholica Doctrina,* Rule 92; Appendix, *Cath. Doctrina,* Formula XXVIII—*AAS,* XV (1923), 431, 432.

[11] Canon 1799, § 2; can. 1980, § 2; *Catholica Doctrina,* Rule 90, (e); *Instructio "Provida,"* Art. 147, § 4.

[12] *Catholica Doctrina,* Rule 92.

[13] Canon 1799, § 2; Canon 1980, § 2; *Catholica Doctrina,* Rule 90 (e); *Instructio "Provida,"* Art. 147, § 4.

[14] E.g., Formula XXVIII of the Appendix, *Catholica Doctrina,* for

It would be of practical value to include in the appointment some mention of the time when the expert is to appear to take his oath of office and secrecy, so that this information may be communicated to the *defensor vinculi* and the parties,[15] who have the right to assist at the expert's oath of office.[16]

ARTICLE II. THE DECREE ACCOMPANYING THE APPOINTMENT

Accompanying the appointment of experts should be a decree in which are explained the purpose, the subject matter, and the canonical requirements concerning the method of the expert examination, as well as the manner in which the reports are to be made, and the time within which the examination and reports must be completed.

SECTION 1. PURPOSE OF THE EXAMINATION

The purpose of the examination must be specified, according to the particular case. a) The obvious object of *peritia* in insanity cases is the determination as to whether or not one of the parties was unable, because of some mental affliction at the time of the marriage, to give true matrimonial consent.[17] The expert should, then, determine whether the insanity was habitual or transitory, and whether lucid intervals intervened.[18]

b) The purpose of the corporal examination in cases of alleged impotence is the ascertainment as to whether or not there is impotence present, and, if so, whether this impotence is absolute or relative, instrumental or func-

the decree appointing the experts in *ratum et non-consummatum* marriage causes.

[15] It should be remembered that in most instances when the right of the parties to do a certain thing, or to be present for a certain act, is mentioned, their advocate or procurator will usually be the one concerned.—*Instructio "Provida,"* Arts. 43, § 1; 44, 45; canon 1647.

[16] Canon 1797, § 2; *Instructio "Provida,"* Art. 146.

[17] Canon 1982.

[18] *Instructio "Provida,"* Art. 147, § 1.

tional, antecedent or subsequent to the marriage, and whether it is perpetual or remediable without grave danger to life.[19]

c) The material object of the physical inspection in causes of claimed non-consummation of a sacramental marriage is the discovery of physical indications which favor or argue against the bodily integrity of the woman.[20] The formal object of the examination is the disclosure as to whether or not the alleged non-consummation in this particular case is confirmed by physical indications.[21]

SECTION 2. SUBJECT MATTER OF THE EXAMINATION

To assure a complete and satisfactory examination and report from the experts, the judge must clearly indicate the subject matter to be examined. After a consideration of the information already obtained in the process, and upon consulting the *defensor vinculi* and the parties, the judge is to define in his decree each and every point (*omnia et singula capita*) with which the experts must concern themselves in their *peritia*.[22]

Doheny complains that the examinations of the experts are ordinarily not satisfactorily detailed or thorough, and that frequently their reports are not sufficiently comprehensive and precise.[23] The judge should take the necessary steps to obviate this difficulty. On the one hand, he must not by overly-detailed instructions insult the intelligence of the professional men who are to serve as experts, and, on the other hand, he must impress upon them that the tribunal needs to obtain a great deal of information from the examination and the report, in order that it may have a

[19] *Instructio "Provida,"* Art. 147, § 1.

[20] *Catholica Doctrina,* Rule 92.

[21] *Catholica Doctrina,* Rule 20; Hickey, "De Processu super Matrimonio rato et non consummato," *The Jurist,* I (1941), 222; Hickey, "Requirements of the *ratum et non consummatum* process," *The Jurist,* V (1945), 16.

[22] Cf. canon 1799, § 1; *Instructio "Provida,"* Art. 147, §§ 1, 3.

[23] Doheny, *Canonical Procedure,* I, 391.

firm basis in reaching a decision. Evidently, the doctor who is for the first time employed to act as expert in an ecclesiastical trial should be given more detailed instructions regarding the matter of the examination than one who has acted in this capacity before. Even the previously employed expert, however, must be at least briefly reminded of the subject matter of the examination and the report, and the relevant circumstances of each case.[24]

By considering the questions asked of the experts in *ratum, non-consummatum* causes when they later appear before the tribunal to testify concerning their reports, we may gather what should be included in the decree of instructions which the judge sends the experts prior to their corporal inspection of the parties. The Sacred Congregation of the Sacraments[25] rules that these questions are to be drawn from, among other sources, the Instruction of the Holy Office given in 1858.[26] This is the most detailed of any of the Instructions mentioned by the Sacred Congregation. That detailed Instruction ruled:

A) for the inspection of the man:

> Animadvertendum autem, ut mediis utantur licitis et honestis, et perscrutandum praecipue utrum illius virilia sint iuxta naturae leges accurate conformata: nimirum an penis naturalem habeat dimensionem, promptamque erectionem ad coeundum necessario duraturam; an aliquo morbo fuerit affectus, a quanto tempore, et cuiusnam characteris; an fibrae compactae et consistentes, seu potius flaccidae lassaeque sint; an testes sani, naturalisque magnitudinis, et utrum aliquo vitio laboraverint vel adhuc laborent; quo in casu morbi characterem, et causas investigabunt; an vetus, vel recens, naturalis, vel acquisitus, et an curabilis, nec absque salutis periculo....

B) for the inspection of the woman:

> Corpus insuper mulieris, sed maxime illius geni-

[24] Lega, (ed. Bart.), *Iudicia Ecclesiastica,* II, p. 754, n. 10.

[25] Appendix, *Catholica Doctrina,* XXX—AAS, XV, (1923), 433. Cf. also XXXII.

[26] *Fontes,* n. 946.

> talia membra a duabus saltem obstetricibus in arte et praxi peritioribus ac bonis moribus imbutis inspiciantur, adhibito prius mulieris balneo, si necessario praemittendum physici et ipsae iudicaverint. Accurate observabunt signa integritatem mulieris constituentia, nimirum conformationem partium, iuncturam, duritiem, rugositatem, et colorem; an hymen sit integrum, vel confractum in totum vel in parte, hoc in casu an et qua naturali causa, seu potius e congressu extranei corporis contigerit; an myrtiformes carunculae inveniantur, earumque magnitudinem, numerum, et conformationem, aliaque signa ab arte tradita integritatem aut corruptionem mulieris constituentia sedulo inspiciant....

In view of the fact that the men and women now employed for the examinations in cases of impotence and nonconsummation are so eminently qualified in their work, and in view of the less detailed wording of the present law when it treats of the matter of physical inspection,[27] it seems to the writer that the judge should ordinarily refrain from decreeing in such great detail the subject matter of the physical examination as he would have done under the Instruction of 1858. Rather, the judge should carefully explain the canonical concept of impotence and consummation,[28] leaving it to the prudence of the experts to ex-

[27] *Catholica Doctrina,* Rule 92, "...Periti autem expleant suum examen, ut distincte referre valeant de singulis signis quae mulieris integritatem inferre sinunt, vel potius eidem refragantur..."; Rule 95, "...periti medici monendi erunt, ut referant...indicia seu argumenta quae potentiam virilem adstruere aut excludere videantur." *Instructio "Provida,"* Art. 147, § 1, as an example of what is meant by "*omnia et singula capita*" has merely: "Whether the impotence is absolute or only relative, whether it is instrumental or functional, antecedent or subsequent to marriage, whether it is perpetual or curable without grave danger to life."

[28] For these notions, cf. pp. 203-204 of this dissertation. For more information, consult such approved authors as: Gasparri, *Tractatus Canonicus de Matrimonio* (2 vols., Typis Polyglottis Vaticanis, 1932), I, nn. 510-551; II, n. 1093 (hereafter cited *De Matrimonio*); Antonius Viscont, *Tractatus Canonicus de Matrimonio Rato et non Consummato* (Romae: Jus Pontificium, 1929), pp. 21-23, 25-38 (here-

amine properly and thoroughly all that must be inspected if the tribunal is to learn whether canonical impotence or non-consummation exists in this particular case. The judge must not, however, omit to inform the expert of all the pertinent facts in the case which might serve as a guide to him in his examination. Thus the proper subject matter of the examination as proposed by the parties should be considered,[29] and even the pertinent acts of the case could be sent to the expert, or examined by him at the tribunal.[30]

These things seem to be more than sufficient for the instruction of the expert. Nonetheless, should any important matter be not amply recorded in the finished reports of the experts, the judicial interrogation of the expert concerning his examination and report will usually bring forth the desired information.

Something similar may be said for cases of insanity. The example given by the *Instructio Provida* in article 147, § 1, regarding the meaning of the *omnia et singula capita* which the judge is to decree for the consideration of the expert is: whether in the case at hand the *amentia* (some form of mental disease or abnormality) is habitual or transitory, and whether it admits of lucid intervals. Moreover, the judge should instruct the psychiatrist that it is his duty to determine the nature and the degree of the mental disease in the case at hand, and that he define what was

after cited *De Matrimonio Rato, non Consummato*). Cf. also J. L. Hammill, "Intention *contra Bonum Prolis*: Its Nature and Proof," *The Jurist*, VIII (1948), 170-195; Rudolph Allers, "Some Medico-Pschological Remarks on Canons 1068, 1081, and 1087," *The Jurist*, IV (1944), 352-358. Of special value because of their wealth of references to Rotal decisions are two articles: 1) Ildefonso P. Lopez, "Nulidad por Impotencia," pp. 433-465; and 2) Ramon B. Serra, "De Matrimonii Inconsummatione et de Processu super Rato," pp. 469-488, in *Las Causas Matrimoniales*, Trabajos de la cuarta semana de Derecho Canonico celebrada en el Monasterio de Nª. Sª. de Montserrat (Salamanca, 1953). Edited under the auspices of the Instituto "San Raimundo de Peñafort." (Hereafter cited Lopez, *Las Causas Matrimoniales*, and Serra, *Las Causas Matrimoniales*).

29 Canon 1799, § 1; *Instructio "Provida,"* Art. 147, § 3.

30 *Instructio "Provida,"* Art. 147, § 2.

the mental state of the contracting party at the time of the external marriage contract.[31]

To obtain this information from the expert, the judge may instruct him to do one of two things, or both of them. He may instruct the psychiatrist 1) personally to examine the party who was allegedly insane at the time of the marriage contract, or 2) to examine the acts of the person which engender the suspicion of insanity.[32]

"The acts (of the person) which engender the suspicion of insanity" will be described in the judicial *acta* of the cause. Thus will be considered medical records of the persons suspected of insanity, as well as the testimony of his spouse and of other witnesses.

It seems to the writer that in every case the judge should first require of the psychiatrist a perusal of the relevant acts of the cause.[33] After that it would be wise for the judge to discuss with the psychiatrist the need of the personal examination. He should not make it a rule of thumb to demand a personal examination in every case.[34] In rare cases the expert may, from a mere study of the acts of the cause, provide a report which clearly manifests to the judge that defective consent was given at the time of the marriage contract. Having thus attained moral certitude in the matter,[35] the judge would with utter futility order a personal examination. Nay, more, it would be an unlawful waste of time, effort, and money.[36]

It must not be forgotten that in this case, as in any other, the parties have the right to submit matters for the con-

[31] S.R.R., *Decisiones*, XXXVIII, (1946), p. 573, n. 3; S.R.R. *Decisiones*, XXIII (1931), p. 464, n. 4.

[32] Can. 1982—Etiam in causis defectus consensus ob amentiam, requiratur suffragium peritorum, qui infirmum, si casus ferat, eiusve acta quae amentiae suspicionem ingerunt, examinent secundum artis praecepta. . . ."

[33] *Instructio "Provida,"* Art. 147, § 2.

[34] Note that in can. 1982 the psychiatrist is to examine the party "*si casus ferat.*"

[35] Can. 1869, § 1; *Instrutcio "Provida,"* Art. 197, § 1.

[36] Can. 1749; *Instructio "Provida,"* Arts. 95, §2; 234, 1°, 2°.

sideration of the experts during the performance of their examination. The judge, however, may reject their suggestions, after consulting the *defensor vinculi.*[37]

SECTION 3. METHOD OF THE EXAMINATION

A) Personal Examination

Since the experts are chosen for their personal qualifications, they cannot delegate someone else to perform the examination. They can, however, delegate someone to assist them in preparatory or subsidiary acts,[38] provided the examination itself is performed personally by the experts.[39] If for some reason they cannot personally perform the examination, they must inform the judge, so that other experts may be appointed.[40]

B) Individual Examination

In all marriage causes of nullity, when more than one expert is employed, each of them must ordinarily conduct his examination individually and separately from the other, not revealing to the other expert the results of his examination.[41] The presiding judge (*praeses*) may, however, for a particular reason (*ex peculiari ratione*) order that the examination take place collegiately,[42] except in regard to special causes, when the law demands a separate and individual examination. Such a separate and individual examination is demanded by law of each of the experts employed for the corporal inspection of women in causes of impotence or non-consummation.[43] No mention is made of the need for the separate examinations of the man. As early as 1840, however, it was demanded that in impotence

[37] Can. 1799, § 1; *Instructio "Provida,"* Art. 147, § 3.
[38] Roberti, *De Processibus,* II, pars I, p. 83, n. 359.
[39] Coronata, *De Processibus,* p. 269, n. 1326.
[40] Reasoning from can. 1803, § 2.
[41] *Instructio "Provida,"* Art. 148, § 1.
[42] *Instructio "Provida,"* Art. 148, § 2.
[43] Can. 1980, § 1; *Catholica Doctrina,* Rule 90 (c).

and non-consummation causes there be separate and independent examinations of the man.[44] Furthermore, in causes of non-consummation, the Sacred Congregation of the Sacraments calls for a separate inspection of the man by each of the experts.[45] In view of this, and in consequence also of the unqualified general rule that in marriage causes of nullity the examination by experts is to take place separately,[46] one may conclude that the old law still binds in its demand that each expert conduct a separate inspection of the man in the causes of impotence and non-consummation.[47]

A collegiate examination of the woman in a *ratum et non-consummatum* cause may be permitted by the judge, when, after the separate and individual examinations and reports, there exists a serious disagreement among the experts concerning their findings in the investigation or in their final conclusions.[48] The writer feels that, under the same condition of a previous unsatisfactory examination conducted separately, a collegiate examination could be permitted by the judge for the examination 1) of the man in non-consummation causes, and 2) of either the man or the woman in impotence causes.[49]

C) Professional Method or Technique

Whereas the judge is to determine the subject matter of the examination and explain its purpose,[50] he should not seek to instruct the expert as to the scientific method or technique of conducting his examination, unless the law itself specifies the method. It is evident that a truly qualified specialist will understand better than the judge what methods he must use to obtain the requested information,

[44] S.C.C., *instr. Cum moneat Glossa—Fontes*, n. 4069. Cf. this dissertation, *supra*, p. 43.

[45] Appendix, *Catholica Doctrina*, XXXII.

[46] *Instructio "Provida,"* Art. 148, § 1.

[47] Can. 20, from the *stylus Curiae Romanae*.

[48] *Catholica Doctrina*, Rule 93, § 2.

[49] By analogy with *Catholica Doctrina*, Rule 93, § 2.

[50] Can. 1799, § 1.

and to draw his conclusions therefrom. Hence the judge should not attempt to give detailed instructions concerning the scientific methods to be used in the examination, but should leave much to the prudent discretion of the expert.[51] Coronata says that, if the judge should determine the means which the experts are to use in the performance of their examinations, he would thereby place upon them a restriction which would destroy almost all efficacy of the *peritia.*[52]

D) Licit Means

While the law grants the expert a wide discretion, according to the suggestions of prudence and the principles of his art or profession, in the determination of the method of his examination, it warns him that he must employ only licit means in his inspection. Thus in causes of impotence and non-consummation the experts are to be warned to conduct their examinations according to morally correct means[53] and the norms of Christian modesty.[54] To assure the observance of these norms, it is further ruled that a

[51] Can. 1982: "...examinent secundum artis praecepta..."; *Instructio Provida,* Art. 150, 1°, by way of omission, for it rules merely "...monendi sunt ut honestis tantum mediis utantur ad impotentiam congnoscendam"; *Catholica Doctrina,* Rule 90 (d): "In exploratione honesta quidem methodus et cautelae adhibeantur, prout scientia ac prudentia opportune suggesserit..." Rule 95: "...ut artis praesidiis utantur licitis et honestis, et referant, iuxta medicinalis doctrinae placita...." *Regulae super Nullitate Sacrae Ordinationis,* n. 68: "...ut artis praesidiis utantur ad dignoscendum statum actoris, et referant, iuxta medcinalis doctrinae placita...." Cf. also Wernz-Vidal, *De Processibus,* p. 454, n. 496; Quintana Reynés *La Prueba,* p. 138; Goyeneche, *De Processibus,* I, pars 2, n. 53 (a), p. 73. Contra: Doheny, *Canonical Procedure,* I, 391; Evans, "*Ratum et non-Consummatum* Procedure: Regulations Concerning Corporal Examination," *The Jurist,* XVI (1956), p. 176, n. 8.

[52] Coronata, *De Processibus,* p. 273, n. 1329.

[53] *Instructio "Provida,"* Art. 150, 1°.

[54] Can. 1979, § 3; *Instructio "Provida,"* Art. 150, 2°; *Catholica Doctrina,* Rule 90, (a), (d).

qualified matron[55] must be present during the entire time of the warm water bath and the individual examinations of the woman party by the two experts.[56]

In regard to the physical examination of the man:

> In instructing the medical experts as to the absolute necessity of employing only licit, proper, and ethical methods in performing the physical examination of the husband in the particular case, the judge and the *Defensor Vinculi* are to be particularly mindful of the decision of the S. Congregation of the Holy Office of August 2, 1929. The Holy Office was asked:
>
> "Whether direct masturbation is permissible for the purpose of obtaining semen for the scientific detection and cure of the contagious disease known as *blenorragia* (blennorrhea)?" To which the reply was: "In the *negative.*"[57]

E) Prevention of Fraud

To guard against the possibility of fraud by the parties in marriage causes, the law has enacted several precautions. In order that the experts will examine the proper party, and not one who poses in his (or her) stead, they must, before beginning the examination, receive from the party a document of identification properly authenticated by the ecclesiastical curia.[58] When the women is to be examined, the judge shall order that she first be subjected to the traditional warm water bath for at least half an hour. If, however, the appointed experts consider that in a particular case the bath would serve no useful purpose whatever, or even prove harmful, the judge, in consideration of these circumstances, and upon consulting with the

[55] Cf. this dissertation, pp. 149-151, for her qualifications and duties.

[56] Can. 1979, § 3; *Instructio "Provida,"* Art. 150, 2°; *Catholica Doctrina,* Rule 90, (b).

[57] Doheny, *Canonical Procedure,* II, 468. For the reply of the Holy Office see *AAS,* XXI (1929), 490.

[58] S.C. de Sacra., *Normae* of 1929, n. 4, §§ 1, 2; n. 1, §§ 1, 2, 3, 4; *Instructio "Provida,"* Arts. 58; 97. Further treatment on pp. 148-149 of this dissertation.

defensor vinculi, shall define what he deems more expedient in that event.[59] In this regulation one sees further deference shown to the experts in their right to determine the method of the examination, though the final decision must come from the judge.

As a final precaution, the judge should carefully forewarn the experts that, since the parties are sometimes less than honest in these matters, the examination of the woman should be thorough enough to detect any possible fraud whereby an apparent bodily integrity is cleverly feigned through the aid of medical adroitness.[60] In this respect, Doheny remarks that "experience has taught the S. Congregation that cunning and artifice are sometimes employed to deceive. It is not the wont of the Holy See to warn about dangers that are merely hypothetical."[61] It has been suggested that plastic surgery might sometimes be used by an unscrupulous woman in an attempt to feign physical virginity.[62]

SECTION 4. METHOD OF THE REPORT

A) Written or Oral Report

In the decree accompanying their appointment, experts should be told the manner in which they are to make their report. This report must always be made in the vernacular.[63]

[59] *Catholica Doctrina,* Rule 92. Cf. pp. 151-152 of this dissertation.

[60] *Catholica Doctrina,* Rule 92.

[61] Doheny, *Canonical Procedure,* II, 454.

[62] "*Ratum et non-Consummatum* Procedure; Regulations Concerning Corporal Examination," Evans, *The Jurist,* XVI (1956), p. 177, n. 10. Because of this possibility, the expert, if he does not treat of the matter in his report, must be questioned as to whether there were any indications that plastic surgery, or any other deceptive means, had been employed by the woman. The experts should be asked to give reasons for their answer, regardless of whether it is affirmative or negative.—Appendix, *Catholica Doctrina,* Formula XXX, question n. 10.

[63] *Instructio "Provida,"* Art. 105, § 1. The earlier *Catholica Doctrina,* Rule 48, simply permitted a vernacular report.

Canon 1801, § 1, states that experts can proffer the report of their examination either in writing, or orally, in the presence of the judge. In this latter case, the notary must immediately write the report and have the expert sign it. Cases in which oral reports are permitted will be rare, however. The law itself demands written reports from the experts in all marriage causes conducted according to a formal judicial procedure,[64] as well as in the matrimonial causes of non-consummation conducted administratively.[65]

In the other type of cause which may be practical, namely, the cause in which the validity of sacred ordination or of the obligations contracted thereby is impugned, there is likewise the requirement of a written report.[66]

B) Separate or Joint Report

Each of the experts is to make his own report, totally distinct from the others, unless, when there is no contradictory law, the judge orders that there be one joint report signed by all. If this joint report is ordered by the judge, any and all differences of opinion among the experts are to be diligently noted.[67]

The law itself demands that there be a separate report from each expert in the causes of impotence and non-consummation.[68] By way of exception, however, the judge may permit a joint report in the causes of non-consummation when the first and separately conducted examinations and reports reveal a serious disagreement among the experts regarding the findings in their investigation or also

[64] *Instructio "Provida,"* Art. 148, § 1.

[65] *Catholica Doctrina*, Rule 93, § 1.

[66] *Regulae super Nullitate S. Ordinationis*, n. 68; Canon 1995, with 1980, §§ 2, 3, and can. 1981. This written report of the expert is the chief source to be used by the *defensor vinculi sacrae ordinationis* in drawing up the questionnaire for the oral interrogation of the expert by the judge.—Appendix, *Regulae super Nullitate S. Ordinationis*, Formula XXIV—*AAS*, XXIII (1931), 492.

[67] Can. 1802, *Instructio "Provida,"* Art. 148, §§ 1, 2.

[68] Can. 1980, § 2; *Catholica Doctrina*, Rule 90, e.

regarding their final conclusion. Before permitting this joint report incident to a joint examination, however, the judge should attempt to resolve the disagreement. This he may do either a) by submitting to each expert the report of the other, or b) by submitting to a *peritior* the reports of the two experts, in order that the source of the contradiction may be explained.[69]

When in a joint report there are differences of opinion either as to the facts or also as to the conclusions derived therefrom must each expert signify which opinion he holds? The present law does not answer this question, for it simply states that the differences must be diligently noted, and that all of the experts must sign.[70] When Lega considered this problem, he remarked that several civil codes forbid the experts, when submitting a collegiate report, to signify which opinion they hold. The reason for this prohibition derives from the fear that the judge could be too easily influenced by the expert of great authority, and accordingly not readily enough by the intrinsic worth of the opinions themselves. It could indeed happen that the expert of lesser fame has sounder arguments at the basis of his conclusions than the expert of greater fame. Lega stated that, although the civil codes had good reason for prohibiting the experts from identifying their opinions in a joint report, such a prohibition did not exist in canon law, unless in some case the judge, for particular reasons, forbade the experts to identify their opinions.[71]

It is true enough that in canon law there is no express prohibition that restrains the experts in a joint report from identifying their opinions. Neither is there any prescription commanding this identification. There is simply no treatment of the question. This being the case, one should not depart from the rule of the Rota, given only eight years prior to the promulgation of the Code, and cited by Cardi-

[69] *Catholica Doctrina,* Rule 93, § 2.

[70] Can. 1802.

[71] Cf. Lega (ed. Bart.), *Iudicia Ecclesiastica,* pp. 766, 767, n. 7.

nal Gasparri in the footnote to canon 1802.[72] This rule of the Rota, forbidding the experts to identify the opinion they held in a joint report, seems to the writer to be the preferable norm even today. The judge must have complete freedom to evaluate the opinions of the experts, being influenced more by the intrinsic value of the reports than by the fame of the experts who signed the report.[73]

Nonetheless, it cannot be said that the judge would be prohibited from asking that in a joint report each expert indicate which of the differing opinions he held, if he felt that there were reason to do so. In fact, there are authors who feel it preferable that each expert identify his opinion even in a joint report, in order that the judge may consider not only the opinion and the arguments of the experts, but also the learning and the probity of the author of the report.[74]

In any event the dispute is of little practical import. In all marriage causes (with which it is that the diocesan tribunal is today chiefly concerned) the court will learn the opinion held by each expert when he appears for his oral interrogatory.[75]

C) *Content of Report*

Whether their report be made orally or in writing, the experts must clearly indicate what means they have used in their examination; the order in which they proceeded during the examination; their findings in the examination (as regards status, quality, condition of the person or thing examined); their conclusions which they have drawn from the facts of the examination, with an explanation, based on their findings and the principles of their profession or

[72] Rota, *Regulae* of 1910, § 125, n. 1, 2°.

[73] Cf. Coronata, *De Processibus*, p. 277, n. 1331, 3°.

[74] Cf. Roberti, *De Processibus*, II, pars I, p. 87, n. 361; Wernz-Vidal, *De Processibus*, p. 457, n. 498, note 25.

[75] Cf. can. 1981; *Catholica Doctrina*, Rule 93, §§ 1, 2; *Instructio "Provida,"* Art. 152.

art, as to why they have been led to such conclusions.[76]

Thus the expert in the non-consummation cause would state whether he had performed the inspection visually and digitally; whether the bath was used; and, if not, why not; whether instruments were employed, and what instruments were they; the order in which he proceeded during his inspection. He would report what indications of virginity or defloration he found. He would then offer his conclusion. If he judged the woman still to be a virgin, he must declare the arguments upon which he based this conclusion, and whether this conclusion indicates non-consummation, and why.[77] If he concludes that she has lost her virginity, he must state whether this loss was likely the result of intercourse, or of some other cause, and then must report why he so judges.

Wanenmacher (1887-1949), writing of the report of experts in matrimonial causes, offered a useful description of the report, which he divided as follows:

> I. An introduction, containing 1) the full name of the expert; 2) degrees received in his branch of science; 3) offices that enhance his authority; 4) the name of the curia and judge requiring the report; 5) the full name of the person examined; 6) the proper reference to identification, by photograph or document or otherwise, of the person examined; 7) the points to be determined by the inspection; and 8) the date and place of the inspection;
>
> II. The body of the report, containing 1) answers to the questions proposed by the judge and the defender together with the discussion on the mode of inspection, and arguments that pertain; 2) observations on the matter, spontaneously made by the expert;
>
> III. Conclusion drawn as to 1) the certain, probable, doubtful existence of impotence, and its nature, absolute or relative, or 2) the fact of non-

[76] Cf. can 1801, § 3; *Catholica Doctrina,* Rules 90, (d); 93, § 1; *Instructio "Provida,"* Art. 148, § 1.

[77] Cf. Appendix, *Catholica Doctrina,* Formula XXIX, in oath of expert. Cf. also p. 210 of this dissertation.

consummation, or 3) the insanity of the party, etc.

IV. Signature of the expert, and date and place of report.[78]

Of the greatest importance in the report is the lucid explanation of the reasons which lead the expert to the conclusion which he holds, The judge, in evaluating the report of the expert, is to consider chiefly the arguments which the expert offers as the basis of his conclusion, rather than the fame of the expert.[79]

SECTION 5. TIME FOR EXAMINATION AND REPORT

A) Time Limit Set

In non-marriage causes the judge may, if he deems it necessary or useful, define the time within which the expert examination is to be performed and the report submitted.[80] In all marriage causes, however, the judge must define the time limit for the completion of the examination and the submission of the report.[81]

These rulings show once more the consideration given to the expert. In non-marriage causes the judge does not necessarily have to set a time limit for the performance of the *peritia*. Obviously this allows the judge to show his utmost dependence upon the services of the expert, acknowledging that a reputable expert will perform his duties within a reasonable time, without being bound by the court to do so. It is likewise an admission that the court appreciates the service of the expert in his acceptance of what is not a compulsory office.

Even in the causes wherein a time limit is set by the judge, it is quite reasonable to suppose that this limit is not set until after consultation with the expert, as well as

[78] Wanenmacher, *Canonical Evidence*, n. 313. For similar descriptions of the report, confer Wernz-Vidal, *De Processibus*, p. 457, n. 498; Quintana Reynés, *La Prueba*, pp. 139-140.

[79] Cf. canons 1801, § 3; 1804, § 2.

[80] Can. 1799, § 2.

[81] *Instructio "Provida,"* Art. 147, § 4; can. 1980, § 2; *Catholica Doctrina*, Rule 90, e.

with the parties, in order to determine the time most convenient for them. This is a requirement not of law, but of prudence.[82] Thus Bottoms writes:

> The judge should bear in mind the attendant circumstances and the nature of the expert's profession. It could not be reasonably expected, for instance, that a busy psychiatrist would cancel his appointments on short order for the convenience of the court ... if a time is set, it should be conveyed to the expert in such a way so as to show him that the court has no reason to doubt that he will expeditiously fulfill the appointment.[83]

Cardinal Lega noted that once the time limit for the completion of *peritia* is established, both the experts and the parties must be informed. Upon receipt of this information, the experts are obliged to perform their work within the period specified, and the parties have a right to demand that the time limit be observed.[84]

B) Extension of Time

The judge may, however, upon consulting the parties, grant an extension of time for the completion of the *peritia,* provided there be a reasonable cause for the prorogation.[85] The expert will ordinarily be the one to seek a prorogation of time, although it may be sought at the instance of the parties, or even ruled *ex officio* by the judge. In any event, the parties must be heard, for they have a right to know why the *peritia* has not been completed, and to object if they think the projected extension of time would unreasonably delay the process.[86]

Only the judge, however, may decide on the reasonableness of the petitioned extension of time. Reasonable considerations for the prorogation of the *peritia* would be such

[82] Cf. Coronata, *De Processibus,* n. 1329; Noval, *De Iudiciis,* II, n. 522, at can. 1799, § 2; Lega (ed. Bart.), *Iudicia Ecclesiastica,* II, p. 757, n. 15.

[83] *Discretionary Authority of the Judge,* pp. 131-132.

[84] Lega (ed. Bart.), *Iudicia Eclesiastica,* II, p. 757, n. 15.

[85] Can. 1799, § 2; *Instructio "Provida,"* Art. 147, § 4.

[86] Arguing from can. 1749.

things as the sickness of the expert, or unforeseen obstacles of a business nature for either the expert or the party to be examined.

Would an extension of time be granted by the judge without hearing the parties be null? It seems that it would not, for the primary purpose of the consultation with the parties is the instruction of the judge on the reasonableness of the petitioned time extension, in view of the conditions of the interested parties. If the judge omits employing this means which is chiefly for his own enlightenment, the omission seems not to affect the validity, but rather the integrity of his act. Hence, in extending the time for the completion of the *peritia* the judge cannot neglect to hear the parties except for a grave necessity.[87]

If the expert, without a legitimate excuse and without obtaining an extension of time, fails to perform his duties within the period designated, he is legally bound to pay the damages that may have resulted.[88] In view, however, of the dignity of the professional persons who are chosen as experts, the judge need not warn them of this. The court may presume that if it has chosen the expert according to the rather rigid requisites of law, there will be no need of invoking canon 1798, for the expert will not unjustifiably fail to execute his office within the allotted time.

The previous consultation with the expert regarding the period of time within which he reasonably foresees that he can execute the *peritia* will in the majority of cases obviate any need for a time extension, and, *a fortiori*, any need to inflict damages upon the expert for any unreasonable delay on his part.

Article III. The Oath of Office

Upon receipt of his formal appointment in the cause, the expert officially signifies his acceptance of the appoint-

[87] Lega (ed. Bart.), *Iudicia Ecclesiastica,* II, p. 757, n. 15. Cf. also can 105, 1°, which does not require for validity that the judge hear the parties.—According to an interpretation recorded in Regatillo, *Institutiones,* I, pp. 159-160, n. 210.

[88] Can. 1798.

ment by taking an oath faithfully to fulfill his office,[89] to be truthful in his report, and to answer any questions that may be asked him by the tribunal.[90] The additional oath to observe secrecy must be taken in marriage causes,[91] as well as in any trial when the nature of the cause or of the evidence is such that from any divulgement of the proceedings and proofs the good reputation of others might be endangered, or when discord, scandal, or other inconvenience might arise.[92]

Until he explicitly or implicitly signifies his acceptance, the expert is under no obligation to undertake the office of judicial expert. By his oath, however, he is considered to accept the office, and thus to bind himself by way of a quasi-contract to fulfill the duties of an expert.[93] Canon 1797, § 1,[94] by its use of the word *"censentur,"* seems not to indicate a mere presumption of acceptance by the expert of his judicial office; but rather a definite point in time after which the expert can be considered subject to the court, and liable for faulty performance of his office.

SECTION 1. NO *Semel pro Semper* OATH

The oath taken must contemplate the proper fulfillment of the office of an expert, not in the abstract, but in this particular cause. It must be made by the expert with full understanding of the duties he is about to undertake. It is for this reason that the judge, besides discussing the matter with him informally, should already have formally instructed the expert, by means of a decree accompanying his appointment, regarding his specific duties in the cause at hand. The expert should know his duties as demanded

[89] Can. 1797, § 1.

[90] Cf. can. 1794; cf. sample oath for experts in *ratum et non-consummatum* causes, p. 210, of this dissertation.

[91] *Instructio "Provida,"* Art. 146; *Catholica Doctrina*, Rule 95.

[92] Can. 1623, § 3.

[93] Can. 1797, § 1; Lega (ed. Bart.), *Iudicia Ecclesiatica*, II, p. 754, n. 10.

[94] "Periti demandatum munus suscipere censentur praestatione iurisiurandi de munere fideliter implendo."

by canon law and the instruction of the Holy See, and as required by the judge in this particular situation. The parties themselves may, as was previously seen, have suggested for the consideration some certain and specific points. Finally, when the judge has deemed it necessary or useful, he may send to the expert certain pertinent acts of the cause for his perusal, depending upon his professional integrity not to reveal the confidential information contained therein.[95]

It is only when these instructions have been received that the appointed expert knows precisely what is expected of him when he accepts the office of expert. It is only when he knows fully what is expected of him that he should take the oath of office. From these considerations it is apparent that an approved expert, often employed by the court for a particular type of cause, could not satisfy the law by simply taking one oath, *semel pro semper*, to perform faithfully the office of expert in all future tasks assigned to him.

In taking the oath, the expert binds himself to use his skill in harmony with the laws of truth and justice, neither affirming a falsehood nor concealing the truth.[96] He swears to use his professional talent to the best of his ability, according to the norms and principles of his art or science, in conducting his examination and in making his report.[97] It was in view of his praiseworthy personal and professional qualifications that he was appointed an expert. Moreover, if the judge in the formula of the oath has specified a time limit for the completion of the *peritia*, the expert must swear to finish his examination and report within the time allotted, unless there should arise some reasonable element for delay.[98]

[95] Can. 1799, § 1; *Instructio "Provida,"* Art. 147, § 2. Such delivery could also be made after the oath of secrecy.

[96] Can. 1794.

[97] Goyeneche, *De Processibus*, I, pars, 2, n. 53, p. 73; cf. also sample oath, p. 210 of this dissertation.

[98] Cf. canons 1622, § 3; 1797, §1, "*de munere fideliter implendo*"; 1799, § 2, with 1798.

SECTION 2. CITING THE PARTIES

The parties have a right to be present when the expert takes his oath, as has also the *defensor vinculi* (or *promotor iustitiae*, if he takes part in the trial).[99] The parties enjoy this right even if they are excluded from assisting at the inspection performed by the experts, or from hearing the report given by them.[100] They must, then, be cited, although they need not necessarily be present.[101]

It seems unlikely that the parties would often use their right to assist at the swearing-in of the expert. Ordinarily they would feel no advantage in assisting at the oath, since they will already have been given full opportunity to bring known exceptions against the expert, and to make suggestions as to the subject matter of the expert examination. Doheny, however, remarks that the presence of the parties at this ceremony "would help to confirm their confidence in the experts and at the same time should duly impress the experts with the serious and sacred nature of their duty."[102]

If a physical examination of the parties will be required, their presence at the oath of the expert would provide an opportunity for the expert's certain identification of the parties, as is at all events demanded by law.[103]

It is absolutely necessary that the oath be taken *coram iudice*, i.e., in the presence of the judge (or *Praeses*, in a collegiate tribunal), and the notary.[104]

SECTION 3. OMISSION OF THE OATH

While the Code does not expressly demand an oath from the experts, it certainly implies it. Thus according to canon 1797, § 1, the experts are thought to have accepted their office *when they have taken their oath "de munere fideliter*

[99] Can. 1797, § 2; *Instructio "Provida,"* Art. 146.

[100] Cf. Noval, *De Iudiciis*, n. 520, at can. 1797, § 2.

[101] Doheny, *Canonical Procedure*, I, 389, at Art. 146.

[102] *Canonical Procedure*, I, 389, at Art. 146.

[103] S.C. de Sacr., *Normae* of 1929, IV, § 2. Cf. also Torre, *Processus Matrimonialis*, p. 296, at Art. 146.

[104] Can. 1797; *Instructio "Provida,"* Art. 146.

implendo." In canon 1797, § 2, the parties are granted the right to assist not only *at the oath of the expert,* but also at the execution of the *peritia,* unless modesty, the nature of the cause, or the prohibition of the law or of the judge rules otherwise. Canon 1798 requires that experts, *after they have taken their oath,* are bound to pay damages if, without a just cause, they do not complete their duties within the time specified.

The general rule for witnesses is that they must take an oath before testifying.[105] The office of the expert is in many ways similar to that of a witness. In marriage causes all who testify—whether parties, witnesses, or experts—must take an oath before testifying.[106]

According to canon 1767, § 3, however, witnesses may be dispensed from taking the oath if the cause relates to purely private rights, and both parties consent to the remission of the oath. Cardinal Lega discussed whether this canon might by analogy be applied to experts, allowing either the judge or the parties to remit the oath in private causes.

> I think that the two causes are not equal, because the expert swears faithfully to fulfill his office, and this directly serves the judge, in order that he might know the conclusions, deduced by the aid of some science or art, concerning some acts of the cause; wherefore it does not pertain to the litigants to remit the oath, since it is not directly related to their benefit. The judge likewise cannot remit it, since the oath is ordained for a safer knowledge of the truth.[107]

The oath, then, must be taken, if the *peritia* is to attain its full juridical value. In the rules of the Rota, promulgated only eight years before the Code, the judge was allowed to omit administering the oath to the expert, especially if the considered judgment (*votum*) to be pronounced by

[105] Canon 1767, § 1.

[106] *Catholica Doctrina,* Rule 39. *Instructio "Provida,"* Art. 96, § 1.

[107] Lega (ed. Bart.), *Iudicia Ecclesiastica,* II, pp. 754-755, n. 11—translation by the writer.

the expert concerned juridico-theological questions, rather than questions of fact.[108] It could happen that the report of these *periti consultores*[109] would contain mention of new circumstances of fact. For this reason, even though he might earlier have dispensed the expert from taking an oath, the judge could, at his discretion, administer an oath to the expert when he presented his report to the court.[110] Such an option is no longer granted to the judge, for he must invariably require the oath from the expert.

SECTION 4. *Post Factum* OATH

Would an oath, taken only after the completion of the *peritia,* that the office has been faithfully fulfilled, satisfy the requirements of the law? Wernz-Vidal were not quite clear on whether a *post factum* oath would suffice, in the event that the appointed expert absolutely refused to take the prior oath to fulfill his office well. Thus, they wrote:

> Si a perito laico, ut non raro evenit, iurata peritia obtineri non potest *nequidem per iuramentum postea in orali periti examine emissum,* talis peritia plenam vim in foro ecclesiastico non sortitur: quare iudicis erit expendere quanti ea sit aestimanda attentis praesertim conditionibus personae.[111]

It is true that the law of the Code does not *explicitly* command that the oath of office be taken before the *peritia* is assumed for execution by the expert, but it certainly implies this.[112] The prior oath is explicitly required in formal marriage causes[113] and in the administrative causes of non-consummation.[114]

Therefore a mere *post factum* oath attesting the faith-

108 Rota, *Regulae* of 1910, § 129, 1°.
109 Rota, *Regulae* of 1910, § 123, 1°.
110 Rota, *Regulae* of 1910, § 129, 2°.
111 Wernz-Vidal, *De Processibus,* p. 454, n. 396; (italics supplied).
112 Cf. canons 1794, 1797, § 1, 1798.
113 *Instructio "Provida,"* Art. 146.
114 *Catholica Doctrina,* Rule 95.

ful completion of the *peritia* would not suffice. It is presumed that the expert will more religiously perform all of his duties in the cause if he has *previously* sworn to do so. Nonetheless, Lega stated that, if for some reason a qualified expert requests that concerning one particular point (*caput peritiae*) he be permitted to delay his oath until after the fulfillment of his office, the judge can, at his own discretion, allow it.[115]

It seems to the writer that the exception which Cardinal Lega envisioned should be permitted only when the expert involved is in all other respects more qualified than other available experts, and has a truly conscientious reason for wanting to defer his oath concerning a particular phase of his examination. Even then that particular part of the *peritia* could not be considered a judicially perfect act. It is much more apparent that, if no oath at all is taken until after the completion of the expert's examination, the *peritia* is not judicially perfect, and a serious exception could be lodged against its lack of judicial form. The *peritia* cannot be said to be absolutely devoid of value, however, for it may have a sound intrinsic worth, and may have been accomplished by experts in good faith (even, perhaps, through the oversight of the court).[116]

If even a *post factum* oath was omitted, then *a fortiori* the *peritia* lacks full juridical force. The value to be afforded to any one of the foregoing three classes of judicially imperfect *peritia* must be determined by the judge, in much the same way as he would evaluate the testimony of witnesses who can afford only adminicular proof.[117]

It is improbable that the court would often have to accept the services of an expert who is unwilling to swear faithfully to perform the work entrusted to him. The judge should, from his informal discussion with the expert prior to the making of a formal appointment, know whether or

[115] *Iudicia Ecclesiastica,* II, p. 755, n. 12.

[116] Cf. Lega (ed. Bart.), *Iudicia Ecclesiastica,* II, p. 755, n. 11.

[117] Can. 1758, with can. 1789.

not the man is willing to take the oath *de munere fideliter implendo.* If the expert is unwilling to take such an oath, the judge should thank him graciously, and set about to appoint some other more co-operative expert.

CHAPTER X

JUDICIAL EXAMINATION

The expert must make his examination and report in accordance with the instructions given him by the judge, and within the time specified.[1] Inasmuch as diocesan tribunals today busy themselves almost entirely with matrimonial causes,[2] it is the legislation that governs the examinations and reports to be made by the experts most frequently employed in martimonial causes which will be treated here.

The general norms, as already discussed, must be followed in the appointment of these experts, in the instructions given to them, in the reception of their oath of office, *et cetera.* Any additional legislation, distinctive of a) the handwriting experts, b) the experts who perform the corporal inspection in causes of impotence or non-consummation, or c) the psychiatric experts used in insanity causes, will also be treated here.

ARTICLE I. HANDWRITING EXPERTS

Because of the importance of public and private documents in all processes, and especially of private notes and letters written under circumstances not open to suspicion (*tempore non suspecto*) in matrimonial processes,[3] it is to be expected that not infrequently handwriting experts will be required if the authenticity of documents is to be duly established.

[1] Cf. pp. 109-126 of this dissertation.

[2] Bartoccetti, noting the diminishing number of non-matrimonial causes handled by ecclesiastical tribunals, points out that, of the decisions edited by the Sacred Roman Rota in the year 1939, fifty-seven of fifty-nine were matrimonial causes; in 1940, seventy-eight of eighty were martimonial; and in 1941, matrimonial causes constituted eighty-six out of a total of ninety.—Lega (ed. Bart.), *Iudicia Ecclesiastica,* III, 1*, 2*, and note 2, page 2*.

[3] *Catholica Doctrina,* Rule 77; *Instructio "Provida,"* Art. 163.

Consequently, Article 149 of the *Instructio "Provida"* states that, when the authenticity of someone's handwriting is to be investigated, the provisions of canon 1800 are to be observed. If, then, some doubt arises as to who is the author of some writing (even if it is simply a signature on a printed or typewritten document), the judge is, at the proposal of the parties, to submit to handwriting experts (*periti calligraphi*), besides the writing in question, other writings[4] with which he may compare it.[5]

The ordinary procedure is to be followed for the appointment of these handwriting experts. One should here note, however, that in order to be assured of the professional competence of the handwriting experts the court should endeavor to employ those (or only one, if the judge is satisfied with one)[6] who have previously been approved by the civil court.

When the parties agree regarding the writing with which the comparison is to be made, Wanenmacher warned of the danger of collusion and dissimulation, and urged the judge not to admit for such comparison any writings composed especially for the purpose of comparison, or written at a time and under circumstances that invite suspicion (*tempore suspecto*).[7]

If the parties disagree on which writings are to be used for the purpose of comparison, the judge shall select those which the party himself acknowledges to be his own, or those which the alleged author of the contested writing

[4] "... vel etiam *unum* tantum scriptum ..."—Lega (ed. Bart.), *Iudicia Eccelsiastica,* II, p. 760, n. 5.

[5] Canon 1800, § 1:—Si dubitetur quis scriptum aliquod exaraverit, iudex praeter scripturam quaestioni obnoxiam assignet peritis, proponentibus partibus, scripturas cum quibus illa comparari *et* conferri debeat.—italics supplied. The "*comparari* ET *conferri debeat*" of the Latin Code is changed to "*comparari* SEU *conferri debeat*" in the Oriental Code, *De Iudiciis,* of 1950, at canon 323, § 1. The changed structure reflects an identity of meaning for the two words, translatable in English with the single word "compare."

[6] Can 1793, § 3.

[7] *Canonical Evidence,* p. 191, n. 310.

drew up in his public capacity and which are kept in archives or in some other public records, or also those which contain his signature as attested by a notary or by some other public official in whose presence the signature was affixed.[8] When the party acknowledges certain writings to be his own, he must do so directly, i.e., in explicit words, because the court cannot be satisfied with a mere conjectural, indirect, or presumptive acknowledgment.[9] The acknowledgment must be, then, directly and judicially made. The basis of the *peritia* in this event is an uncontroverted writing which may be compared with a controverted one, in order that it may be determined whether one and the same hand produced both writings.[10] Obviously, the simple non-objection of the party when a writing allegedly his was exhibited in another trial (or even in the same trial, before there arose any question of the need of his acknowledging the writing) does not constitute an acknowledgment so strong that the judge must consider the writing incontrovertibly that of the silent party.

If, however, the writings designated by the parties and by the judge for the purpose of comparison do not, in the estimation of the experts, suffice for the investigation, then the judge, either at the instance of the parties or even *ex officio,* is to cite him (if he is still living) to whom the controverted writing is attributed, in order that he may, in the presence of the judge or his delegate, write in his own hand whatever the experts, the judge himself, or his delegate may dictate.[11]

Moved by the fear of deceit on the part of the parties, Wanenmacher remarked that, when the experts request that new writings be made in the judge's presence (*coram iudice*), the judge should not let the author know the purpose of the writing.[12] There seems to be no legal require-

[8] Can. 1800, § 2.

[9] Lega (ed. Bart.), *Iudicia Ecclesiastica,* II, p. 760, n. 5.

[10] From can. 1800, § 1.

[11] Can. 1800, § 3. The delegate here spoken of is a delegated judge.

[12] *Canonical Evidence,* p. 191, n. 310.

ment to withhold this purpose from the party concerned, and it strikes the writer as being a rather unfair method of dealing with the party. It is quite true that there is danger in using for a comparison in handwriting the lines written in court, at the dictation of the judge or expert, and with the party's knowledge of the reason for the writing. That danger is present on two counts: 1) that the party may deliberately seek to deceive the experts, and 2) that the writing with which the present lines are to be compared may have been made several years earlier, and the manner of writing was perhaps somewhat different from what it now is. It is not unusual that over the course of the years one's handwriting should change considerably.[13]

Nevertheless, the writer has great confidence in the knowledge, uprightness, and scientific methods now employed by handwritings experts in tribunals of the state. Such men, duly appointed as experts in tribunals of the Church, and given their freedom to conduct the comparison according to whatever licit, scientific means their talent dictates, could to a large degree discover whether the handwriting made *coram iudice* was done in a normal way, or with some abnormality that might indicate an intent to deceive.

If there were lacking the authenticated writings, or such as are acknowledged by the party as his own,[14] then other writings, entirely private, could serve for the comparison, if the experts requested it, and the judge allowed it. Since, however, the law attributes no particular value to such documents, the judge invariably would have to determine the worth to be accorded to such a comparison.[15]

When one is cited by the court to write something dictated by the judge or the experts, his refusal to write, if no legitimate cause for the refusal be proved, is considered as a confession of the authenticity of the controverted writ-

[13] Cf. Wern-Vidal, *De Processibus*, p. 456, n. 497.

[14] According to canon, 1800, § 2.

[15] Cf. Wernz-Vidal, *De Processibus*, p. 456, n. 497.

ing, to his own prejudice.[16] The judge is left no discretion to evaluate this refusal, as he is when considering the refusal of a party to answer a question proposed by the court,[17] but is bound by the present canon, 1800, § 4, to judge the refusal to write as tantamount to a confession that the disputed writing is that of the unco-operative party.

Handwriting experts in formal matrimonial causes must make written reports,[18] and must appear in court to identify and confirm their reports, and to answer any questions furnished by the *defensor vinculi* to the judge.[19] In other causes the handwriting experts may be permitted to make simply an oral report,[20] and do not necessarily have to appear in court even if they make written reports.[21]

Article II. Experts in Impotence and Non-Consummation Causes

In causes of impotence or non-consummation it is required that experts make a corporal inspection of one or both spouses, unless from circumstances such an examination is evidently useless.[22]

Section 1. Omission of Examination

The physical examination of the spouses, but especially of the woman, is to be omitted as useless:

1) If the records reveal that because of a lack of time, place, and opportunity, consummation of the marriage was impossible. In such an event, if only the claim of non-consummation is made, and not the claim of impotence, neither party is to be physically inspected.

[16] Can. 1800, § 4.
[17] Can. 1743, § 2.
[18] *Instructio "Provida,"* Art. 148, §1.
[19] *Instructio "Provida,"* Art. 152.
[20] Can. 1801, § 1.
[21] Can. 1801, § 2.
[22] Can. 1976.

This is the so-called *casus inconsummationis tempore coarctatae.*[23]

2) If it is already established that the woman has (through sexual intercourse) lost her bodily integrity, she is not to be physically examined.[24]

This rule clearly does not intend that the inspection of the woman is to be omitted because of the mere fact that the hymen is no longer physically intact. A gynecologist may sometimes be able to determine that the rupture was due not to sexual intercourse, but to some other factor, which factor may have been indicated in the testimony of the woman herself. Furthermore, the present law obviously intends to follow the previous and more precise ruling of an Instruction of the Holy Office, as mentioned in the opening paragraphs of the *Qua singulari* of 1942.[25]

That Instruction made it clear that the inspection of the woman was to be omitted when her loss of physical virginity was attributable to sexual intercourse, and not when it was attributable to other factors.

Of course, the knowledge of such previous sexual experience on the part of the woman would have to be known from the acts of the cause. It would generally appear from the judicial confession of the woman herself, giving this as the reason for her refusal to undergo a judicial exam-

[23] *Catholica Doctrina,* Rule 86, (a); *Qua singulari* of 1942, n. 1, (a); "Si coniuges operam dare rei matrimoniali non potuerunt quia coniuges ne per brevissimum tempus quidem soli fuerunt, vel saltem impossibile eis fuit carnaliter commisceri. Tunc dicitur adesse casus inconsummationis tempore coarctatae."—Viscont, *De Matrimonio Rato et non Consummato,* p. 47.

[24] *Catholica Doctrina,* Rule 64, § 1: "Argumentum ex corporis mulieris inspectione deductum, per se, semper requiritur, nisi ex adiunctis inutile evidenter appareat (Can. 1976; cf. *infra,* sub n. 85), vel aliunde haberi non possit, prouti si mulier sit vidua aut corrupta." *Catholica Doctrina,* Rule 86 (b): "Inspectio corporis uxoris omittitur, utpote inutilis ... si certo iam constet de mulieris defloratione." See also *Qua singulari* of 1942, n. 1, (b).

[25] S.C.S. Off., instr. (ad Ep. Rituum Orient.), a. 1883, Pars II, Tit. VI, Art. 5, at *Haec mulieris inspectio.*—*Fontes,* n. 1076; *supra,* p. 48.

ination by experts. It could also be known through the reliable testimony of witnesses in the cause, or even through the testimony of a reliable doctor who had examined the woman previously.[26]

The law presumes that, when a widow had cohabited with her former husband, the previous marriage was consummated.[27] This presumption of law, however, does not of itself give proof of defloration, as is required before the physical examination can be omitted as useless.[28] Hence the physical examination in conjunction with a claim of the non-consummation of the second marriage is not to be omitted simply in view of the fact that the woman is a widow, and therefore *presumptively* is no longer a virgin. If, however, to this presumption is added the testimony of the woman herself that her earlier marriage was *de facto* consummated, then her physical examination is to be omitted as not serving any useful purpose. If she claims that even her previous marriage was not consummated, or if she says nothing about its consummation or non-consummation, then a physical examination of her would be required, for the simple presumption of consummation does not establish an evident inutility of such an examination.

3) If, in view of the moral excellence of the parties and the witnesses, and in serious consideration of their dispositions and all other supporting evidence, the ordinary judges that the fullest (*plenissima*) proof of impotence or non-consummation is already had,

[26] *Catholica Doctrina,* Rule 88.

[27] Can. 1015, § 2.

[28] *Catholica Doctrina,* Rule 86, (b): "*Inspectio corporis uxoris omittitur, utpote inutilis ... si certo iam* CONSTET *de mulieris defloratione.*" Cf. also *Qua singulari* of 1942, n. 1, (b). The wording of *Catholica Doctrina,* Rule 64, § 1, which treats of the omission of the physical examination when it is useless, "*prouti si mulier sit vidua aut corrupta,*" refers to the widow simply as one who is *presumably* no longer a virgin. The later Rule 86 makes it clear that the defloration must be more than simply presumed, since it needs to stand acknowledged as a fact.

then the bodily inspection of both parties is to be omitted.[29]

It seems that this *"plenissima . . . probatio de impotentia vel de inconsummatione"* will rarely be had without the corroborating force of evidence obtained from a physical inspection of the parties. Thus Hickey wrote:

> I feel sure that few Ordinaries, unless the case be a really outstanding and exceptional one, will be inclined to assume the responsibility of dispensing from the physical examination of the woman on the score that the fact of non-consummation has indeed been fully proven on the basis of moral evidence. Moreover, in practice, it is usual to make the decision regarding the examination of the woman before all the other proofs have been compiled (usually during the judicial interrogatory of the woman party),[30] though of course there is no rule why it may not be deferred.[31]

4) If from the inspection of the man it is fully established that he is incapable of consummating the marriage, then too the inspection of the woman will be omitted.[32]

The most obvious cases would be those wherein the inspection reveals a lack of the male organs necessary for consummation.[33]

Except for the one case (number 3, above) wherein the ordinary must reach the decision regarding the futility of the corporal examination, the judge will decide whether there exists one of the reasons in consequence of which the

[29] *Qua Singulari* of 1942, n. 1, (c).

[30] Cf. question n. 25 in the sample interrogatory of the woman petitioner in a non-consummation cause.—Appendix, *Catholica Doctrina,* Formula XIX.

[31] Hickey, *The Jurist,* V (1945), 15; (parenthesis supplied by writer).

[32] *Qua singulari* of 1942, n. 1 (d).

[33] "Vir impotens est: a) si membro virili careat, vel tale sit, ut erigi non possit, vel in erectione tantum distendi nequeat, quantum requiritur ad vaginam mulieris perforandam."—S.R.R. *Decisiones,* IX (1917), p. 217, n. 2.

examination is considered useless. If he has a positive doubt whether one of the factors indicative of the futility of an examination is present, he must consult the *defensor vinculi* before deciding.[34]

SECTION 2. CORPORAL EXAMINATION OF THE WOMAN

Unless there exist one of the foregoing four reasons for the omission of the corporal inspection, the woman party is always to be examined.[35] Once it is determined that the inspection is necessary, the court must appoint two experts to perform the examination.

A) Preferred Experts

The determination as to the order of preference in the appointment of these experts is not an easy matter. It is simple enough to indicate the experts most preferred in the matter, and those least preferred, i.e., the minimum with which the court can be satisfied. It is difficult, however, because of apparently contradictory rulings of the Sacred Congregation of the Sacraments[36] and of the Holy Office,[37] to determine the hierarchy of preference if the most desirable experts cannot be obtained for the inspection. The writer, after considering the pertinent legislation, will submit what he considers to be the order of preference in the selection of experts for the examination of the woman in causes of impotence or non-consummation.

In the year 1918:

> Ad mulierem vero inspiciendam duae obstetrices, quae legitimum peritiae testimonium habeant, ex officio designentur; nisi maluerit mulier a duobus medicis ex officio pariter designandis inspici vel id Ordinarius necssarium habuerit.[38]

[34] *Catholica Doctrina,* Rule 85.

[35] Can. 1976; *Catholica Doctrina,* Rule 64, § 1: "Argumentum ex corporis mulieris inspectione deductum, *per se, semper* requiritur, nisi . . ." (Italics by the writer).

[36] *Instructio "Provida,"* Art. 150, 2°.

[37] *Qua singulari* of 1942, nn. 3, 4.

[38] Can. 1979, § 2.

In the year 1923:

> Ad mulierem vero inspiciendam duae obstetrices, quae legitimum peritiae testimonium habeant debitaque in arte sua experientia polleant, *ex officio* designentur. Integrum est tamen mulieri inspiciendae expetere ut loco obstetricum, a duobus medicis, pariter ex officio designandis, inspiciatur; quod et Ordinarius, si necessarium duxerit, decernere potest, audito vinculi defensore, praecipue ob aliquod dubium fraudis, scilicet quod praesidia artis adhibita sint ad reparandas partium laesiones (Can. 1979, §§ 1, 2).[39]

In the year 1936:

> In causis impotentiae... ad inspiciendam mulierem deputentur duae mulierers, si adsint, quae in arte medica laurea doctorali et experientia sint praeditae, vel, ex mulieris consensu aut ex decisione collegii, duo medici, sin minus duae obstetrices vere peritae....[40]

In the year 1942:

> Quoties ad necessariam probationem assequendam requiritur coniugum inspectio corporalis... ad mulierem vero inspiciendam designentur (ad mentem Can. 1979, § 2) duae mulieres quae laurea doctorali in arte medica, vel saltem legitimo peritiae in arte obstetricia testimonio praeditae sint.[41]
>
> Si vero praefatae mulieres ad inspectionem perficiendam haberi nequeant, tunc licitum erit Ordinario, de consensu mulieris inspiciendae, examen peragendum committere viris, qui tamen non tantum medica arte sint insignes, sed etiam religionis et honestatis laude commendati, moribus atque aetate graves, ab ipso Ordinario vel iudice moniti de christianae modestiae regulis sancte servandis; quique ad inspectionem ne deveniant nisi adstante honesta matrona ex officio designanda (Can. 1979, § 3).[42]

In the year 1950:

> Ad mulierem vero inspiciendam designentur

[39] *Catholica Doctrina*, Rule 89, § 1.

[40] *Instructio "Provida,"* Art. 150, 2°.

[41] *Qua singulari* of 1942, n. 2.

[42] *Qua singulari* of 1942, n. 3.

> duae mulieres quae laurea doctorali in arte medica, vel saltem legitimo peritiae in arte obstetricia testimonio praeditae sint. Si vero tales mulieres ad inspectionem perficiendam haberi nequeant, tunc licitum erit Hierarchae, de consensu mulieris inspiciendae, examen peragendum committere viris, qui non tantum medica arte sint insignes, sed etiam religionis et honestatis laude commendati, moribus atque aetate graves.[43]

As to the meaning of the word *obstetrices,* the translation *midwives* is literally accurate, but in its proper sense is rather unknown to the United States. In this regard, Doheny remarked:

> It is to be noted that these midwives must have legitimate certificates as proof of their competency and sufficient experience to assure the court of their ability . . . the law does not refer to untrained and unlicensed midwives, as are sometimes found in the United States and other countries. In Italy, France, and some other European countries, midwives are not infrequently graduates of special schools or universities, or otherwise well versed in their science. They are required to pass stringent examinations before they are licensed by the state. It is to such well-trained and thoroughly qualified persons that Rule 89 (of *Catholica Doctrina,* as well as the other canons and instructions mentioned) refers.[44]

In the regulations recorded above there is noticeable an increasing demand for greater skill in the examining experts. Even more evident, especially in the Decree of the Holy Office in 1942, is the concern of the Church that Christian modesty be observed. It is only to be expected that such vigilance in Christian modesty should come from the Holy Office, for to it is entrusted, under the leadership of its presiding head, the pope, the duty of safeguarding faith and morals.[45] As custodian of morality, it has in this Decree increased the number of reasons for which the cor-

[43] Oriental Code, *De Iudiciis,* can. 486, § 2.

[44] Doheny, *Canonical Procedure,* II, 448 (parentheses supplied by writer).

[45] Can. 247, § 1.

poral inspection of the parties may be omitted.[46] It demands that the woman's consent to be examined—even by women experts—must always be had.[47] It allows *only* the ordinary, with the woman's consent, to appoint men experts for the physical examination of the woman party.[48] In the judicial interrogation of the woman, it is not the judge, but a doctor appointed by the ordinary, who is to question the woman party concerning the delicate matters of her conjugal life.[49] As a final indication of its vigilance over modesty, the Holy Office instructs the judges to refrain from minute and prolix descriptions in drawing up their sentences; rather, they are simply to record the facts and the arguments in restrained terms (*"castigatis verbis"*).[50]

From a careful consideration of all the preceding, it seems that the order of preference in the appointing of experts for the corporal inspection of the woman party should be:

1) If available and agreeable to the woman party, female gynecologists and skilled general practitioners enjoy priority.
2) Of second choice, if they are available and agreeable to the party, are truly qualified and licensed midwives provided, however, that there be no special reason compelling the ordinary, with the woman's consent, to appoint eminently qualified male gynecologists or general practitioners.[51]

[46] *Qua singulari* of 1942, n. 1.
[47] *Qua singulari* of 1942, nn. 3, 4.
[48] *Ibidem*, n. 3.
[49] *Qua singulari*, n. 6.
[50] *Qua singulari*, n. 7.
[51] Can. 1979, § 2: "...nisi...id Ordinarius necessarium habuerit..."; *Catholica Doctrina*, Rule 89, § 1: "...quod et Ordinarius, si necessarium duxerit..."; *Qua singulari*, n. 2: "...ad mulierem vero inspiciendam designentur (*ad mentem* Can. 1979, § 2) duae mulieres quae laurea doctorali in arte medica, vel saltem legitimo peritiae in arte obstetricia testimonio praeditae sint."—Italics supplied by the writer.

The ordinary must not make it a standing rule to appoint male gynecologists in place of qualified female general practitioners or midwives.[52] Although there is a requisite that the women experts be well qualified, at least to the extent of being licensed as midwives, there is no requisite that the judge invariably use the very best available expert, male or female. Indeed, the Decree of 1942,[53] confirmed, it seems, by the Oriental Code of 1950,[54] makes it quite clear that, in order to safeguard Christian modesty, the general norm is: women are to be examined by women experts (be they gynecologists, general practitioners, or qualified midwives), and men are to be examined by men experts.

Only for a special reason, then, should the ordinary depart from this general rule. Such a reason would be:

a) Physical necessity, viz., the unavailability of women doctors or midwives,[55] and
b) moral necessity, viz., when in a particular cause, in order to detect a suspected simulation of physical integrity, the ordinary feels compelled to appoint mature and enlightened male experts, outstanding for their moral and professional qualifications, rather than to appoint the less qualified women experts available.[56]

The consent of the woman, however, must always be had.[57] If she refuses to be examined by men doctors, their employment must not be urged. If she refuses altogether to be

[52] Cf. *Qua singulari*, n. 3, where the expression "*praefatae mulieres*" refers to the unavailability of the female physicians, as well as of the midwives mentioned in n. 2.

[53] *Qua singulari*, n. 2.

[54] *De Iudiciis*, can. 486, §§ 1, 2.

[55] *Instruction "Provida,"* Art. 150, 2°; *Qua singulari*, n. 3.

[56] Can. 1979, § 2; *Catholica Doctrina*, Rule 89, § 1; *Qua singulari*, n. 3, *ad mentem* Can. 1979, § 2.

[57] *Qua singulari*, n. 3. This demand obtains despite the apparently contradictory *Instructio "Provida"* of 1936, at Art. 150, 2°: "ad inspiciendam mulierem deputentur duae mulieres, si adsint... vel, ex mulieris consensu *aut ex decisione collegii*, duo medici, sin minus duae obstetrices vere peritae...."—Italics by the writer.

inspected, even by women experts, no inspection is to be urged. Rather, it will suffice to warn her of the juridical consequences of her refusal, or of the increased difficulty, or even of the probable impossibility of obtaining proof of her allegation of impotence or non-consummation.[58]

3) If, however, the woman requests male gynecologists or general practitioners for the examination, the ordinary may appoint them, even if female gynecologists are available.[59]

4) If, however, on account of particular local circumstances, it would sometimes be impossible or very difficult to find two skilled midwives or physicians (male or female), it could be tolerated that the inspection be performed by one expert male physician and one midwife. If, because of the same circumstances, not even this could be done, it could be tolerated that the inspection be conducted by two morally acceptable matrons (or married women) of mature age who also otherwise are suited for the task.[60]

This ruling, while it is explicitly for use in non-consummation causes, is applicable, by analogy, in causes of impotence when the wife is to be examined. As regards the toleration that one male physician and one midwife conduct the examination, the Rule itself contains a reference to an Instruction of the Holy Office as its source. This Instruction[61] dealt with impotence causes exclusively.

The generous concessions granted in this rule are given in view of conditions that exist in missionary countries, or in sparsely settled and mountainous districts. The Sacred Congregation does not permit use of this rule unless the circumstances therein described are truly verified.

[58] *Catholica Doctrina,* Rule 64, § 2; *Qua singulari,* nn. 3, 4.

[59] Can. 1979, § 2; *Catholica Doctrina,* Rule 89, § 1; *Instructio "Provida,"* Art. 159, 2°; *Qua singulari,* nn. 2, 3 (*ad mentem* Can. 1979, § 2).

[60] *Catholica Doctrina,* Rule 89, § 2.

[61] S.C.S. Off., instr. (ad Ep. Rituum Orient.), a. 1883, tit. VI, art. 5, n. 49.—*Fontes,* n. 1076. Cf. this dissertation, pp. 47-49.

As regards the last concession, that the inspection may be made *"a duabus matronis seu mulieribus nuptis,"* Doheny stated the following:

> This final concession is granted for districts where truly primitive conditions obtain. The judge would be obliged to inform the S. Congregation why it was impossible to secure the services of physicians and midwives.[62]

Fortunately, in the United States today, there would seldom, if ever, be a need to invoke the concession of Rule 89. It is not likely that in any place there will be great difficulty in obtaining qualified female gynecologists or general practitioners. If there should be difficulty in obtaining women doctors, the writer knows of no place where male physicians could not be had.

B) The Examination Proper

1° Place of Examination

The judge must designate the place for the inspection.[63] In doing this, however, he should consult the woman party, and especially the experts, in order to designate a place suitable and convenient for the examination. Generally, he will designate a hospital or a clinic for the inspection.

2° Identification of the Party

At the designated place, and before beginning the physical inspection, the experts must be assured, by means of a court-authenticated document of identification, that they are about to examine the proper party, and not someone who poses in her stead.[64] If it does not contain all the marks of personal identification, this document (the original from the judicial acts, or a copy of it) must nevertheless unequivocally distinguish one person from another, as is done, e.g., by means of a good, recent photograph.[65] If the

[62] Doheny, *Canonical Procedure,* II, 449.

[63] *Catholica Doctrina,* Rule 92.

[64] S.C. de Sacr., *Normae* of 1929, n. 4, § 1.

[65] S.C. de Sacr., *Normae* of 1929, nn. 1, § 2; 4, § 1.

tribunal accepts a recent driver's license, with an accurate and complete description of the person, then the experts must be satisfied with such identification. Regardless of what the court accepts as satisfactory identification, there must be some seal or notation on the document establishing that it has been properly entered in the acts. Such identification would ordinarily be sent by the court to the experts along with the instructions regarding the subject matter of the examination. It may be personally handed to the experts by the party herself, or it may be presented to the experts when they appear in court to take the oath of office.

If, however, the woman party is known personally by the examining experts (as, for example, if they were introduced to the woman when they took the oath), there is no need to present a document of identification. This circumstance must, however, be noted in the judicial acts.[66]

3° The Matron

An upright matron (*honesta matrona*) must be appointed by the court as the guardian of Christian modesty throughout the entire inspection of the woman party. She is to be appointed regardless of whether male or female experts conduct the physical examination.[67]

The woman appointed as matron should be of mature age, esteemed for her religious character and probity of life. She must not be easily liable to dishonesty or deception. She must fully understand her rather simple, but serious duties, and be able to report to the tribunal the rightful discharge of her duties. By her oath of office[68] she must swear to observe the norms of law and the instructions of the judge, especially in taking care that during the examination no fraud is committed and that the rules of Christian

[66] S.C. de Sacr., *Normae* of 1929, n. 4, § 2.

[67] Can. 1979, § 3; *Catholica Doctrina,* Rule 90 (b). This matron is not simply one of the two matrons or married women who, as a last resort, are employed by the court to inspect the woman when no other more qualified experts are available.—Cf. *Catholica Doctrina,* Rule 89, § 2.

[68] *Catholica Doctrina,* Rule 91.

modesty are perfectly observed. She further swears that she will be truthful in replying to the oral interrogatory of the court (held after the inspection), and will likewise observe secrecy.[69]

Doheny notes that, if the matron is esteemed for her religious character and probity of life, she may be presumed to be unsusceptible to subornation or bribery. "However," he adds, "she should not be of an ingenuous type, lest she be imposed upon and deceived."[70]

It is advisable, whenever possible, to secure as matron someone who possesses not only fine moral qualifications, but also high professional ability, e.g., a mature, experienced registered nurse. Even though she might be eminently well qualified for the task, it would be unbecoming (and, one would think, rather embarrassing to the woman party) to allow a woman religious (sister) to serve in the capacity of matron.[71]

If she is otherwise qualified, the assisting nurse employed by the gynecologist would be a convenient choice as matron.

The matron is not a judicial expert, but is an instrument of the court acting in the capacity of a special sort of witness. Hence she is not required to make a written report upon the completion of her duties, but is merely required to answer truthfully to the oral interrogatory of the tribunal. No mention of a written report is made in the Rules of *Catholica Doctrina.*

That the matron need present no written report is more obvious when one considers the oath which she must take[72] and the interrogatory to which she must reply in court.[73]

[69] *Catholica Doctrina,* Rule 94; Appendix, *Catholica Doctrina,* Formulae XXIX, XXXI. Cf. p. 211 of this dissertation.

[70] *Canonical Procedure,* II, 451, at Rule 91.

[71] Cf. Doheny, *Canonical Procedure,* II, 450, at Rule 90 (b), citing S.C.C., *Parisien., Matrimonii,* 3 augusti, 1889.—*Thesaurus,* CXLVIII (1889), 659.

[72] Appendix, *Catholica Doctrina,* Formula XXIX. Cf. p. 211 of this dissertation.

[73] Appendix, *Catholica Doctrina,* Formula XXXI. Cf. pp. 180-181 of this dissertation.

In her oath of office nothing whatever is said of a written report; nor in her oral interrogatory is there any request that she confirm a written report. On the other hand, the experts in taking their oath of office swear to be truthful in drawing up their *written* report;[74] and when they appear before the court for their oral interrogation, they must confirm under oath the report previously written by them.[75]

There seems, then, to be no justification for demanding a written report from the matron.[76]

4° The *Balneum*

When she has been properly identified, the woman is, before being examined in non-consummation causes, to be subjected to the *balneum*. This warm water bath was originally introduced not so much as a hygienic measure, but rather in order to dissolve any foreign substance which might have been inserted into the vagina with the intent of simulating physical integrity.[77]

According to the ruling which obtains today, the bath is to be taken by the woman in lukewarm water for at least half an hour,[78] in the presence of the court-appointed matron. Since she is appointed by the court as the guardian of modesty for the entire time of the corporal inspection, she must

[74] Appendix, *Catholica Doctrina*, Formula XXIX, p. 210, of this dissertation.

[75] Cf. n. 3 of the sample questionnaire for the examining experts, Appendix, *Catholica Doctrina*, Formula XXX. Cf. p. 178 of this dissertation.

[76] *Contra* Evans, *The Jurist*, XVI (1956), p. 178, n. 11. In his English form of the oath to be taken by the matron, Doheny in one volume demands a written report (*Canonical Procedure*, II, 452). In another volume, however, his English form of the oath does not require such a written report. Cf. Doheny, *Practical Manual for Marriage Cases* (2. ed., The Bruce Publ. Co.: New York, Milwaukee, Chicago, 1947), p. 183.

[77] Sanchez, Lib. 7, disp. 113, n. 11. Cf. p. 30-31 in the historical section of this dissertation.

[78] *Catholica Doctrina*, Rule 92.

also be present throughout the duration of the *balneum.*[79]

If the appointed experts, men or women, think that in the cause at hand the *balneum* would be altogether useless, or even harmful, the judge can permit its omission. He must, however, first consult the *defensor vinculi,* and consider the particular circumstances in the cause.[80]

It is probably true that in the majority of cases today truly skilled experts will judge the *balneum* to be superfluous, since they can readily detect fraud by means of a thorough visual and digital inspection. Generally, then, they will request the omission of the *balneum.* And the judge should ordinarily accede to this request.

Nonetheless, the proper procedure should be followed in each recurring case, namely: a) the judge should mention the judicial requisite of the *balneum,* and ask the experts whether they think it harmful or useless; b) if the experts inform him that they consider it useless, the judge should consider the attendant circumstances and consult the *defensor vinculi,* and c) if his decision is favorable, the judge should decree the omission of the *balneum.*

In the rare instance that the judge deems the experts not sufficiently skilled to detect a simulated integrity without the aid of the *balneum,* he must not accede to the request of the experts for its omission. Better, when he is forced to employ these less skilled experts, he should not mention to them the possibility of omission of the *balneum.*

5° Method of Examination

Immediately after the *balneum* (if it is used) the experts should, one at a time, conduct their examination of the woman party.[81] They should perform the examination according to the instructions received from the judge. These instructions must contain an explanation of the canonical concept of impotence or of non-consummation, suited to the extant demand, in language understandable to the doc-

[79] Cf. *Catholica Doctrina,* Rule 90, (b).

[80] *Catholica Doctrina,* Rule 92.

[81] Can. 1980, § 1; *Catholica Doctrina,* Rule 90, (c).

tors.[82] The instruction should indicate the subject matter of the examination,[83] and an admonition that only proper and licit means may be employed in pursuing the examination.[84]

Generally, however, the instruction should not attempt to give a detailed explanation of the scientific techniques to be utilized.[85] Rather, the judge should depend upon the ability and ingenuity of the experts to apply their professional knowledge and skill in a manner most suited to discovering any and all of the physical indications of impotence or non-consummation, or of the absence of such signs.[86] Thus Torre,[87] noting the progress of medical science, especially in more recent times, urges that the experts be left free to determine the most adequate scientific technique available for discovering the truth. He mentions that on at least one occasion a radiological examination was successfully utilized by the experts for their discovery of evidence.

"It should be remembered that the aid of the expert (in non-consummation causes) is enlisted not so much to ascertain whether the woman examined possesses all the usual signs of virginity (the material object of the examination), but rather to discover whether *in the particular case under discussion* the alleged fact of non-consummation is con-

82 The reader may look to pp. 203-204 of this dissertation for such an explanation of non-consummation, as it appeared in *The Linacre Quarterly*, the Official Journal of the Federation of Catholic Physicians' Guilds in the United States of America. Cf. Paul V. Harrington, J.C.L., and Joseph B. Doyle, M.D., "Indications and Proofs of Non-Consummation," *The Linacre Quarterly*, XIX (1952), 61-76. Cf. especially p. 65 (hereafter cited Harrington-Doyle, *The Linacre Quarterly*).

83 Cf. pp. 110-115 of this dissertation.

84 *Catholica Doctrina*, Rule 90 (d). Cf. pp. 117-118 of this dissertation.

85 Cf. pp. 116-117 of this dissertation.

86 *Catholica Doctrina*, Rule 92.

87 *Processibus Matrimonialis*, p. 300, at Art. 150.

firmed by the examination (the formal object of the examination)."[88]

While as a general rule the judge should refrain from a very minute instruction as to the matter of the corporal inspection,[89] yet there could arise some occasion for such detailed instruction. Thus, if in some locality the judge can obtain the services of only meagerly qualified experts, he may feel compelled to outline very thoroughly the matter of the examination. In this manner he could more probably elude the irksome necessity of requesting a repetition of the corporal examination, in the event that these less skilled experts produced only an incomplete and unsatisfactory report.

Again, the experts themselves, even eminently qualified persons, could possibly request a more precise instruction. This might be expected, for example, of conscientious Catholic doctors the first time they are engaged by the tribunal for such service.

For whatever laudable reason, if the judge desires to furnish the experts with complete directions regarding the matter (or even the procedure) of the examination, he might find useful for that purpose an appended pattern for such instruction.[90]

SECTION 3. CORPORAL EXAMINATION OF THE MAN

A) Omission of Examination

Before treating of the causes wherein there is required a physical examination of the man, one may well point out the two instances when such an examination can be omitted as useless: 1) In cases wherein non-consummation is the manifest result of a restrictive time limit (*in consummationis tempore coarctatae*), i.e., when it is contestable that there was no opportunity for the consummating of the

[88] Hickey, *The Jurist,* V (1945), 16. Italics and parentheses by the writer.

[89] Cf. pp. 116-117 of this dissertation.

[90] Cf. pp. 205-209 of this dissertation.

marriage,[91] and 2) in other cases when, in proper heed to the moral excellence of the parties and the witnesses, and in sober consideration of their dispositions and of all the other corrobative evidence, the ordinary judges that there already exists the fullest possible (*plenissima*) proof of impotence or of non-consummation.[92]

B) Necessity of Examination

It is obvious that, with the exceptions noted above, the man must be examined in nullity causes when it is alleged that he is relatively or absolutely impotent.[93] Even in certain causes of non-consummation the man must be physically examined, since this examination very often contributes greatly toward safely establishing the fact of non-consummation. Thus the physical examination must not be omitted when the non-consummation is attributed to his relative or absolute impotence, and when on the other hand there is no full proof of his wife's physical integrity.[94]

If the examination of the woman does not reveal a completely integral hymen, and if proof of non-consummation is not otherwise had,[95] then the allegedly impotent husband must be examined.[96]

In a non-consummation cause, however, would an allegedly impotent husband still have to be examined, even if his

[91] *Catholica Doctrina*, Rule 86, (a); *Qua singulari* of 1942, 1, (a).

[92] *Qua singulari* of 1942, 1, (c).

[93] Can. 1976.

[94] "Viri corporalis inspectio quae, ut plurimum, valde confert ad tute adstruendum factum inconsummationis, non est praetermittenda cum inconsummatio tribuatur eius impotentiae absolutae vel relativae, et aliunde de uxoris physica integritate plena non habeatur probatio."—*Catholica Doctrina*, Rule 84, § 2.

[95] E.g., in the judgment of the ordinary, from the moral excellence of the parties and the witnesses.—*Qua singulari* of 1942, 1, (c).

[96] "Ad eruendam veritatem in certis casibus insuper multum confert *inspectio viri*... Item condicio aliciuius hymenis non amplius intacti aliquando ea est ut matrimonii inconsummatio, non obstante hymenis laceratione, ex cognito perimetro membri mariti certo statui possit."—S.R.R. *Decisiones*, XXV (1933), p. 88, n. 2.

wife's physical integrity had already been established by means of her physical inspection? Rule 84, § 2, worded negatively as it is, does not treat of this situation. Consequently, unless the ordinary should intervene by declaring that a *plenissima probatio* was had from all the evidence thus far gathered,[97] it would be left to the judge, upon consultation with the defender of the bond (*audito defensore vinculi*), to determine whether the examination of the allegedly impotent husband was to be required as necessary, or to be omitted as useless.[98] It seems that in the case under discussion (physical integrity of the wife; alleged impotence of the husband) the judge would ordinarily demand the physical examination of the allegedly impotent husband, and this for two reasons:

1) While it is true that a completely integral hymen, revealing not the slightest evidence of laceration or rupture, commonly constitutes an efficacious argument for non-consummation,[99] it does not always do so. It is possible, in an admittedly rare case, that a very elastic hymen would allow a partial penetration and an accompanying semination, without sustaining any discernible rupture or laceration of the hymeneal membrane, and without a stretching of the hymeneal ring to the point where there is definite evidence of a real relaxation.[100]

[97] *Qua singulari* of 1942, 1, (c).

[98] Cf. can. 1976; *Catholica Doctrina*, Rule 85.

[99] "Porro, prouti penetratio penis in vaginam est elementum substantiale copulae, et incapacitas penetrandi est impotentiae argumentum; ita integritas hymenis, qui per penetrationem laceratur, est *commune et efficax argumentum* matrimonii inconsummationis." —S.R.R. *Decisiones*, XXXIII (1941), 3, n. 6. (Italics by the writer.)

[100] "Nihilominus hymenis condicio non semper praebet certum argumentum; id est nequit in unoquoque casu ex hymenis laceratione certo deduci consummatio, et ex eius integritate inconsummatio matrimonii. Nam . . . sunt mulieres, quarum hymen adeo elasticus est, ut introductione penis non laceretur . . . Siquidem membrum virile, quando extraordinarie parvum est, vaginae penetrationem cum seminatione intra ipsam absque laceratione hymenis perficere valet, praesertim si hymen satis mollis et perforatus est."—S.R.R. *Decisiones*,

2) Furthermore, since the husband is allegedly the cause of the non-consummation by reason of his impotence, the Holy See would not likely be content to give a dispensation *super rato* without some advertence to the claimed impotence. It may be that *de facto* the man is absolutely and incurably impotent, and hence must be forbidden to remarry. If there should be serious doubt regarding his absolute impotence, the Holy See would, as is its custom, append a clause prohibiting his remarriage *"inconsulta Sancta Sede."*

C) Refusal of Examination

It is not infrequent that allegedly impotent men refuse to submit to a judicially ordered physical examination. At times they will even swear that they are not impotent.[101] Since the inspection of the man often affords very valuable evidence, the court should endeavor in whatever way possible to persuade the man to submit to the examination. Thus, if the man at first refuses, the judge should again make the request,[102] or employ other and more efficacious means to urge the inspection. He might ask a friend of the man, or a person in authority, to serve as an intermediary in order to convince the man to be examined.[103]

If desipte all persuasion the man absolutely refuses to be examined, the probable reasons for his refusal must be recorded in the acts, and supplementary proofs are to be obtained, if available.[104] The probable reasons for this refusal will be drawn from the other evidence in the case, e.g., the testimony of the man himself, of his wife, of others as witnesses, and from medical records.[105]

XXV (1933), p. 88, n. 2. Cf also Harrington-Doyle, "Indications and Proofs of Non-Consummation," *The Linacre Quarterly,* XIX (1952), 72. Cf. also pp. 207-208 of this dissertation.

101 S.R.R., *Decisiones,* XX (1928), p. 326, n. 4.

102 Analogy with can. 1843, § 2.

103 *Catholica Doctrina,* Rule 38, § 3; *Instructio "Provida,"* Art. 115.

104 *Catholica Doctrina,* Rule 84, § 3.

105 "Pertinax recusatio ista, si confertur cum ratione confessa, gravem aliam constituit praesumptionem pro existentia impotentiae

D) *Examination Proper*

When the man agrees to be examined, his identity must first be ascertained by the experts in accord with the instructions of the tribunal.[106] The experts appointed for the examination should preferably be urologists or pyschiatrists, according as the alleged impotence is organic or functional.[107] The examination must be conducted by each expert separately.[108] Following the instructions given them by the judge, the experts are to employ only licit means in their examination, but are left freedom to utilize whatever scientific techniques they deem opportune.

Doctors should be informed that impotence, canonically considered, is any natural, or accidental defect in the man or the woman which makes them incapable of carnal intercourse (*copula*).[109] This is termed *impotentia coeundi,* and is not to be confused with *impotentia generandi.*[110]

With this information, the expert will be able to give a detailed report of any and all indications which seem to establish or disprove virile potency,[111] and it is not likely that the judge must be specific in telling the doctors what to examine.[112]

viri; saepius enim homines, qui tali vitio etiam absque culpa afficiuntur, ad dedecus vitandus, humano respectu moti, non dubitant veritatem ac iustitiam offendere."—S.R.R. *Decisiones*, XX (1928), p. 326, n. 4.

[106] Cf. pp. 148-149 of this dissertation.

[107] Serra, *Las Causas Matrimoniales*, p. 487.

[108] Cf. pp. 115-116 of this dissertation.

[109] The proper canonical meaning of *copula* is succinctly indicated in a response of the Holy Office, given Feb. 12, 1941. The question was put: "Utrum ad copulam perfectam et ad matrimonii consummationem requiratur et sufficiat ut vir aliquo saltem modo, etsi imperfecte vaginam penetret, atque immediate in ea seminationem saltem partialem naturali mode peragat, an tanta vaginae penetratio requiritur, ut glans tota intra vaginam versetur," and the answer was: "Affirmative ad primam partem, negative ad secundam partem." —cited in S.R.R. *Decisiones*, XXXIII (1941), pp. 182-183, n. 2.

[110] Cf. Wernz-Vidal, *Ius Canonicum*, V (*Ius Matrmoniale*), p. 261, n. 219.

[111] Cf. *Catholica Doctrina*, Rule 95.

[112] Cf. pp. 116-117 of this dissertation.

E) Licit Means

The judge, however should make it clear that the experts are not permitted to induce an erection in the man whom they examine, nor may they suggest to the man that he do so himself.[113] This may seem to raise a problem as to how the doctor will be able to find out "*an penis naturalem habeat dimensionem, promptamque erectionem ad coeundum necessario duraturam,*" for he may be required to report on this in writing or during his oral interrogation by the court.[114] This he may find out by whatever scientific conjecture or judgment he may derive from an examination of the male member in its quiescent state, and by elicting pertinent information from the man during the examination. He is not expected to make his report entirely from physical findings. Thus, certain things upon which the doctor is to report he learns only by questioning the patient, or by referring to medical records. He will be asked during his oral interrogation by the court, for example: Has the man suffered from any disease which might have had an influence upon his conjugal relations? How long has the diseased lasted?[115]

A fortiori the doctors are to be reminded that masturbation must not be employed with a view to obtaining a sample of the sperm[116]. Indeed, such a sample would ordinarily serve little if any purpose at all. In general reference to this matter Pope Pius XII said:[117]

> The *peritia* required by the ecclesiastical tribunal in processes of nullity because of impotence

[113] Acts inherently (*per se*) productive of venereal pleasure (*delectatio*) are licit only when directed and ordered to their correct end. Cf. Regatillo-Zalba, *Theologiae Moralis Summa* (3 vols., I (1952), II (1953), III (1954), Madrid: La Editorial Catholica, S.A.), II, n. 306, pp. 324-326.

[114] Cf. p. 111 of this dissertation.

[115] Cf. Appendix, *Catholica Doctrina,* XXXII, esp. nn. 3, 4, and the reference to Formula XXX, in which cf. question n. 14.

[116] Cf. p. 118 of this dissertation.

[117] Allocution to a group of urologists, given on Oct. 10, 1953, and appearing in *AAS,* XLV (1953), 677, 678.

> generally consists in establishing not the *impotentia generandi,* but the *impotentia coeundi.* The *impotentia generandi,* as distinguished from the *impotentia coeundi,* does not suffice, according to constant jurisprudence, for obtaining a judgment of nullity. One is permitted, then, in the majority of cases, to omit the microscopic examination of the sperm. It can be demonstrated in another manner, if such a manner be of any avail, that the seminal tissue still possesses a certain functional capacity, and likewise that the ducts which connect the glands or organs of ejaculation are still functioning, so that they are not entirely atrophied or definitely obstructed.

The Pope next adverted to a reply of the Holy Office in which it was maintained and defined that *"masturbatio directe procurata ut obtineatur sperma"* is not licit.[118] He then continued:

> It is quite another thing if the doctor should obtain the sperm . . . in another manner which is licit, in an instance wherein this will really be possible, and when without his own intervention he becomes the recipient of the matter bearing on the examination. He is not responsible for the acts of another, and the examination and use of such things when given are not morally reprehensible. If the ecclesiastical tribunal many times ignores or expressly rejects the expert reports based upon such a procedure, it does this in order that it may not seem, through the utilization of such things, to favor an abuse.

In this regard Pinna remarks that, if masturbation is employed for the purpose of determining the presence or the absence of *verum semen,* the conclusions of the experts in the matter are not even to be considered.[119]

ARTICLE III. EXPERTS IN DEFECTIVE CONSENT CASES

> Even in cases of lack of consent by reason of insanity, the opinion of experts is required. These

[118] p. 118 of this dissertation.

[119] Joannes M. Pinna, *Praxis Iudicialis Canonica* (Romae: *Officium Libri Catholici,* Catholic Book Agency, 1952), p. 76, n. 5.

shall, according to the norms of their art, examine the person, if the case demands it, or his acts when they arouse the suspicion of insanity. Moreover, experts who previously attended the allegedly insane person are to be heard in the capacity of witnesses.[120]

In cases of insanity one or, in line with the gravity of the case, two doctors are to be appointed, who are particularly versed in the science of psychiatry. Nevertheless, there must be carefully excluded those who do not profess sound (Catholic) doctrine in the matter.[121]

SECTION 1. MEANING OF *Amentia*

In cases of a defective consent in consequence of mental abnormality (*amentia*), distinguished psychiatrists must be utilized by the court. The term *amentia* is not to be understood in any strict, scientific sense, but in a very broad sense. Rudolf Allers, in a splendid article concerning the annulment of marriage because of defective consent,[122] says of the Code meaning of *amentia*: "This is the general term for all kinds of mental ailments causing an incapacity of responsible action and correct thought."[123] So general is the term that it would embrace not only the many types of mental illness, as one generally understands them, but also characteristic types of mental deficiency. Thus, feeblemindedness may be of such a pronounced degree that it renders a person absolutely ignorant of the meaning of

[120] "Etiam in causis defectus consensus ob amentiam, requiratur suffragium peritorum, qui infirmum, si casus ferat, eiusve acta quae amentiae suspicionem ingerunt, examinent secundum artis praecepta; insuper uti testes audiri debent periti qui infirmum antea visitaverint."—Can. 1982.

[121] "In causis amentiae unus vel, pro casus gravitate, duo medici deputentur, qui in scientia psychiatrica peculiariter sint versati, cauto tamen ut excludantur qui sanam (catholicam) doctrinam hac in re non profiteantur."—*Instructio "Provida,"* Art. 151.

[122] "Annulment of Marriage by Lack of Consent because of Insanity," *The Ecclesiastical Review* (*ER*), CI (1939) 325-343.

[123] *Ibid.*, p. 340, at III.

marriage, even in its minimum canonical sense.[124] Since the will quite generally follows the intellect, this defective knowledge and understanding can readily give rise to a defective consent.

From these considerations the writer concludes that the proper interpretation of *amentia* in canon 1982 points to some form of mental disorder or abnormality which may render a person incapable of giving a true matrimonial consent. It is in this very general sense that the word *amentia,* and its English equivalent, "insanity," will henceforth be used.

SECTION 2. NECESSITY OF *Peritia*

When from the introductory charge (*libellus*), or from evidence produced during the trial, there arise at least probable arguments or serious indications of *amentia,*[125] the judge must employ one or, if the case merits it, two experts particularly versed in psychiatry. It is not true to say that the judge is sometimes allowed to omit the *"suffragium peritorum"* in cases of insanity. If experts are available, they must be employed, no matter how evident the insanity which vitiates the consent might be, in the eyes of the judge, through the testimony gathered from winesses. The law requires this in view of the fact that the judge is not expected to be able to evaluate mental ab-

[124] Expert psychiatrists sometimes require of the parties more knowledge than is necessary for the marriage contract. *De facto,* the contractants need not know all the social and ethical implications of marriage; nor need they have a juridical knowledge of the marriage contract itself. All that is needed by way of knowledge is stated in canon 1082, "which canon is virtually contained in canon 1081, § 2."—S.R.R. *Decisiones,* XXXVIII (1946), p. 263, n. 8. Canon 1081, § 2, reads: "Consensus matrimonialis est actus voluntatis quo utraque pars tradit et acceptat ius in corpus, perpetuum et exclusivum, in ordine ad actus per se aptos ad prolis generationem." Canon 1082 reads: "Ut matrimonialis consensus haberi possit, necesse est ut contrahentes saltem non ignorent matrimonium esse societatem permanentem inter virum et mulierem ad filios procreandos."—§ 1.
"Haec ignorantia post pubertatem non praesumitur."—§ 2.

[125] S.R.R. *Decisiones,* XXVII (1935), p. 696, n. 4.

normalities without the aid of a psychatrist. Rotal causes are cited which terms the use of experts "not absolutely necessary" for passing a judgment regarding the lack of consent resulting from insanity.[126] It is clear, however, that in such cases the Rota simply treats of the *validity* of a sentence pronounced without the use of experts. It is certainly illicit to neglect the *suffragium peritorum* when experts are available.[127]

On an equal basis (*ceteris paribus*), the psychiatrists who are chosen should be Catholics, uninfected with any psychiatric "doctrine" contrary to the Catholic faith, such as any false determinism, which in effect denies free will.[128]

SECTION 3. OBJECT OF *Peritia*

The experts employed must report to the court their opinion regarding the nature and the degree of the mental disease in the particular case. They should define what was the mental state of the contracting party at the time of the marriage ceremony.[129] The judge should, then, instruct them to report whether the insanity (*amentia*) was

[126] Eudoxio Castañeda Delgado, *La Locura y el Matrimonio* (*Psiquiatría y Jurisprudencia de la Sagrada Rota Romana*), (Cantarranas 16, Valladolid, and Dr. Fourquest, 5, Madrid: Editorial Sever-Cuesta, 1955), p. 137, (hereafter cited Castañeda, *La Locura*). This very excellent book is the more valuable because of its copious references to decisions of the Roman Rota, with the avowed intention of pointing out areas of agreement and of disagreement between canonists and psychiatrists. An earlier article by the same author treats the same topic summarily, "Nulidad por Vicio de Consentimiento," pp. 491-535 of the already cited *Las Causas Matrimoniales* (hereafter cited Castañeda, *Las Causas Matrimoniales*).

[127] S.R.R. *Decisiones*, XV (1923), pp. 133-134, n. 15. Cf. also Pickett, *Mental Affliction*, p. 157.

[128] Cf. can. 1982; *Instructio "Provida,"* Art. 151; pp. 90-91 of this dissertation. Cf. also S.R.R., *Decisiones*, XXIII (1931), p. 275, n. 2: "Quod vero est ad defectum internae libertatis, crebro a peritis assertum peculiaris cautela requiritur in eorum conclusionibus admittendis. Nimis facile plures psychiatri hanc animi morbis vim tribuunt, ut voluntatem libertate privent."

[129] S.R.R. *Decisiones*, XXXVIII (1946), p. 573, n. 3; S.R.R. *Decisiones*, XXIII (1931), p. 464, n. 4.

permanent or transitory, and whether lucid intervals may have intervened.[130]

It is, however, outside the province of the expert to give his opinion regarding the validity of the marriage consent. Rather, this is the duty of the judge,[131] who is sometimes called the *"peritus peritorum."*[132] Speaking to urologists, but in a vein applicable to all judicial experts, Pope Pius XII said that "the conclusions which are drawn from the medical *peritia* for (pronouncing) the *judicial* sentence are not within the competence of the *peritus* or of the *peritissimus.*"[133]

The judge, then, instead of asking the experts whether they consider the marital consent to have been given validly or invalidly, should rather ask whether the defendant was fully responsible for his actions. "If the expert's answer does not seem definite enough, the case may be made clearer by asking the expert whether he would consider the defendant responsible had he committed a crime, or whether he would deem him capable of attending to his personal affairs. The judge is a layman in psychiatry, but the expert is usually entirely unacquainted with the spirit and terminology of the law."[134]

[130] *Instruction "Provida,"* Art. 147, § 1.

[131] "Cum medici sit morborum naturam gradumque declarare, requiritur his in causis suffragium peritorum (can. 1982). Sed unius iudicis tandem est definire, an actus positus ab eo, qui infirmitate mentis laborat, habendus sit invalidus."—S.R.R. *Decisiones*, XXIII (1931), p. 464, n. 4.

[132] "... nam peritus peritorum semper iudex manet ..."—a Rotal decision of May 22, 1956, reported in *Monitor Ecclesiasticus*, An. LXXXI, Series VII Fasc. II—An. 1956, p. 267, n. 6 (Desclée—Romae).

[133] "Les conclusions qui découlent de l'expertise médicale pour la sentence *judiciaire* ne sont pas de la compétence du *peritus* ou *peritissimus.*"—*AAS*, XLV (1953), 675.

[134] Allers, "Annulment of Marriage by Lack of Consent because of Insanity," *E.R.*, CI (1939), 341. Msgr. John J. Hayes is of the opinion that the expert should be asked to determine not only whether the party was sane at the time of the contract, but also whether a then-existing mental disease was of such a nature and character

Castañeda observes that *de facto* the experts sometimes trespass their bounds by declaring their opinions concerning the validity of the consent in the particular case at hand. Sometimes tribunals ask too much of the experts in this regard.[135]

SECTION 4. *Suffragium Peritorum*

Since "the examination of an insane person at the time of a suit for nullification of marriage often reveals nothing of the eventual reason for assuming or suspecting incapacity of consent at the time of the wedding,"[136] the Code does not always require an inspection of the person allegedly insane. It does require, however, the *suffragium peritorum*. Sometimes, then, it may suffice to have the expert carefully examine the judicial *acta*, (e.g., testimony of parties and witnesses; medical records admitted judicially) in order to learn from them the behavior of the person which indicates a suspicion of insanity.[137]

A) Examination of the Acts

Allers notes that the first serious "outbreak" of insanity in generally not the true beginning of a mental disease, but simply represents a crisis which made the disease manifest.[138] Therefore it is important for the psychiatrists to investigate the behavior of the person not only from the time of the "outbreak," but also for the time beforehand. The person's manner of acting prior to the outbreak Allers terms the "prepsychotic personality," and considers it of great value in arriving at a knowledge of the true state of the disease at the time of the marriage.

> To form his opinion the expert needs as much data on the prepsychotic personality as possible,

as to render its victim incapable of validly contracting marriage. —"Mental Disease and the Ecclesiastical Courts," *The Jurist*, XVI, (1956), 280.

[135] *La Locura*, p. 144; *Las Causas Matrimoniales*, p. 257.

[136] Allers, *ibid.*, p. 325.

[137] Can. 1982. Cf. also p. 167 of this dissertation.

[138] *Ibid.*, p. 326.

> and he needs data which refer precisely to those points which will enable him to get a clear idea of the mental state at that time. The expert, however, is not allowed to collect this material himself. He cannot put questions to the plaintiff and witnesses. He must rely on the data supplied to him by the acts of the matrimonial curia, the brief of the plaintiff and the depositions made before the instructing judge. Whether the expert may form an opinion with a greater or lesser certainty depends upon the ability of the judge to collect sufficient evidence.[139]

Clearly, then, the auditing jüdge should have no scruple in sending the expert all the acts which he (the judge, who may prudently consult the expert) thinks necessary and timely.[140] The professional integrity of the psychiatrist chosen will guarantee the safety and secrecy of the acts, if they are sent to the expert along with his appointment, but prior to his oath of office. There will be greater assurance of this if the expert views the acts only after his formal acceptance of the office by means of the oath to perform his office well and to observe secrecy.[141]

Not only may the judge send the already gathered *acta* to the expert, but he may even, at the suggestion of the expert, and after hearing the *defensor vinculi,* call in more witnesses, recall these already heard, obtain previous medical records, and in general amplify the evidence enough to give the expert a sufficient basis for study.[142] Such is the practice of the Roman Rota.[143]

It should be noted that the expert bases his opinion upon his study of the acts *as they are recorded.* It is not his office to investigate the truth of the testimony of the witnesses, the deposition of the plaintiff, or the medical rec-

139 *Ibid.*, p. 327.

140 Cf. *Instructio "Provida,"* Art. 147, § 2.

141 Can. 1797, § 1; *Instructio "Provida,"* Art. 146.

142 Cf. can. 1749; 1781; 1786; *Instructio "Provida,"* Arts. 95; 107.

143 S.R.R. *Decisiones*, XXIX (1937), p. 769, nn. 15, 16. Cf. also Castañeda, *La Locura*, pp. 141-142.

ords. He assumes, and rightly, that the acts afforded him by the judge for study have already been properly admitted into the judicial record.[144]

B) Examination of the Person

If the judge deems it necessary, he may order a personal examination of the party of whom it is alleged that he gave a defective matrimonial consent.[145]

Allers points out that in most cases "a personal inspection of the defendant does not reveal anything bearing immediately on the pending decision. The one thing a personal examination will show is the diagnosis, of which there is as a rule no doubt, since the expert may in most cases rely on the diagnosis made in the hospital for the insane or by the specialists who advised the patient's confinement. A personal examination is indeed necessary only in cases where there is some real doubt about the diagnosis. Notwithstanding the progress made in psychiatry, there are of course still cases in which the diagnosis may be doubtful. The exact diagnosis is often not of a decisive importance.[146] . . . The question of diagnosis, however, cannot be neglected, because in certain cases much may depend on what it reveals."[147]

A judicially ordered personal examination is, then, not so important as one might at first think. The judge would be wise to consult the psychiatrist before ordering a personal examination.[148] Knowledge concerning the allegedly insane person's mental state *at the time of the marriage* is ordinarily of supreme importance. For this reason the

[144] Castañeda, *La Locura,* p. 145; *Las Causas Matrimoniales,* p. 528; Allers *art. cit., ER,* CI (1939), 342.

[145] Can. 1982.

[146] In one Rotal case a judgment of nullity was given when, although the experts differed in their diagnosis of the disease, they agreed that it made the party incapable of giving consent at the time of the marriage.—S.R.R. *Decisiones,* XXIX (1937), p. 770, n. 17.

[147] Allers, *ibid.,* pp. 325-326.

[148] Cf. pp. 106-108 of this dissertation.

law demands that there always be summoned *as witnesses* those who earlier examined the persons extrajudicially, even though they are forbidden to serve as experts.[149]

Often it is impossible to secure the personal examination when it is desirable.[150] Perhaps the person supposedly insane at the time of the marriage cannot be located. Or perhaps, in a rare case, he is now said to be completely cured of his mental affliction, and refuses to be examined. Finally, an interview with the person may be impossible even when his whereabouts is known, and when he is willing to be examined. "The modern tendency, at least in the United States, is to exclude rigorously all persons from examining the patients in insane asylums.... Whenever such an impasse is reached in a trial, it might be advisable for the court to [try to] secure the service, as experts, of the officials of the particular institution where the insane person is interned."[151]

If a personal examination is advisable and possible, the psychiatrist is to be left freedom in the choice of the scientific methods employed.[152] If he chooses to employ mental tests (e.g., the Rorschach test) which must be administered by skilled clinical psychologists, it seems that these latter must also be appointed by the court as experts.[153] They are today highly qualified men, to some degree versed in psychiatry,[154] and are quite frequently employed in mental institutions as the necessary complement of the psychiatrist. They could hardly be said to perform merely secondary, or subsidiary acts, as would be said, e.g., of a nurse

[149] Can. 1982; *Instructio "Provida,"* Art. 143.

[150] "Personal examination of the feeble-minded is more important than the evidence collected from the witnesses.... If careful examination shows a person to be feeble-minded today, it proves that this person was feeble-minded before and will not improve."—Allers, *ibid.*, p. 340.

[151] Doheny, *Canonical Procedure,* I, 392.

[152] Can. 1982—"...qui infirmum, si casus ferat...examinent secundum artis praecepta..."; cf. also pp. 116-117 of this dissertation.

[153] Cf. can. 1792.

[154] Cf. *Instructio "Provida,"* Art. 151.

who prepares the implements and in a general way assists the doctor.[155] A simple "I.Q." test, however, requires little training on the part of the one who administers it, and its results can be ascertained by the psychiatrist without the need of any interpretation by a trained psychologist. Those who administer such uncomplicated tests would not have to be sworn in as experts.

[155] Cf. p. 115 of this dissertation.

CHAPTER XI

JUDICIAL REPORT AND ORAL INTERROGATORY

ARTICLE I. JUDICIAL REPORT

After completing their examination the experts must report their findings to the court in accord with the instructions received from the judge, and within the time specified.[1] In matters dealing with the status of a person (in matrimonial causes, and those which deal with the nullity of sacred orders or its obligations), these reports must be written, not oral.[2] They must chiefly contain an account of the examination, the method employed, the facts discovered, the conclusions drawn from the examination, and the reasons which lead the experts to such conclusions.[3] There is no need for any member of the tribunal to witness the signing of the report. If, however, the judge has reason to fear that some exception might be raised against the authenticity of the written reports, he can demand that the reports be signed by the experts in the presence of an ecclesiastical notary.[4]

Sometimes the court is forced, by reason of the truly primitive conditions of the locality, or because of the refusal of the woman to be examined by any other more qualified experts, to employ two older married women for the corporal inspection of the woman party in causes of non-consummation[5] and impotence.[6]

[1] Cf. pp. 119-126 of this dissertation.

[2] Cf. p. 120 of this dissertation.

[3] Can. 1801, § 3; *Catholica Doctrina,* Rule 93, § 1; *Instructio* "Provida," Art. 148, § 1.

[4] Lega (ed. Bart), *Iudicia Ecclesiastica,* II, p. 767, n. 8.

[5] *Catholica Doctrina,* Rule 89, § 1. The refusal of the woman to be inspected by the more qualified experts is not mentioned in this rule as a reason allowing the examination by the "*honestae matronae.*" But it is logical to permit it, since the intent of the rule is obviously that of obtaining at least some kind of evidence from a corporal examination, even if the woman refuses to be examined by the more qualified and available experts. Cf. also *Catholica Doctrina,* Rule 89, § 2.

[6] Analogy with *Catholica Doctrina,* Rule 89, §§ 1, 2.

In such unusual instances it is advisable, though not obligatory in the law itself, to instruct the women examiners before they begin their inspection. This could more effectively be done by qualified male physicians, if they are available, though not acceptable to the woman for inspection.[7]

When the two examining matrons have completed their inspection, their reports are not to be accepted by the court as sufficient in themselves. Rather, the court must submit those reports to the study of one or two male experts, even if such experts can be found only in another locality. These experts are in turn to relay to the court their opinion about the findings and conclusions reported by the matrons.[8]

Article II. Oral Interrogatory

Section 1. Necessity

The expert, especially if he has submitted a written report, may be called upon by the judge to appear in the tribunal for the purpose of explaining certain parts of his report.[9] In the few instances wherein an oral report is given[10] there will be practically no need to recall the expert, since during his oral report he can be fully questioned by the court upon any point that is not quite clear, e.g., the meaning of techincal terms employed.

When, however, the report has been submitted in writing, it is quite understandable that often an explanation and clarification will be necessary. It is for this reason that the law itself demands that in all marriage causes[11] the experts must appear in court for the threefold purpose of

[7] The woman party must always consent to the examination, and is not to be compelled to be inspected by either men or women.—*Qua singulari* of 1942, n. 4.

[8] *Catholica Doctrina,* Rule 89, § 2.

[9] Can. 1801, § 2; can. 1981; *Catholica Doctrina,* Rule 93, § 1; *Instructio "Provida,"* Art. 152.

[10] Can. 1801, § 1; Cf. p. 120 of this dissertation.

[11] Can. 1981; *Catholica Doctrina,* Rule 93, § 1; *Instructio "Provida,"* Art. 152.

1) identifying their reports; 2) confirming them by oath, and 3) answering any questions proposed to them by the court. These experts are always to be interrogated one at a time, even in the exceptional cases when a joint report has been allowed.[12]

Since the expert is sworn to fulfill his office faithfully, he is bound to answer the call to appear in court, This "call" to appear in court may be made by way of a formal citation, if the judge thinks that the gravity of the case or the character of the expert demands it. More often, however, the call will be made in the form of an invitation, as befits the dignity of the professional men ordinarily appointed as experts.[13]

Generally, before his acceptance of the office,[14] the expert will have agreed to appear in court in order to confirm and elucidate his report. In keeping with the note of courtesy that should prevail throughout the judicial process, especially in the court's dealings with the expert, the judge should consult the convenience of the expert before assigning a time for the confirmation of the written report. If necessary, the invitation should be diplomatically worded so as to express some obligation on the part of the expert to appear for this confirmation and oral interrogatory.

SECTION 2. NATURE OF THE INTERROGATION

In marriage causes, the oral interrogatory will be prepared by the defender of the bond (*defensor vinculi*),[15] who relies chiefly upon the written report of the experts. The questions will concern the general and particular circumstances and difficulties of the cause in question.[16] Thus

[12] Can. 1981; *Catholica Doctrina,* Rule 93, § 2; *Instructio "Provida,"* Art. 148, § 2, together with Art. 152.

[13] Cf. Lega (ed. Bart.), *Iudicia Ecclesiastica,* II, p. 765, n. 4.

[14] Cf. pp. 106-108 of this dissertation.

[15] Can. 1981; *Catholica Doctrina,* Rule 93, § 1; *Instructio "Provida,"* Art. 152.

[16] Appendix, *Catholica Doctrina,* Formula XXX; similarly in causes involving the nullity of sacred orders.—Cf. Appendix *Regulae*

the more complete the report of the experts, the shorter and less detailed will be the interrogatory of the *defensor vinculi*. Often technical phrases will have to be explained, and a further elucidation of the arguments upon which the expert based his conclusions will be needed. One great advantage of the oral interrogatory is that it allows for spontaneity, a quality always desirable in depositions and testimony, but seldom obtained in a written report.

In causes of non-consummation and, by analogy, of impotence, the *defensor vinculi* should be mindful of the following Instructions, as suggested by the Sacred Congregation of the Sacraments, in drawing up his questionnaire:[17]

1) The Instruction of the S.C. of the Holy Office, *Iudex ad hoc deputatus*, of 1858;[18]
2) the Instruction of the S.C. of the Council, *Cum moneat glossa*, of August 22, 1840;[19]
3) the Instruction of the S.C. of the Holy Office (to the Bishops of the Oriental Rites), *Quemadmodum matrimonii foedus*.[20]

It is likewise suggested that, if some particular difficulty should arise, the *defensor vinculi* might consult other experts as advisors in the formulation of the interrogatory.[21]

The experts must never be informed beforehand of the questions to be proposed to them.[22]

SECTION 3. INTERROGATION PROPER

When the experts appear in the tribunal, they are to

super Nullitate Sacrae Ordinationis, Formula XXIV (*AAS*, XXIII (1931), 473-492).

[17] Appendix, *Catholica Doctrina*, Formula XXX; XXXII, "... prout eruuntur ex Instructionibus a S. Sede typis editis, quae supra memoratae sunt, n. XXX, iuxta casus adiuncta."

[18] Cf. pp. 45-47 of this dissertation.

[19] Cf. pp. 42-45 of this dissertation.

[20] Cf. pp. 47-49 of this dissertation.

[21] Appendix, *Catholica Doctrina*, Formula XXX.

[22] Can. 1776, § 1; *Instruction "Provida,"* Art. 103, § 1, (a).

swear to the truth of the answers they are about to make.[23] This oath can, at the discretion of the judge, be omitted if in their oath of office the experts have already sworn to be truthful in the oral interrogatory.[24] But in such a case, when the oath is omitted, the judge should remind the experts that they are still under oath to speak truthfully.

The experts must answer the questions orally, not reading from an already written account.[25] They are not forbidden, however, to bring in notes as an aid to their memory, especially when they testify concerning complex matters, or concerning an examination conducted quite some time past.[26]

If the expert who is being interrogated has inspected one of the parties involved in a marriage cause, he will be asked by the court to identify that person. For this reason the person examined will have already been cited to appear in court at the time of the oral interrogation of the experts.[27] If, however, the person is not willing to appear, or is not able to do so, identification must be made in some other way. Thus the expert could be asked to describe the person; or, better, he could be presented with the photograph or other document or identification (which he should have seen when he inspected the party) and asked whether the person described is the one he examined. And if the expert had been introduced by the tribunal to the person

[23] Analogy with can. 1767; can. 1981; *Catholica Doctrina,* Rule 93, § 1; *Instructio "Provida,"* Art. 152.

[24] Cf. form of oath in non-consummation causes, p. 210 of this dissertation. Cf. also the Appendix, *Catholica Doctrina,* Formula XXX: "... Iudex instructor, perito vel obstetrici *iterum* delato, *si ita existimet,* iureiurando de veritate dicenda ..."; Formula XXXII: "... Fit autem orale examen singulorum medicorum, in quo, *si iudici videatur,* post *rursus* praestitum iusiurandum de veritate dicenda. ..." (Italics supplied by the writer.)

[25] Analogy with can. 1777; *Catholica Doctrina,* Rule 43, § 2; *Instructio "Provida,"* Art. 103, § 1, (b).

[26] Can. 1777; *Catholica Doctrina,* Rule 43, § 2; Bartoccetti, in Lega (ed. Bart.), *Iudicia Ecclesiastica,* III, 161*, at Art. 103, § 1 (b).

[27] Cf. S.C. de Sacr., *Normae* of 1929, n. 4, § 3. Cf. also "*Instructio "Provida,"* Art. 58.

prior to the examination it would suffice that the *peritus* tell the court whether the person he examined was, in fact, the same he later examined.[28]

Regardless of who proposes the questions, they will always be asked by the judge.[29] Most of the questions asked will be the ones in the interrogatory formulated by the *defensor vinculi,* but to this the judge may add other questions which he deems opportune.[30] Doheny suggests that in marriage causes of nullity the three judges of the collegiate tribunal should be present at the interrogation of the experts. If they have read the written reports earlier, they will be prepared to propose pertinent questions.[31]

Only by an extraordinary concession of the judge will the parties or their advocates be allowed to assist at the interrogation of the experts.[32] If they are present they may propose questions to be asked by the judge, just as they are permitted, before the experts begin the inspection, to suggest certain points to be considered by the experts in their inspection and report.[33]

In certain cases, male physicians may propose questions (through the judge) to women experts. The law requires that a doctor of honorable personal and professional reputation, truly skilled in matters of gynecology, be always present during the oral interrogation of women experts who have conducted the physical inspection of the woman party in causes on non-consummation or impotence. This male doctor may make opportune remarks and propose any questions which he deems useful or necessary.[34] To be of use in the cause, the male physician must know something of the particular cause. Hence the court should brief

[28] Cf. S.C. de Sacr., *Normae,* of 1929, n. 4, § 4.

[29] Can. 1773, § 2; *Catholica Doctrina,* Rule 41; *Instructio "Provida,"* Art. 96, § 1.

[30] Cf. can. 1742, § 2; *Catholica Doctrina,* Rule 44, § 3; *Instructio "Provida,"* Art. 101.

[31] Doheny, *Canonical Procedure,* I, 396, at Art. 152.

[32] Can. 1771; *Instructio "Provida,"* Art. 128.

[33] Can. 1799, § 1; *Instructio "Provida,"* Art. 147, § 1.

[34] *Qua singulari* of 1942, n. 5.

him on the case, or even allow him to read the pertinent acts.

This ruling that male physicians assist at the interrogatory of women experts must be observed regardless of how well qualified the women experts are. Onerous as it seems,[35] this ruling must be observed even when outstanding female gynecologists have inspected the woman party.

This male physician who assists at the interrogation of the women experts does not in so doing act in the capacity of an expert, strictly so considered.[36] He should, however, as an instrument of the tribunal, take an oath of office and secrecy.[37] While it is not necessary that this physician be in any other capacity employed by the tribunal in this particular cause, it may often happen that he has been otherwise engaged in the trial. Thus, because he is already acquainted with the case, the expert who has already conducted the physical examination of the man party to the cause may be employed for the interrogation of the women experts, or perhaps the doctor appointed may be the one who previously inspected the woman party in the customary extrajudicial inspection made before the requesting of permission to construct a non-consummation cause, or who was privately consulted by the party in either an impotence or a non-consummation cause.[38] The doctor who assists at

[35] Bartoccetti in Lega (ed. Bart.), *Iudicia Ecclesiastica,* III, 184*, at Art. 150, prefaces the Decree of the Holy Office of 1942 with this remark: "The norms of the following decree of the S.C. of the Holy Office are to be religiously observed, even if their observance sometime seems burdensome."

[36] Cf. p. 59 of this dissertation for the definition of an expert.

[37] Argument from cans. 1621, § 1; 1623, §§ 2, 3; *Catholica Doctrina,* Rule 19; *Instructio "Provida,"* Arts. 20; 104, § 2.

[38] Cf. *Catholica Doctrina,* Rule 9, § 1: Hickey wrote of this private examination that "it frequently happens that the *oratrix* in presenting the petition for the dispensation exhibits, as evidence that the marriage was not consummated, a physician's certificate attesting her state of virginity. In instances wherein the *oratrix* contends that she is in complete possession of her physical integrity, but has no certificate from a reputable physician to attest this fact, it is the

the oral interrogation of the women experts may be the same mature, honorable physician who, in the causes of impotence and non-consummation, was appointed by the ordinary to interrogate the woman party regarding the delicate matters of her conjugal life.[39]

It should be noted that, whereas the appointment of the doctor who interrogates the woman party can be made only by the ordinary,[40] there is no such limitation of the judge's authority for the appointment of the doctor who is to be present during the court's oral interrogation of the women experts.[41] Further, whereas the male doctor

custom of some curias to suggest, before the forwarding of the petition to Rome, that she be examined by a physician and obtain from him an appropriate certificate.

"While the *Regulae* nowhere suggest it, and although this examination can in no sense be styled or be accepted as a substitute for the *inspectio canonica*, there is much practical wisdom to recommend the practice. Firstly, by bringing out from the very beginning the full facts, it protects the court against possible surprises revealed by the *inspectio canonica*. Secondly, it serves a useful purpose in the protection, so to speak, of the evidence derived through the *argumentum physicum*, for in the interval between the sending to Rome of the petition and the formal construction of the process, many things may happen to affect the condition of the petitioner. Accidents may occur, or serious illness may develop, the treatment of which may require various sorts of remedies or even operations impairing the probative value of the canonical inspection. It will greatly add to the force of the certificate if this suggested private examination be performed by a reputable physician familiar with the conduct of examinations of this sort, as well as with the canonical concept of consummation, who can later give valuable testimony as a witness in the case. Finally, for obvious reasons, it will be well to suggest that the identity of the person examined be well established by the physician at the time of the examination."—"De Processus super Matrimonio rato et non consummato," *The Jurist*, I (1941), 215.

[39] *Qua singulari* of 1942, n. 5. Cf. Schmidt, "Interrogation of the Woman Party in the *Super Rato* Process," *The American Ecclesiastical Review*, CXXVI (1952), in two parts, Feb., pp. 109-119, and March, pp. 217-227. Cf. especially p. 223.

[40] *Qua singulari* of 1942, n. 6.

[41] *Qua singulari* of 1942, n. 5.

interrogates the woman party *directly*,[42] the physician present at the interrogation of the women experts questions them only *indirectly*, i.e., through the judge.[43]

As was previously seen, the questions to be asked of the experts during their oral interrogatory will differ in each concrete case. Nonetheless, the following questionnaires, suggested in the model formulae of the Appendix to *Catholica Doctrina* will prove helpful in composing the interrogatory for the experts in non-consummation causes.[44]

A) Interrogation of the experts who have examined the woman party:

1. Is the expert related in any way to the woman examined or to her husband? Or is the medical expert related to, or in any way interested in, a third party who may be keeping company, with a view to marriage, with either consort?[45]
2. How long has he known the consorts and how did he become acquainted with them?
3. Does he confirm under oath all the portions of the report which he wrote concerning the bodily inspection of the woman?
4. Has he anything to add to the report, to correct, or to modify?

[42] *Qua singulari* of 1942, n. 6: "... *coram* Tribunali, sed *a* medico..."; cf. also Schmidt, in the article cited, p. 119: "The employment of a physician to interrogate the woman directly introduces an exception into the procedure. For the rule is that all questioning is to be executed only by the judge himself." He cites cans. 1742, § 1, 1773, § 2; *Catholica Doctrina,* Rule 41; *Instructio "Provida,"* Art. 101.

[43] *Qua singulari* of 1942, n. 5: "... earum orale examen fiat *ab ipso Tribunali*...."

[44] Appendix, *Catholica Doctrina,* Formulae XXX, XXXI, XXXII. The translation will be that of Doheny, *Canonical Procedure,* II, 458-460, and p. 467. The questions to be asked of the matron will be appended as they are found in Doheny, *op. cit.,* II, 464.

[45] Doheny here specifies and enlarges the wording of the Formula, which reads simply "1. An perito aliqua sit necessitudo cum muliere inspecta, vel eius viro?" This accords with his common sense warning, as indicated on pp. 94-95 of this dissertation.

5. Has he performed the physical examination and written his report independently of, and separately from, the other expert?
6. Was the person subjected to the special bath, and for what length of time?
7. In what manner and method did the expert proceed in the inspection?
8. Did he examine the signs recognized by medical science as indications of bodily integrity or of loss of virginity?[46]
9. On what arguments does he principally rely in formulating the opinions expressed in the report?
10. Is there any suspicion of fraud, and especially is there any reason to suspect that artifices of medical science may have been employed in an effort to simulate integrity?
11. Has the woman suffered, and especially while living with her husband, from some illness, physical defect, or abnormality, which might have had an influence on the marital relations? And could or could not these aliments be cured?
12. (*If found necessary.*) How can the opinion of the expert be reconciled with the contrary opinion of the other expert, of the physician, or with a contrary statement of one or of both consorts? These statements are then read to the expert (i.e., the statements of others which are contrary to the report of the expert being questioned).

[46] This is the material object of the examination. To determine the formal object of the examination, namely, whether or not in this particular case, on the basis of inspection of the genital apparatus, there was consummation of the marriage, Bartoccetti says the question usually asked of the experts, "*ex stylo S.C. de Sacramentis,*" is the follwoing: "Utrum bene perspectis et fori hymenealis mensura et forma et hymenealis membranae natura et qualitatibus (extensibilis vel minus) excludenda prorsus sit in casu quaecumque etiam partialis penetratio glandis in vaginam mulieris, vel una tantum vice peracta, cum qualibet seminis, effusione in eadem." Lega (ed. Bart.), *Iudicia Ecclesiastica,* III, 335*, note 1.

13. What has the expert observed as to the general constitution of the woman examined, of her temperament and of her psychic state?
14. Has the expert received any relevant information from the woman herself? What information?
15. (*If considered relevant to the case.*) Does the expert know anything that is relevant about the physical condition of the other consort, that is, of the husband? Is this opinion really corroborated or weakened by the information learned during the process about the physical condition of the husband? The relevant portions of the testimony (about the state of the husband) are then read.
16. To what cause does the expert think the alleged non-consummation of the marriage is to be attributed in the case?
17. Whether other tests should be employed to ascertain the truth? And what type of tests should be used?
18. After the deposition is read to him, the expert is to be asked whether he wishes to add, omit, correct, or modify anything.

B) Interrogation of the experts who have examined the man party:
1. Did the physician employ only licit and ethical methods in the inspection? (Precisely what methods were employed)?[47]
2. What reason or indications did he discern which would tend to prove or exclude virile potency?
3. Has the man suffered from any disease which might have had an influence on conjugal relations? What was the nature of the disease?
4. Has this disease existed for a long time or is it of recent origin? Is it natural or acquired? Is it curable without danger to health?

C) Interrogation of the Matron:
1. Was the matron present, without any interruption,

[47] Parenthesis by the writer.

during the entire time of the bodily inspection?

2. Was the bath properly prepared, and how taken? How long did the bath continue? (If the bath was not given, this question is obviously omitted).
3. Did the medical experts observe the rules of modesty and did they perform the examination according to the special directions given them? (Insofar as these directions were previously made known also to the matron.[48]
4. Could any fraud or deception have taken place?
5. Has the matron any remarks to make about the matter?
6. Has the matron anything to add, omit, correct, or modify?

The interrogation of the experts in other than non-consummation causes will follow lines similar to the interrogation of the experts recorded above. That is, when a written report has been submitted, it must be confirmed in all its parts by means of an oath; questions necessary in the concrete case should be asked; the expert should hear his completed testimony read to him, and should be given the opportunity to add, suppress, or change any parts of his testimony.[49] He should be asked if he has any additional remarks to make about any matter pertinent to his examination, his report, or the parties with whom he came in contact during the course of the trial.

When the interrogation is finished, the expert takes a final oath that he has spoken the truth, and that he will observe secrecy until the publication of the acts, or even perpetually, if the judge deems it necessary. Lastly, he should sign the deposition, being followed by the *defensor vinculi* or *promotor iustitiae* (when they are present), the judge and the notary.[50]

[48] Parenthesis by the writer.

[49] Can. 1780, § 1; *Catholica Doctrina,* Rule 46; *Instructio "Provida,"* Art. 104, § 1.

[50] Cf. cans. 1623, § 3; 1769; 1780; *Catholica Doctrina,* Rule 46; *Instructio "Provida,"* Art. 104, § 2.

SECTION 4. RE-EXAMINATION OF EXPERTS

After they have completed their testimony, the experts may sometimes be recalled for a re-examination,[51] upon the request of the parties, of the *defensor vinculi* or the *promotor iustitiae,* or even upon the *ex officio* issued order of the judge, after he has consulted the *defensor vinculi.* At the re-examination the experts may be interrogated further about matters to which they have already testified, or about new facts or questions which have arisen during the process.[52]

ARTICLE III. UNSATISFACTORY REPORTS

There may even be occasion for a confrontation of the experts,[53] especially when there is disagreement in their reports. If need be, there can even be confrontation not only between the experts, but also between the experts and the parties or witnesses.[54] Such a confrontation between experts to discuss their differences in reports might well be the easiest way to resolve the differences and to arrive at the truth. Ordinarily it could be conducted in such a manner as to avoid all danger of injured feelings, ill-will, scandal, or dissension.[55]

If the judge does not wish to have a confrontation of the experts, or if after such confrontation there should still exist disagreements among the experts regarding the findings in their investigations or in their final conclusions, the judge may do one of several things in an attempt to resolve the differences.

[51] This re-examination may, for a grave reason, take place even after the publication of the reports.—Cf. can. 1786; *Instructio "Provida,"* Art. 135.

[52] Can. 1781; *Catholica Doctrina,* Rule 47, § 2; *Instructio "Provida,"* Art. 107, § 1.

[53] Analogy with can. 1772, § 2; *Catholica Doctrina,* Rule 47, § 1; *Instructio "Provida,"* Art. 133.

[54] Bottoms, *Discretionary Authority of the Judge,* p. 140.

[55] Cf. can. 1772, § 3; *Catholica Doctrina,* Rule 47, § 1; *Instructio "Provida,"* Art. 133.

First, if he judges that the experts were superiorly equipped for their task and have conscientiously conducted their examination and have given an objective and clear report, he may choose to do nothing further. He may judge that the disagreement is insoluble, and that the employment of further means would be an unlawful waste of time, effort, and money.[56] Obviously, it would very seldom happen that the judge would be completely convinced that a disagreement among the experts is truly insoluble.

Of the means available for the resolving of the differences and the obtaining of a satisfactory report, there is no hierarchial preference stated in law. The writer herewith submits what he thinks should be the order of preference in resolving the disagreements of expert reports:

1) The judge should submit the written reports of each expert to the other, in order that they themselves may explain the source of the difficulty.[57]
2) The reports of both may be submitted to the study of a *peritior*, who will strive to resolve the difficulty.[58]
3) If the *peritior* is unable to resolve the difficulty by means of a mere study of the reports of the first experts, he may be permitted to conduct his own examination of the person or the object.[59]
4) If the cause requires it, the judge may order a reexamination to be conducted jointly by the originally

[56] Cf. can. 1803, § 1: "... *licet* iudici ..."; *Catholica Doctrina*, Rule 93, § 2, "... iudex *poterit* ..."; *Instructio "Provida,"* Art. 153, "... praeses alium, quem vocant peritiorem, designare *poterit*. ..." Regarding the unlawful employment of useless means, cf. can. 1749; *Instructio "Provida,"* Art. 95, § 2.

[57] *Catholica Doctrina*, Rule 93, § 2.

[58] Cans. 1803, § 1; 1980, § 3; *Catholica Doctrina*, Rules 89, § 2; 90, (f); 93, § 2; *Instructio "Provida,"* Art. 153. *Contra*, Doheny, *Canonical Procedure*, I, 397, at Art. 153, where he states that in cases of nullity an examination of the spouse must always be made by the *peritior*, and that the judge cannot be content with his mere study of the reports of the first experts.

[59] Can. 1803, § 1; *Catholica Doctrina*, Rule 93, § 2; *Instructio "Provida,"* Art. 153.

appointed experts. In this event, although they will submit a joint report, they will again be interrogated separately.[60]

5) Finally, if the differences in the reports seems irreconcilable, or if for any other reason the reports are unsatisfactory, the judge may appoint new experts to perform anew the entire *peritia,* i.e., to conduct an examination and give a report such as was required of the first experts.[61]

In deciding which of these means he should use to obtain a satisfactory report, the judge should especially consider the convenience and preference of the parties. The woman party in a non-consummation cause, for example, may prefer to be re-examined by the experts originally employed, rather than by a different expert. Nor should any second corporal inspection be required if a satisfactory report can be obtained without it, not only for reasons of modesty, but also to eliminate needless effort and expense.

Bottoms wisely notes that, when the judge deems it necessary to employ a *peritior,* he is presented with a practical difficulty. "The judge will have chosen the best available experts for the initial examination, and will usually be rather nonplussed in his task of securing a more qualified expert. In such a case, the judge could select another expert at least as well qualified.... Generally, the securing of an expert truly better qualified than those first chosen would involve great expense in bringing one from another section of the country."[62]

In the same vein, Castañeda in treating of expert psychiatrists, calls the term *"peritior"* an unhappy choice of words. "Ordinarily, the judges are directed in their first intention to the most skilled psychiatrists of the locality, and so this new expert is usually *less skilled* than the first

[60] Can. 1802; *Catholica Doctrina,* Rule 93, § 2; *Instructio "Provida,"* Art. 148, § 2.

[61] Can. 1803, §§ 1, 2; *Catholica Doctrina,* Rule 93, § 2; *Instructio "Provida,"* Art. 153.

[62] Bottoms, *Discretionary Authority of the Judge,* p. 136.

experts. He ought rather to be termed a *new expert,* or a *third expert.*"[63]

At any rate, if the judge carefully selects truly outstanding experts from the very beginning, and instructs them well, there will not often arise a need to appeal to the services of a new expert or a *peritior.* Even less likely will be the need of requiring a third or a fourth *peritia,* although the judge could allow this if he considered it truly necessary or useful.[64]

If a *peritior* is chosen, Evans reminds us that secrecy should be strictly observed, for "one doctor could easily be offended if he learned that another more skilled than he was called to pass judgment on his work."[65]

ARTICLE IV. PUBLICATION OF THE REPORTS

In non-consummation causes, there is no publication of the process.[66] Hence there is no publication of the experts' reports. Nevertheless, if after the conclusion of the process one or both of the parties should for a grave reason request permission to be shown the experts' reports, their request may be granted, under certain conditions. Thus, before conceding this permission the judge a) must consult the *defensor vinculi,* and, if need be, the interested party, in order to ascertain the need of such perusal of the reports, and b) must be assured that the danger of collusion and dishonesty is averted. Finally, if this permission is granted, express mention of the publication must be made in the acts.[67]

In other causes, once all the experts have confirmed their reports and have been orally examined, their reports and

[63] *La Locura,* p. 139, note 15.

[64] Note the use of the word "*quoties*" in canon 1803, § 2. Cf. also Coronata, *De Processibus,* II, p. 278, n. 1332.

[65] Evans, "*Ratum et non-Consummatum* Procedure: Regulations Concerning Corporal Examination," *The Jurist,* XVI (1956), 179.

[66] Can. 1985; *Catholica Doctrina,* Rule 97, § 1.

[67] *Catholica Doctrina,* Rule 97, § 2.

testimony may be immediately published.[68] If, however, he thinks it best, the judge may defer publication until the other proofs have been completed.[69]

After the publication of the reports the parties may raise objections against the manner in which the expert inspection was made, or may point out discrepancies in the reports and the testimony.[70] They can no longer raise an exception against the very person of the expert unless the reason for the objection was non-existent or unknown earlier.[71]

[68] Analogy with can. 1782, § 1.

[69] Analogy with can. 1782, § 2; *Instructio "Provida,"* Arts. 134; 175.

[70] Cf. can. 1783, 2°. The conclusions of the expert cannot be directly impugned.—Cf. pp. 98-99 of this dissertation.

[71] Cf. cans. 1783, 1°; 1764, § 4.

CHAPTER XII

PENALTIES; REMUNERATION OF THE EXPERTS

ARTICLE I. PENALTIES AGAINST DELINQUENT EXPERTS

> It is the duty of the experts to execute their *peritia* according to the laws of truth and justice, neither affirming a falsehood, nor concealing the truth. If they are delinquent in this, they are to be punished according to the norm of canon 1743, § 3.[1]

If in good faith and using his skill to the best of his ability, the expert should wrongly interpret the cause, the nature, or the effects of the facts observed, he is not guilty of a falsehood, but has simply committed an error, and is not to be punished. If he lies, or deliberately conceals the truth when testifying to the facts observed, or deliberately misinterprets their cause, their nature, or their effects, he is to be punished.

This punishment is, however, to be inflicted only when the experts have, according to the norm of canon 2195, § 1, committed a true delict, i.e., an external and morally imputable violation of a law to which is attached at least an indeterminate canonical sanction. The sanction attached to the willful violation of canon 1794 is the same as that which is attached to canon 1743, § 3, viz., if the sworn expert is a layman, he will be personally interdicted;[2] if he is a cleric, as will rarely occur, he may be punished with a *ferendae sententia* suspension "*generaliter lata.*"[3]

Once the expert has taken his oath he is bound faithfully to perform his examination and to report to the court the results of that examination.[4] These things he is bound to do not only in heed to the virtue of religion, but also

[1] Can. 1794.

[2] Can. 2275.

[3] Cf. can. 2278, § 2.

[4] Cf. can. 1798, § 1.

and fundamentally in heed to the virtue of justice.[5] Therefore canon 1798 states that "if the experts, after they have taken the oath, fail to fulfill their mandate within the prescribed time, or if without a just cause they elude its execution, they are bound to pay damages."[6]

Thus, if the expert without a just cause fails to complete his examination within the assigned time, he must pay damages. He is likewise bound if, even though he has completed the examination in time, he unjustifiably fails to report on time. Certainly he is bound to pay damages if without a justifying reason he does absolutely nothing toward the execution of his expert duties.

He likewise is bound to pay damages who has been substantially negligent in performing his examination, even though he may have concluded a very cursory examination and reported within the time specified. If the expert who performs his examination well and who makes a satisfactory report is bound to pay damages simply for his failure to observe the time limit, then certainly the expert who observes the time limit but fails substantially in his examination is bound also.[7]

It is left to the prudent discretion of the judge to determine in the individual case whether there exists a reason-

[5] Lega (ed. Bart.), *Iudicia Ecclesiastica,* II, p. 755, n. 13.

[6] "Post iusiurandum praestitum, si periti intra praefinitum tempus mandato non paruerint aut sine iusta causa exsecutionem defugiant, tenentur damnorum."Can. 1798.

[7] Wanenmacher furnished an example of an exception raised against what was suspected to be a substantially unsatisfactory report. "In an unpublished case of non-consummation at X., the wife who had been examined by two physicians, both of whom rendered their certain conclusion that the hymen was intact, brought a letter to the Curia in which she pointed out that one of the physicians had very carefully and at great length examined her, while the other had completed the inspection in a moment. She did not know that both physicians had pronounced in her favor, but suspected the one of having concluded contrarily. She was within her right when she thus objected to the method of examination, but she did not promote her case by it."—*Canonical Evidence,* pp. 183-184, n. 298.

able and a justifying cause excusing from the proper and timely fulfillment of the mandate of *peritia.*

Damages to be paid by a negligent expert include not only the expense of hiring the expert, but also any other expenses which were needlessly incurred by reason of his negligence. The expert is bound to pay nothing, however, until the judge has by sentence condemned him to damages. This sentence may be pronounced *ex officio* by the judge, or at the instance of the parties, depending on the nature of the cause. The expert may be altogether relieved of paying damages if the party who must pay for the needless expense is willing to condone the damages.[8]

Article II. Remuneration of the Experts

The expert should be compensated for his services. There is no statement in law regarding the definite amount to be paid to the expert. There is rather a very general and prudent rule, namely: the fees and expenses of the experts are to be equitably determined by the judge (the *praeses* in a collegiate tribunal), using as a norm the custom prevailing in civil courts of the locality for similar services.[9]

Although there is a difference between *"expensas et honoraria"* in the canon and article cited, ordinarily no practical distinction is made in the remuneration of the expert. He is paid in one lump sum, which will include not only the fee, but also an adequate coverage of ordinary expenses. Due allowance should be made, however, for extraordinary expenses, e.g., the cost of transportation, food, and lodging when an expert from another locality is employed.

The value of the expert's time should be remembered by the judge in his assessing of the fee. A busy psychiatrist, for example, must be amply reimbursed for time spent in examination, in writing his report, and in appear-

[8] Cf. Lega (ed. Bart.), *Iudicia Ecclesiastica,* II, p. 756, n. 13.

[9] *Instructio "Provida,"* Art. 234, 2°. Cf. also can. 1805, which adverts not precisely to the custom of *the civil courts,* but to the custom of *the locality.*

ing for the oral interrogatory. Had he not been so engaged, he would usually have been profitably occupied in treating clients.

Care must be taken by the court, however, lest the parties be unjustly burdened with the fees and expenses of the experts.[10] The particular case, then, should be considered. One case might require a long, arduous examination and a detailed report, whereas another case of the same nature might entail only a short, uncomplicated examination and report. It would be unfair to exact of the parties an equal fee in the two cases. Likewise to be considered is the financial condition of the party who will be obliged to pay.[11]

If the sum fixed by the judge seems unreasonable to either the parties or the experts, recourse can be had to the same judge within ten days. Thus the judge may, if he see fit, change the assessment.[12] An appeal from the sentence of the principal cause carries with it an appeal from the ruling concerning the expenses.[13]

Generally the expenses of the *peritia* are to be paid by him who petitions it. If, however, the judge acts *ex officio,* the plaintiff of the main trial is to pay, for he is considered responsible for the entire process, with its necessary incidentals.[14] Nevertheless, in marriage causes the collegiate tribunal may determine that the expenses of the *peritia* be borne by both parties.[15] More frequently than not, both parties to a marriage cause are in fact, if not in law, plaintiffs jointly seeking a declaration of nullity, and the *defensor vinculi* is the only true "defendant" of the marriage bond.

[10] *Instructio "Provida,"* Art. 234, 2°.

[11] Cf. *Instructio "Provida,"* Art. 236, § 2; cf. also Roberti, *De Processibus,* II, pars I, p. 84, n. 359.

[12] Can. 1913, § 1; *Instructio "Provida,"* Art. 236, § 3.

[13] Can. 1913, § 2; *Instructio "Provida,"* Art. 236, § 4.

[14] Arguing from can. 1909, § 2. Nevertheless, it may be argued that when the *reus* brings the petition for the *peritia,* he must pay; from the rule, *Reus excipiendo fit actor.*

[15] *Instructio "Provdia,"* Art. 236, § 1.

In order to guarantee financial compensation for the experts, the judge, and even the experts themselves,[16] can demand that the responsible party deposit with the tribunal a sum of money, or at least a sufficient security of payment.[17]

The method of paying the experts is left to the discretion of the judge. The writer knows of at least one diocese where, in causes requiring corporal inspection, the judge instructs the medical expert that he is to send to the party examined the usual bill for a thorough physical examination. If the doctor is instructed to add to that bill an extra charge to cover his additional service of reporting and appearing in court, this manner of remunerating the expert seems satisfactory. Perhaps the experts will generously and of their own initiative condone any expenses beyond the usual fee.

Whatever, method is employed, the court must exercise control over the payment of the experts. On the one hand, the experts must not receive a niggardly sum, or feel that he must accept only a minimum fee because he is assisting an ecclesiastical tribunal. On the other hand, the court must not grant excessive fees to the expert at the unjust expense of the parties.[18]

If need be, the court may itself pay the expert, granting the right of gratuitous assistance to the needy parties; or it may partially compensate him when the parties are able to contribute a limited amount to the *honoraria et expensas*.[19]

Experts who perform their *peritia* in an improper or negligent manner forfeit their fees, and may even be punished.[20] The experts do not forfeit their fees for the reason simply that their *peritia* seems to the judge insufficient, and that a substitute expert must be appointed.

[16] Coronata, *De Processibus*, p. 279, n. 1334.
[17] Can. 1909, § 2; *Instructio "Provida,"* Art. 235, § 1.
[18] Cf. *Instructio "Provida,"* Art. 234, 2°.
[19] Can. 1914; *Instructio "Provida,"* Art. 237.
[20] Arguing from can. 1798.

The court has the obligation of investigating the qualifications of the experts. If an appointed expert is inadequately qualified for the particular task assigned him, but in no way has deluded the court as to his ability, and performs his job as best he can, then not the expert, but the court itself, is to blame for the unsatisfactory *peritia,* and cannot deprive him of his *honoraria.* Of course, if the appointed expert has deceived the court into thinking him to be qualified, or if while qualified he performs a cursory and incomplete examination, he certainly does not deserve any financial compensation.

CHAPTER XIII

PROBATIVE VALUE OF *PERITIA*

The probative value of expert testimony is concisely fixed in the expression of the Rota that "the judge is the expert of experts."[1] This phrase implies that the judge is superior to the experts, not being bound by their conclusions even when they give concordant reports.[2] It implies that the testimony of experts represents only one type of proof among many, and must be so regarded by the judge.

Since the judge is to pronounce his sentence only when he has achieved moral certitude,[3] and since that moral certitude must be drawn from *all* the acts and proofs in the cause,[4] it is evident that the value of *peritia* will differ from cause to cause in a court. In one instance it may supply the vital part which welds together the other bits of evidence into a tightly coherent picture of moral certitude. In another it may be one of the small, rather inconsequential contributors to the completed portrait of certitude; or it may contribute absolutely nothing. Yet, in still another instance, the testimony of experts may be of itself conclusive.[5]

Roman law seemed to require the judge to pronounce sentence according to the majority opinion of the experts engaged.[6] The practice in the Church, however, varied, sometimes demanding that sentence be pronounced in accord with the majority opinion of the experts, but more often leaving the judge free to evaluate the worth of these

[1] *Nullitatis matrimonii,* 22 maii 1956, coram R.P.D. Pericle Felici, Ponente. Recorded in *Monitor Ecclesiasticus,* An. LXXXI, Ser. VII, Fasc. II, 1956, p. 267, n. 6.

[2] Can. 1804, § 1; *Instructio "Provida,"* Art. 154, § 1.

[3] Can. 1869, § 1; *Instructio "Provida,"* Art. 197, § 1.

[4] Can. 1869, § 2; *Instructio "Provida,"* Art. 197, § 2.

[5] This would obtain, for example, when the inspection reveals physically certain signs of impotence. Cf. Reiffenstuel, Lib. IV, tit. 15, n. 42, cited at pp. 33-34 of this dissertation.

[6] Cf. *supra,* pp. 1-3.

opinions. The Code has crystallized in a wonderful fashion the previous teaching and practice concerning the probative value to be afforded to the *peritia*. On the one hand, the supremacy of the judge is shown in that he is not bound to pronounce sentence according to the majority, or even the unanimous opinion of the experts.[7] On the other hand, respect and deference is shown to the opinions of the experts, for the judge, in giving his decision, must state the reasons and arguments which motivated him in his rejection or acceptance of the conclusions reached by the experts.[8]

If the types of proof are considered objectively, without relation to a particular case, it can be said that the evidence gained from experts is nobler than that afforded by witnesses, but it is nevertheless more fallible. Although the effects of physical laws are certain (unless a miracle intervenes), man does not know these laws with exactitude, nor does he fully know their effects. Especially then is there the possibility of error when, in investigating these laws and their effects, one seeks at the same time to capture some human trace or imprint.[9]

[7] Can. 1804, § 1; *Instructio "Provida,"* Art. 154, § 2. When the parties submit their dispute to arbitration, the opinion of an expert arbiter is absolute, for then he acts as a true judge, and not simply as the judicial expert here treated.—Cf. cans. 1929-1932.

[8] Can. 1804, § 2; *Instructio "Provida,"* Art. 154, § 2; Lega (ed. Bart.), *Iudicia Ecclesiastica,* II, p. 770, n. 12. Augustine is singular in his interpretation of canon 1804, § 2, for in speaking of the judge's appraisal of the expert report he said that "if he decides to give the reasons for his decision (which, however, he is not bound to do, because the text only says *cum reddit, when* or *if* he does), he should explain why he admitted or rejected the conclusions of the experts." —*A Commentary,* VII, 248, at can. 1804, § 2. This seems a strained interpretation, especially in view of canons 1840, § 3, and 1873, § 1, 3°. In marriage causes there is no doubt that the judge *must* explain the arguments motivating his acceptance or rejection of the experts' opinions: "Tribunal *debet* in rationibus decidendi exprimere, quibus motum argumentis peritorum conclusiones vel admiserit vel reiecerit."—*Instructio "Provida,"* Art. 154, § 2.

[9] Cf. Muñiz, *Procédimientos,* p. 275, n. 342.

Article I. Rejected Experts

After the completion of his *peritia,* inclusive of the oral interrogatory, an expert may be rejected, if it is proved that he was juridically unqualified for the office from the very beginning, or that he became disqualified after being appointed.[10] In such an event the conclusions reported by that expert are substantially vitiated, and cannot serve as even an indication or support of truth.[11]

Such an expert, by reason of the suspicion that caused his dismissal, cannot be considered credible, especially as regards the conclusions that he draws from facts discovered in his examinations. Inasmuch as it is more difficult to detect erroneous and false conclusions in the report of the expert than to detect such error or falsity in the testimony of a suspect witness, the conclusions of the expert may not be conceded even that adminicular value which one may attach to the testimony of a suspect witness.[12]

It cannot, however, be said that the entire report of the rejected expert is wholly useless, for the *facts* as witnessed in a particular cause may be corroborative of other testimony gathered during the course of the trial. In this sense, then, the report of a rejected expert may, as an extrajudicial document, sometimes serve as adminicular proof, somewhat as the testimony of a suspect witness may provide supporting evidence.

Article II. Effect of Second *Peritia* on First

If the first experts appointed are discordant in their reports, or if they have failed to solve the questions propsed for their examination and report, then a *peritior* or new experts may be appointed.[13] If the *peritior* merely examines and explains the reports of the first experts, obviously these first reports do not lose their juridical value; nor do the first reports lose their juridical value simply because a *peritior*

[10] Can. 1803, §2.

[11] Cf. Lega (ed. Bart.), *Iudicia Ecclesiastica,* II, p. 769, n. 10.

[12] Cf. can. 1758.

[13] Can. 1803, § 2.

or new experts have been appointed for a new examination and report. Rather, there will attach to the reports such worth as they have intrinsically. That is, reports are valuable in proportion to the knowledge and the skill of their author, to the accuracy of the facts and principles stated, and to the soundness of the reasoning as based upon such facts and principles. Thus the second, third, or even a fourth report is of greater worth than the first only insofar as it is intrinsically superior to the first.[14]

ARTICLE III. GENERAL NORMS

> The direct findings of experts have a greater value as proof than the conclusions drawn from their findings. When the report of an expert contains merely the recountal of what he has observed in the course of his inspection, his testimony to these facts has at least the same value as the testimony of any direct witness. Thus, an expert's report on the condition in which he has found the hymen, or on the condition in which he has found the mental conditions of a person, must not be easily set aside. However, when the expert's report goes on to draw inferences from these observations made, these inferences must be accorded such deference as the ability and logic of the expert rightly demand. . . .[15]

Concordant reports and testimony of the experts are of greater value than singular or individual testimony.[16] When two or more absolutely trustworthy experts agree upon facts witnessed during their expert inspection, their testimony in regard to such facts is generally conclusive.[17] While the testimony of one expert may sometimes prove conclusive because of the physical finding which it reports, or may be the decisive factor of proof as related to the other evidence collected, it does not of itself constitute full

[14] Cf. Lega (ed. Bart.), *Iudicia Ecclesiastica,* II, p. 769, n. 11.

[15] Bottoms, *Discretionary Authority of the Judge,* p. 203.

[16] Cf. can. 1789, 4°, with can. 1791, § 2.

[17] Cf. can. 1791, § 2.

proof, for the expert is not by law a specifically qualified witness (*testis qualificatus*).[18]

The testimony of experts who have performed their examinations extrajudicially is not of juridical value as a canonical *peritia*. It may, however, be of extreme importance as the testimony of a trustworthy witness who testifies through his own personal knowledge (*de scientia*), especially if it concerns an examination made at a time not open to suspicion (*tempore non suspecto*).[19] It is for this reason that such experts must be called as witnesses in insanity causes,[20] and should be called in non-consummation and impotence causes.[21]

> The conclusions, inferences and opinions of experts should be based upon facts judicially proved, i.e., documentated [sic] properly witnessed in court, or discovered by the experts . . . in the course of official inspection. If they are founded on facts not judicially proved, they are not, strictly speaking, classified as expert's proofs. Thus the Rota in a case of impotence has rejected expert opinion founded on the extraneous medical history of a case.[22]

The credible reports of experts often establish the basis of important presumptions in marriage causes. Thus the report that the hymen is still physically integral, while not an absolute sign that there has been no consummation of marriage, establishes a factual presumption (*presumptio hominis*) to that effect.[23] When it is established, through the reports of experts or other evidence, that there existed

[18] Cf. can. 1791, § 1.

[19] Cf. *Catholica Doctrina*, Rule 70, *Instructio "Provida,"* Art. 116.

[20] Can. 1982; *Instructio "Provida,"* Art. 143.

[21] Can. 1978; *Catholica Doctrina*, Rule 88 with Rule 58: "In his causis *debet* uterque coniux testes . . . inducere . . . alioquin de re edoctos, qui iurare possint . . . praesertim de veritate circa rem deductam in controversiam."—Italics by the writer. Cf. *Instructio "Provida,"* Art. 143.

[22] Wanenmacher, *Canonical Evidence*, p. 200, n. 325, citing S.R.R. *Decisiones*, V (1913) p. 673, n. 23.

[23] Cf. S.R.R. *Decisiones*, XXXIII (1941), 3, n. 6, as quoted in part on p. 156, note 99, of this dissertation.

before and after the marriage contract a type of insanity which of its nature is perpetual and incurable, there is a presumption that the insanity existed also at the time of the marriage contract.[24]

Properly to apply this principle of presumption in insanity causes, the judge must know which diseases are to be classed as *natura sua* perpetual and irremediable, and must know also the more evident symptoms of such diseases. Schizophrenia, or dementia praecox, the most prevalent of all mental diseases in the United States,[25] is generally considered incurable. In a rare case, however, there can be some improvement in the condition of a schizophrenic person, to the extent namely that he could validly enter a marriage contract.[26]

[24] "Si constet de amentia antecedenti et subsequenti, deducitur et amentia concomitans. Mentecapti namque habent et quae vocantur lucida intervalla, in quibus possunt etiam quandoque valide contractus inire et proinde etiam matrimonium, etsi hodie iuxta complures medicos etiam in ipso lucido intervallo habeatur latens quaedam amentia. Quare cum amentia sit morbus natura sua perpetuus et insanabilis, in dubio, num matrimonium tempore amentiae initum fuerit, an in lucido intervallo, censetur fuisse tempore amentiae contractum."—S.R.R. *Decisiones*, XXIII (1931, p. 153, n. 8. Cf. also Gasparri, *De Matrimonio*, II, n. 785; also a summary of his teaching employed in a recent case in which the marriage was declared null because of psychasthenia. "Adducatur denique principium a cl. Gasparri ... idest, cum morbus est certus, et certe matrimonium antecendens, et certe facultates mentis laedens, defectus consensus etiam in casibus apparentis normalitatis praesumi debet, donec contrarium stricte probetur."—*Nullitatis Matrimonii*, coram R.P.D. Boleslao Filipiak, *Ponente*. Recorded in *Monitor Ecclesiasticus*, An. LXXXI, Ser. VI, Fasc. III, a. 1956, p. 456, n. 4.

[25] McGowan, "Fundamentals of Psychiatry in Relation to the Ecclesiastical Tribunal," *The Jurist*, XVI (1956), 253.

[26] McGowan, *The Jurist*, XVI (1956), pp. 257, 259.

SCHOLION

REGARD FOR EXPERTS

Quintana Reynés vehemently complained of the extremist position of certain judges who, "in a manner certainly unbecoming their apparent education, place almost no confidence in expert proof... relying altogether on what they call their 'enlightened common sense' and regarding as of equal inconsequence the mastery of every kind of science, including those which they have not so much as greeted in their already rancid studies."[1]

Fortunately the attitude which Quintana Reynés so scathingly criticized is today rare. There is a healthy regard for the knowledge and skill of experts, especially for psychiatrists and other medical specialists. At the same time, the Rota's not infrequent rejection of the opinions of experts serves as a reminder that the experts are not infallible, despite their learning.

The evident conclusion from such observations is that the judge should have at least some basic scientific knowledge of the cases which he will more commonly encounter. Thus, besides keeping abreast of the Rotal decisions in cases of non-consummation, impotence, and insanity, the officials of the tribunal should familiarize themselves with certain fundamental scientific notions necessary in their work.

> In view of the fact that ecclesiastical tribunals are requested to investigate and adjudicate cases of alleged nullity of marriage because of insanity, it is necessary that the officials of the tribunal, especially the judges, have a knowledge of the latest psychiatric teaching concerning at least those kinds of insanity which most frequently affect the mental competence of human individuals. I refer especially to those psychoses or species of

[1] Quintana Reynés, *La Prueba,* p. 141.

insanity known as Schizophrenia (or Dementia Praecox) and Manic Depressive Psychosis.[2]

In consideration of the increasing incidence of functional impotence,[3] a knowledge of its more common causes—whether they be of a nervous, neurasthenic, or psychic nature[4]—should be had by members of the tribunal.

[2] McGowan, *The Jurist,* XVI (1956), 251.

[3] Quinn, *Rotal Jurisprudence with Regard to Functional Impotence in the Male,* a paper delivered on Oct, 23, 1956, to the Canon Law Society of America. (Published for Limited Distribution by the Canon Law Society of America, The Catholic University of America, Washington, D.C., 1957), p. 5.

[4] Quinn, *ibid.,* p. 6.

CONCLUSIONS

1. Experts have been employed in judicial processes of the Church at least since the year 249.
2. A well-conducted informal interview with the expert whom the court wishes to employ is an excellent means of avoiding an unsatisfactory *peritia*.
3. It is not required by law to appoint the very best experts available. The experts, however, must be truly and adequately skilled for the task assigned to them, and if it is possible they should also be specialists.
4. In causes of functional impotence both a urologist and a psychiatrist or neurologist should be appointed as experts.
5. The ruling of Article 150, 2°, of the *Instructio "Provida"* no longer avails as allowing the collegiate tribunal to appoint male experts for the corporal inspection of the woman. It is overruled by n. 3 of the Decree *Qua singulari* of the Holy Office, which restricts the making of such an appointment to the ordinary, with the consent of the woman party.
6. In exceptional circumstances more experts may be appointed than the number specified by law.
7. Experts must invariably take an oath of office before beginning their examination. This oath cannot be taken once for all the future (*semel pro semper*).
8. The word *censentur* in canon 1797, § 1, indicates not a mere presumption of the expert's acceptance of his judicial office, but rather it defines the point of time after which the person employed is to be considered a judicial expert, subject to the court, and liable for any faulty performance of his duties.
9. Experts are to be left free to perform the judicial examination according to the scientific techniques which

they deem appropriate and adequate, in line however with the judge's warning that they employ only licit means.

10. In impotence and non-consummation causes there must be a separate examination of the man by each of the experts.
11. No written report is required of the matron who assists at the physical examination of the woman who is a party in the cause.

APPENDIX I

Canonical Notion of Consummation[1]

"The jurisprudence of the Sacred Roman Rota has always held that a marriage is consummated by a true sexual union in which the husband, with an erect male organ, penetrates, *at least imperfectly,* the vagina of his wife and therein deposits semen. In one particular decision, the judges of the Rota declared that 'in order to have perfect copula, it is not necessary to have complete penetration by the male organ, i.e., that the entire male organ enter the vagina of the woman, but only that penetration is required by which, after the erection of the male organ has ceased, there is excluded mere semination *ad os vaginae* (near the introitus). It is sufficient to have partial penetration so that some of the male organ enters through and beyond the hymeneal membrane and into the vaginal canal and to have at least a partial semination within the canal.'[2] In other words, intra-vaginal deposition of semen is essential although penile penetration need not be complete. A decision of the Holy Office[3] . . . consonant with Rotal jurisprudence, stated that for perfect copula and consummation of the marriage, it is required and suffices that 'a man in some fashion, even though imperfectly, penetrates the vagina and immediately effects in a natural manner a semi-

[1] According to Harrington-Doyle, "Indications and Proof of Non-Consummation," *The Linacre Quarterly*, Vol. 19, No. 3 (August, 1952), 64-65.

[2] S.R.R. *Decisiones*, XXII (1930), 412-414, nn. 7, 8, 9; XXIII (1931), 452, n. 6.

[3] While Fr. Harrington lists this decision as of March 1, 1941, a Rotal decision dates it as of Feb. 12, 1941. Cf. S.R.R. *Decisiones*, XXXIII (1941), 182-183, n. 2.—cited in note 109, p. 158 of this dissertation.

nation, at least partial, within the vagina, with this reservation that the entire male organ need not enter the vagina.'

"It is clear from the above that the minimum, which is required and suffices for true consummation, is to be found between the two extremes of mere vulvar penetration, on the one hand, and complete penetration of the entire male organ, on the other. There must be verified a true entrance through the hymeneal membrane and into the vaginal canal, so that part of the male organ can be truly said to be enveloped by the vagina. Juxtaposition of the glans penis against the hymeneal orifice with the result that only the tip of the *glans* enters beyond the hymeneal membrane, and this without in any way stretching or tearing it or loosening the hymeneal ring, is not sufficient. For in this instance, it could not be said that any *penetration* had occurred. Rather must there be realized the apposition of an erect male organ against the hymeneal orifice with a definite pressure which will cause the membrane to be pushed aside and to be stretched, at least momentarily, so that part of the male organ can actually enter the vagina. This minimum penetration, coupled with a simultaneous semination, will constitute proper consummation."

APPENDIX II

Subject Matter and Method of the Physical Examination[1]

"The corporal inspection, as it is sometimes called, should be concerned exclusively with the female genitalia; there is no need to record the temperature, blood pressure, pulse, previous medical history, etc., unless this last is necessary to explain some present physiological phenomena. Attention should be centered on the labia maiora and minora, the hymeneal membrane and the hymeneal ring. Special note should be made of any swelling or scars on the labia maiora and minora, the presence or absence of an anatomically intact hymen, any evidence of hymeneal tears, fissures or carunculae myrtiformes, the relative snugness of the hymeneal ring and finally, indications of vaginismus, i.e., reaction of the woman to the examination—whether it was the normal reaction a doctor would expect, i.e., a very slight fleeting contraction of the sphincter cunni, or whether it was abnormal and unusual—viz., a true spasm. In addition, any other abnormal or unusual anatomical or physiological findings should be recorded.

"The examination should take place under the best possible medical conditions, in good light and with the use of a regulation examining table. Anaesthesia should not be administered, since it would destroy any evidence of vaginismus, if such exists, and would make it impossible for the doctor to determine the reaction of the patient to the entire procedure.

"If the hymeneal membrane is noticeably absent, the doctor should try [by his own examination and by prudent in-

[1] According to Harrington-Doyle, "Indications and Proof of Non-Consummation," *The Linacre Quarterly*, Vol. 19, no. 3 (August, 1952), 71-73.

terrogation to account for this fact—was it congenital or][2] was it lost by a hymenotomy or a hymenectomy. If the latter, then the name of the doctor who performed the surgery should be recorded, along with the name of the hospital and the approximate date of the operation. This is necessary and useful, so that these records might be obtained to verify these facts.

"If old hymeneal scars, tears, fissures or carunculae myrtiformes are witnessed, then some explanation should be sought by the doctor. Can their presence be satisfactorily explained by trauma, resulting from falls or sharp objects, by the forceful stretching and tearing of the membrane by reason of violent athletic exercising, such as riding horseback, in which the patient was accustomed to participate, by the habitual use of menstrual tampons, or by reason of a past history of autoeroticism, where either a digital manipulation or the insertion of objects into the vaginal canal was resorted to?

"The elasticity and size of the hymeneal ring should be carefully computed. In the past, many doctors measured this factor in terms of the number of fingers which could be inserted easily into the orifice. Unless one could observe the size of the fingers or have their dimensions, a report, stating that one or two fingers could be easily inserted, would mean little to the one who was reviewing it. It is suggested that a more accurate and objective measurement could be easily obtained by inserting a standard gauge Hanks uterine sound through the hymeneal orifice until the largest size, that penetrates easily, is determined.

"If there is any indication of vaginismus, its extent must be carefully noted, especially if its severity would have made it impossible for any penetration to have occurred.

"With all this factual information before him, the doctor is expected to make a conscientious judgment as to

[2] The bracketed material represents a printer's oversight in the article as it originally appeared in the *Linacre Quarterly*. The proper material was graciously supplied by Father Harrington from his manuscript copy.

whether the marriage in question has or has not been consummated. This opinion is to be reached only after a careful consideration of the minimum penetration and semination required by the norm described above.[3]

"As is evident, it is always much easier to establish a positive fact—that something did occur—than to try to prove a negative fact—that something did not occur.

"A very specific norm was set forth by the S.C. de Discip. Sacram. on December 18, 1950, in a private reply to the Tribunal of the Archdiocese of Boston, which should be of great value in aiding the doctor in arriving at his decision: 'If due consideration is given to the measurement and form of the hymeneal ring and the nature of the hymeneal membrane with its characteristic extensibility, can there be excluded, in this particular case, even the slightest penetration on one occasion of the male organ into the vagina with an accompanying partial semination?'[4]

"*Usually,* by conducting a vaginal examination, doctors can differentiate between a virgin and a woman who has had some sexual experience. For, in most cases, where even the minimum penetration . . . has taken place, there will be some evidence remaining for the examiner to detect; e.g., carunculae myrtiformes, tears, scars and fissures of the hymeneal membrane, definite relaxation or stretching of the hyemneal ring, etc. If the doctor finds these present and they cannot be accounted for or explained in any of the ways mentioned above, then he must conclude that the marriage in question had been properly consummated.[5] If, on the other hand, the examining physician finds a hymen which is completely intact and absolutely integral and a hyemneal ring which is snug and tight and shows no evi-

[3] Cf. Appendix I of this dissertation, pp. 203-204.

[4] This seems identical with the suggestion of Bartoccettii, cited in note 46, p. 179 of this dissertation.

[5] It would seem more accurate to say that in such a case the doctor must conclude that *serious attempts* at consummation were made; it remains for the court to infer from this the consummation or nonconsummation of the marriage.

dence of ever having been stretched, then he will be justified in judging that the marriage had never been properly consummated and in so reporting to the Tribunal. It is true that in some rare and exceptional instances, sufficient penetration could have taken place without in any way rupturing the hymeneal membrane or without stretching the hymeneal ring to the point where there is definite evidence of a real relaxation. This possibility merely points up the fact that the doctor's report is not entirely conclusive and by itself would not be sufficient to establish the fact of non-consummation with the moral certitude demanded and required by the various Roman Congregations.

"There would seem to be definite evidence of non-consummation in the cases, admittedly rare indeed, where the hymeneal orifice was so minute or where a condition of vaginismus was so severe or where there was such disproportion between the size of the male organ and the female introitus that the minimum penetration could not possibly have occurred.

"In this analysis, it is clear that all of the emphasis has been placed on the question of penetration without any consideration of the factor of *semination.* It is true, as was stated above, that a marriage remains unconsummated, if the minimum of semination has not occurred, even if minimum or maximum penetration has been definitely established. But this is theoretical and has little, if any, practical value, since it is nigh on impossible to prove that sufficient semination has not taken place, especially if we recall that once penetration has been established, minimum semination is *presumed.* The only seeming exception to this rigid conclusion would appear to be instances where, in the man, *both* testes are entirely absent, or completely undeveloped or absolutely atrophied and thus cannot manufacture male sperm or where a double vasectomy had been performed prior to the marriage and had perdured throughout the entire duration of the marriage, so that the sperm, which had been manufactured, could not be transmitted.

Verification of these facts could not only be had by having the husband submit to a corporal inspection and in cases, where surgery had intervened, to receive copies of hospital records and medical reports."

APPENDIX III

Suggested Formulae of the Oath to be Taken by the Medical Experts and the Matron in Non-Consummation Cases[1]

OATH OF THE EXPERT

"I, *N.N.*, appointed as the medical expert to conduct the physical examination of Mrs. (Mr.) ________, do hereby solemnly swear that I will faithfully fulfill this office; that I will investigate thoroughly all that medical science demands should be examined in order to infer the consummation or non-consummation of the marriage in question, and that I will observe especially the prescriptions contained in the Rules of the Sacred Congregation of the Sacraments as given in the Decrees of May 7, 1923, chapter XIII; of March 27, 1929; and of the Decree of the Holy Office of June 12, 1942, as well as the special instructions given me by the court.

"Moreover, I swear to be entirely truthful in both my written report and in my oral testimony, and that I will observe strict secrecy concerning my examination and report.

"So help me God and these His holy Gospels which I touch with my right hand."

Given this ______ day of __________, 19____.

Signed ______________________________

(medical expert)

N.N. __________________, Auditing judge

N.N. __________________, Notary

[1] From the Appendix, *Catholica Doctrina,* Formula XXIX, with slight revisions.

OATH OF THE MATRON

"I, *N.N.*, officially appointed to assist at the physical examination of Mrs. ________, do hereby solemnly swear that I will faithfully fulfill this office, observing especially the prescriptions contained in the Rules of the Sacred Congregation of the Sacraments as given in the Decrees of May 7, 1923, chapter XIII; of March 27, 1929; and of the Decree of the Holy Office of June 12, 1942, as well as the special instructions given me by the court.

"I swear that I shall be particularly attentive that no fraud be committed and that the rules of Christian modesty shall be perfectly observed; and, furthermore, that in my oral interrogation I will relate all the facts truthfully, and will respond truthfully to the questions which the court shall see fit to propose to me. Finally, I will observe absolute secrecy concerning this entire matter.

"So help me God and these His holy Gospels which I touch with my right hand."

Given this ______ day of ____________, 19____.

Signed ______________________________

(matron)

N.N. ____________________, Auditing judge
N.N. ____________________, Notary

BIBLIOGRAPHY

Sources

Acta Apostolicae Sedis, Commentarium Officiale, Romae, 1909-1929; Civitate Vaticana, 1929-

Acta Sanctae Sedis, 41 vols., Romae, 1865-1908.

Bouscaren, T. Lincoln, *The Canon Law Digest,* 3 vols. and Supplements through 1953, 1954, and 1955, Milwaukee: Bruce & Co., 1934-1949-1953-1954-1955-1956.

Codex Iuris Canonici, Pii X Pontificis Maximi iussu digestus, Benedicti Papae XV auctoritate promulgatus, Praefatione, Fontium Annotatione et Indice Analytico-Alphabetico ab Emo Petri Card. Gasparri Auctus, Romae: Typis Polyglottis Vaticanis, 1917; reimpressio, 1946.

The Civil Law, a translation by S. P. Scott, 11 vols., Cincinnati, 1932.

Codicis Iuris Canonici Fontes, cura Emi Petri Card. Gasparri, editi, 9 vols., Romae (postea Civitate Vaticana): Typis Polyglottis Vaticanis, 1923-1939 (Vols. VII-IX, ed. cura et studio Emi. Iustiniani Card. Serédi).

Collectio Omnium Conclusionum et Resolutionum S. C. Concilii ab anno 1564 ad annum 1860, ed. S. Pallottini, 17 vols., Romae, 1868-1893.

Corpus Iuris Canonici, ed. Lipsien. 2. post Aemilii Ludovici Richteri curas... instruxit Aemilius Friedberg, 2 vols., Lipsiae: Tauchnitz, 1879-1881. Editio anastatice repetita, Lipsiae: Tauchnitz, 1928.

Codex Theodosianus, ed. P. Kreuger, T. Mommsen, 3 vols., Berolini, 1905.

Corpus Iuris Civilis, 3 vols., Vol. I, *Institutiones,* quas recognovit P. Krueger; *Digesta,* quae recognovit T. Mommsen et retractavit P. Krueger, ed stereotypa 15.; Vol. II, *Codex Iustinianus,* quem recognovit et retractavit P. Krueger, ed. stereotypa 10.; Vol. III, *Novellae Constitutiones,* ed. stereotypa 5, a R. Schoell; opus Schoellii morte interceptum absolvit G. Kroll; Berolini; apud Weidmannos, 1928-1929.

Corpus Scriptorum Ecclesiasticorum Latinorum, editum consilio et impensis Academiae Litterarum Caesareae Vindobonensis, Vindobonae, 1866—

Decisiones Sacrae Rota Romanae coram Olivatio, Romae, 1785.

Decretales D. Gregorii Papae IX, suae integretati una cum glossis restitutae cum privilegio Gregorii XIII, Pont. Max., et aliorum Principum, Romae, 1582.

Decretum Gratiani, emendatum et notationibus illustratum, una cum glossis, 2 vols., Romae, 1582.

Jaffé, Philippus, *Regesta Pontificum Romanorum ab condita Ecclesia ad annum post Christum natum MCXCVIII*, ed. 2 correctam et auctam auspiciis G. Wattenbach, curaverunt F. Kaltenbrunner, P. Ewald, S. Loewenfeld, 2 vols., Lipsiae, 1885-1888.

Liber Sextus Decretalium D. Bonifacii Papae VIII, suae integritati cum Clementinis et Extravagantibus, earumque Glossis restitutis, Romae, 1582.

Mansi, Joannes, *Sacrorum Conciliorum Nova et Amplissima Collectio*, 53 vols. in 60, Parisiis, 1901-1927.

Potthast, Augustus, *Regesta Pontificum Romanorum inde ab anno post Christum naturm MCXCVIII ad annum MCCCIV*, 2 vols., Berolini, 1874-1875.

S. R. Rotae Decisiones Nuperrimae (1684-1706), 10 vols., Romae, 1751-1763.

S. Romanae Rotae Decisiones seu Sententiae quae . . . prodierunt anno 1909—, Romae, Typis Vaticanis, 1912—

Thesaurus Resolutionum Sacrae Congregationis Concilii, 1718-1908, 167 vols., Vols. I-V, Urbini, 1739-1740; Vols. VI-CLXVII, Romae, 1741-1909.

Reference Works

Aretinus, (Franciscus de Aretio, or de Accoltis), *Consilia Domini Francisci de Aretio, magnifici equitis . . . ac summariis novissime ornata.* Bound with the *Consilia* of Joannes Calderinus, 1546.

Augustine, Charles, *A Commentary on the New Code of Canon Law*, 8 vols., Vol. VII, 2. ed., St. Louis: B. Herder Book Co., 1923.

Baldus de Ubaldus, *Super Decretalibus*, Lugduni, 1547.

Beste, Udalricus, *Introductio in Codicem*, 3. ed., Collegeville, Minn.: St. John's Abbey Press, 1946.

Blat, A., *Commentarium Textus Codicis Iuris Canonici*, 6 vols., Lib. IV, *De Processibus*, Romae: Ex Typographia Pontificia in Instituto Pii X, 1927.

Boich, Henricus, *In Quinque Libros Commentaria*, Venetiis, 1576.

Bottoms, Archibald M., *The Discretionary Authority of the Ecclesiastical Judge in Matrimonial Trials of the First Instance*, The Catholic University of America Canon Law Studies, n. 349, Washington, D.C.: The Catholic University of America Press, 1955.

Castañeda Delgado, Eudoxio, *La Locura y el Matrimonio* (Psiquiatría y Jurisprudencia de la Sagrada Rota Romana), Valladolid and Madrid: Editorial Sever-Cuesta, 1955.

Coronata, Matthaeus Conte a, *Institutiones Iuris Canonici*, 5 vols., Vol. III, 4. ed., 1956, Taurini, Romae: Marietti.

Decius, Philippus, *Super Decretalibus*, Lugduni, 1559.

De Luca, Joannes B., *Theatrum Veritatis et Justitiae*, 16 vols., Venetiis, 1734.

Doheny, William J., *Canonical Procedure in Matrimonial Cases*, 2 vols., Vol. I, *Formal Judicial Procedure*, 2. ed., 1948; Vol. II, *Informal Procedure*, 2. printing, 1948; Milwaukee, Bruce Publ. Co.

———, *Practical Manual for Marriage Cases*, 2. ed., 1947; Milwaukee, Bruce Publ. Co.

Dorna, Bernardus, *Die* SUMMA LIBELLORUM *des Bernardus Dorna*, Vol. I of *Quellen zur Geschichte des Römisch-Kanonischen Processes in Mittelalter*, edited by L. Wahrmund; Innsbruck, 1905.

Durandus, Gulielmus, *Speculum Iuris*, Venetiis, 1577.

Engel, Ludovicus, *Collegium Universi Iuris Canonici*, 9. ed. a Caspare Barthel, Beneventi, 1760.

Gasparri, Petrus Card., *Tractatus Canonicus de Matrimonio*, ed. nova ad mentem Codicis Iuris Canonici, 2 vols., Romae: Typis Polyglottis Vaticanis, 1932.

Gonzales-Tellez, Emmanuel, *Commentaria Perpetua in Singulos Textus Quinque Librorum Decretalium Gregorii IX*, 5 vols., Lugduni, 1673.

Goyeneche, S., *De Processibus*, breves adnotationes ad Lib. IV Codicis Iuris Canonici, 1 vol., 2 parts, Romae: ad s. Ioannis Lat., 1947.

Guido a Baiiso, *Rosarium seu in Decretorum Volumen Commentaria*, Venetiis, 1577.

Hostiensis, Cardinalis (Henricus de Segusio), *Commentaria in Quinque Decretalium Libros*, 6 vols. in 4, Venetiis, 1581.

———, *Summa Aurea*, Lugduni, 1568.

Innocentius IV, (Sinibaldus Fliscus), *Commentaria in V Libros Decretalium*, Venetiis, 1570.

Lega, M. (ed. V. Bartoccetti), *Commentarius in Iudicia Ecclesiastica iuxta Codicem Iuris Canonici*, 2. ed., 2 vols., Romae: Azienda Libraria Cattolica Italiana, 1950.

Martin, Michael, *The Roman Curia*, London, 1913.

Miguélez, Lorenzo Dominguez; Alonso, Sabino Morán; Cabreros, Marcelino De Anta, *Código de Derecho Canonico y Legislación Complementaria*, 5. ed., Madrid: La Editorial Católica, 1954.

Muñiz, T., *Procedimientos Eclesiasticos,* 2. ed., 3 vols., Barcelona, 1925.

Noval, J., *Commentarium Codicis Iuris Canonici,* Liber IV, *De Processibus,* Pars I, *Le Iudiciis,* Augustae Taurinorum-Romae: Marietti, 1920.

Panormitanus, Abbas (Nicholaus de Tudeschis), *Commentaria in Quinque Libros Decretalium,* 5 vols. in 7, Venetiis, 1588.

Paucapalea, *Die* SUMMA *des Paucapalea uber das* DECRETUM GRATIANI, herausgegeben von Dr. J. Friedrich von Schulte, Giessen, 1890.

Pickett, R. Colin, *Mental Affliction and Church Law,* Universitas Catholica Ottaviensis, series canonica, tom. 25, Ottawa, Ontario: The University of Ottawa Press, 1952.

Pinna, Joannes M., *Praxis Iudicialis Canonica,* Romae: Officium Libri Catholici (Catholic Book Agency), 1952.

Quinn, Joseph J., *Rotal Jurisprudence with Regard to Functional Impotence in the Male.* Published for Limited Distribution by the Canon Law Society of America, Washington, D.C.: The Catholic University of America, 1956.

Regatillo, Eduardus, *Institutiones Iuris Canonici,* 2 vols., 4. ed., Santander: Sal Terrae, 1951.

Regatillo, E. F., et Zalba, M., *Theologiae Moralis Summa,* 3 vols., Vol. II, *De Mandatis Dei et Eccliesiae,* 1953, Madrid: La Editorial Católica.

Reiffenstuel, Anacletus, *Ius Canonicum Universum,* 5 vols. in 7, Parisiis, 1864-1870.

Repetitiones in Iure Canonico, Venetiis, 1587.

Reynés, Lorenzo Quintana, *La Prueba en el Procédimiento Canónico,* Barcelona: Bosch, 1942.

Roberti, Franciscus, *De Processibus,* 2 vols., Romae: Vol. I, 4 ed., 1956; Vol. II, 1926.

Rufinus, *Die* SUMMA DECRETORUM, herausgegeben von Dr. H. Singer, Paderborn: Schöningh, 1902.

Sanchez, Thomas, *De Sancti Matrimonii Sacramento Disputationum Libri Decem,* 3 vols., Venetiis, 1726.

Sandeus, F., *Commentaria in V Libros Decretalium,* 3 vols., Venetiis, 1570.

Schmalzgrueber, Franciscus, *Ius Ecclesiasticum Universam,* 5 vols. in 12, Romae, 1843-1845.

Schmier, Farnciscus, *Iurisprudentia Canonico-Civilis,* 2 vols., Venetiis, 1754.

Tiraquellus, Andreas, *De Legibus Connubialibus, et Iure Maritali,* Lugduni, 1569.

Torre, Joannes, *Processus Matrimonialis,* 3. ed., Neapoli: M. D'Aurea, Pontificius Editor, 1956.

Van Hove, Alphonsus, *Commentarium Lovaniense in Codicem Iuris Canonici,* 1 vol. in 5 toms., Tom. I, *Prolegomena,* 2. ed., Mechliniae-Romae: H. Dessain, 1945.

Verano, Cajetanus F., *Iuris Canonici Universi Commentarius Paratitlaris,* Monachii, 1703-1708.

Viscont, Antonius, *Tractatus Canonicus de Matrimonio Rato et non Consummato,* Romae: Ius Pontificium, 1929.

Wanenmacher, Francis, *Canonical Evidence in Marriage Cases,* Philadelphia: Dolphin Press, 1935.

Wernz-Franciscus X.,-Vidal, Petrus, *Ius Canonicum ad Codicis Normam Exactum,* 7 vols. in 8, Vol. V, *Ius Matrimoniale,* 3. ed., 1946; Vol. VI, *De Processibus,* ed. altera, Romae: Apud Aedes Universitatis Gregorianae, 1949.

Whalen, Donald W., *The Value of Testimonial Evidence in Matrimonial Procedure,* The Catholic University of America Canon Law Studies, n. 99, Washington, D.C.: The Catholic University of America Press, 1935.

Willet, Robert A., *The Probative Value of Documents in Ecclesiastical Trials,* The Catholic University of America Canon Law Studies, n. 171, Washington, D.C.: The Catholic University of America Press, 1942.

Woywod, Stanislaus,-Smith, Callistus, *A Practical Commentary on the Code of Canon Law,* rev. ed., 2 vols., New York: Joseph F. Wagner, Inc., 1948.

Articles

Allers, Rudolf, "Annulment of Marriage by Lack of Consent Because of Insanity," *The Ecclesiastical Review,* CI (1939), 325-343.

———, "Some Medico-Psychological Remarks on Canons 1068, 1081, and 1087," *The Jurist,* IV (1944), 351-380.

Castañeda Delgado, Eudaxio, "Nulidad por Vicio de Consentimiento," *Las Causas Matrimoniales* (Salamanca, 1953), pp. 491-535.

Evans, George R., "*Ratum et non-Consummatum* Procedure: Regulations Concerning Corporal Examination," *The Jurist,* XVI (1956), 170-180.

Hammill, J. L., "Intention contra *Bonum Prolis*: Its Nature and Proof," *The Jurist,* VIII (1948), 170-195.

Harrington, Paul V., and Doyle, Joseph B., "Indications and Proof of Non-Consummation," *The Linacre Quarterly,* Vol. XIX (1952), pp. 61-76.

Hayes, John J., "Mental disease and the Ecclesiastical Courts," *The Jurist,* XVI (1956), 267-284.

Hickey, Joseph A., "De Processu super Matrimino Rato et non Consummato," *The Jurist,* I (1941), 210-224.

———, "Requirements of the *Ratum et non Consummatum* Process," *The Jurist,* V (1945), 1-19.

Lopez, Ildefonso P., "Nulidad por Impotencia," *Las Causas Matrimoniales* (Salamanca, 1953), pp. 433-465.

McGowan, John E., M.D., "Fundamentals of Psychiatry in Relation to the Ecclesiastical Tribunal," *The Jurist,* XVI (1956), 251-266.

Schmidt, John Rogg, "Interrogation of the Woman Party in the *Super Rato* Process," *The American Ecclesiastical Review,* CXXVI (1952), in two parts; Part I, pp. 109-119; Part II, pp. 217-227.

Serra, Ramon B., "De Matrimonii Inconsummatione et de Processu super Rato," *Las Causas Matrimoniales* (Salamanca, 1953), pp. 469-488.

Periodicals

American Ecclesiastical Review, The, Vols. I-XXXII, Philadelphia, 1889-1905; from 1905: *The Ecclesiastical Review,* Vols. XXXIII-CIX, Philadelphia, 1905-1943; from 1944: *The American Ecclesiastical Review,* Washington, D.C.: Vol. CX, 1944—

Jurist, The, Washington, D.C., 1941—

Linacre Quarterly, The, St. Louis, Mo., 1934—

Monitor Ecclesiasticus, Romae, 1876—

Unpublished Thesis

Arthur, E. Robert, *Expert Witnesses, an Historical Study,* Typewritten licentiate dissertation, School of Canon Law, (archives' unique copy is #3283), The Catholic University of America, Washington, D.C., 1940.

Abbreviations

AAS—Acta Apostolicae Sedis.

ASS—Acta Sanctae Sedis.

Can.—Canon of the *Codex Iuris Canonici.*

Catholica Doctrina, Rule—S.C. de Sacramentis, decr., *De Processibus in causis dispensationis super matrimonio rato et non consummato,* with the appended *Regulae Servandae,* 7 maii 1923.

Fontes—Codicis Iuris Canonici Fontes.

Instructio "Provida," Art.—The indicated Article of the S.C. de Sacramentis, *Instructio servanda a tribunalibus dioecesanis in pertractandis causis de nullitate matrimoniorum,* 15 aug. 1936.

Qua singulari of 1942—S.C.S. Officii Decretum, *De Quibusdam Cautelis Adhibendis in Causis Matrimonialibus Impotentiae et Inconsummationis,* 12 iunii, 1942.

Rota *Regulae* of 1910—*Regulae Servanda in Iudiciis apud Sacrae Romanae Rotae Tribunal,* 4 aug. 1910.

S.C. Sacr., *Normae* of 1929—*Normae Observandae in Processibus Super Matrimonio Rato et Non Consummato ad Praecavendum Dolosam Personarum Substitutionem,* 27 mart. 1929.

BIOGRAPHICAL NOTE

William M. Pickard was born on January 22, 1930, in Port Arthur, Texas. He received his elementary and secondary education in the same city at St. James' Parochial and High Schools. In 1947 he enrolled at St. Mary's Seminary, La Porte, Texas, where he pursued his studies in philosophy and theology. He was ordained to the priesthood on May 29, 1954, at Kirwin Memorial Chapel, St. Mary's Seminary, by His Excellency, the Most Reverend Wendelin J. Nold, S.T.D., Bishop of Galveston. In October of the same year he was admitted to the School of Canon Law of the Catholic University of America, from which he received the degree of the Baccalaureate in Canon Law in June, 1955, and the degree of the Licentiate in Canon Law in June, 1956.

APHABETICAL INDEX

CANON LAW STUDIES*

375. Kelleher, Rev. Francis T., A.B., J.C.L., Judicial expenses.
376. Bantigue, Rev. Pedro N., J.C.L., The Provincial Council of Manila of 1771. (Its text followed by a commentary on *Actio* II, *De Episcopis*)
377. Burns, Rev. Dennis J., J.C.L., Matrimonial indissolubility: contrary conditions.
378. Deutsch, Rev. Bernard F., J.C.L., Jurisdiction of pastors in the external forum.
379. Dunnivan, Rev. John P., A.B., J.C.L., Prejudicial attempts in pending litigation.
380. Ernst, Rev. Albert C., A.B., J.C.L., Free admission to church for sacred rites.
381. Frattin, Mr. Peter Louis, J.C.L., The matrimonial impediment of impotence: occlusion of the spermatic ducts and vaginismus.
382. Henry, Rev. Charles W., O.S.B., A.B., S.T.L., J.C.L., Canonical relations between bishops and abbots at the beginning of the tenth century.
383. Hoffman, Rev. Lawrence J., A.B., S.T.B., J.C.L., Clergy conferences: Canon 131.
384. Markham, Rev. James, A.B., S.T.L., J.C.L., The Sacred Congregation of Seminaries and Universities of Studies.
385. McGrath, Rev. John J., A.B., LL.B., J.C.L., A comparative study of crime and its imputability in ecclesiastical criminal law and in American criminal law.
386. McGuire, Rev. James D., O.R.S.A., J.C.L., The postulancy.
387. Munday, Rev. James E., J.C.L., Ecclesiastical Property in Australia and New Zealand.
388. Murphy, Rev. Joseph P., A.B., J.C.L., The laws of the State of New York affecting church property.
389. Pickard, Rev. William M., J.C.L., Judicial experts: a source of evidence in ecclesiastical trials.
390. Ruddy, Rev. James, J.C.L., The Apostolic Constitution *Christus Dominus*: text, translation and commentary, with short annotations on the Motu Proprio *Sacram Communionem*.
391. Vanyo, Rev. Leo. V., A.B., J.C.L., Requisites of intention in the reception of the sacraments.

* For a complete list of the available numbers of this series apply to the Catholic University of America Press, 620 Michigan Avenue, N.E., Washington (17), D.C., for a general catalogue.

www.ingramcontent.com/pod-product-compliance
Lightning Source LLC
LaVergne TN
LVHW050247080826
844660LV00012B/606

* 9 7 8 0 8 1 3 2 2 5 4 9 4 *